CHARMING
SMALL HOTEL
GUIDES

France

CHARMING SMALL HOTEL GUIDES

France

Edited by Chris Gill

DUNCAN PETERSEN

HUNTER
PUBLISHING INC

300 Raritan Center Parkway,
CN 94, Edison, N.J. 08818

Conceived, designed and produced by
Duncan Petersen Publishing Ltd,
Edited by Fox and Partners, The Old Forge,
Norton St Philip, Bath, U.K.

Editor	Chris Gill
Assistant editors	Amanda Crook, Ian Stratford, Kate Targett
Proofreader	Edward Hunt
Production editor	Nicola Davies
Art director	Mel Petersen

This edition published in the UK and Commonwealth 1994 by
Duncan Petersen Publishing Ltd,
54 Milson Road, London W14 OLB,
and distributed by
Automobile Association Publishing,
c/o Exel Logistics MS,
Invicta Warehouse, Sir Thomas Langley Road,
Medway City Estate, Rochester, Kent

ISBN 1 872576 30 3

A CIP catalogue record for this book is available
from the British Library

AND

Published in the USA 1994 by
Hunter Publishing Inc.,
300 Raritan Center Parkway, CN 94, Edison, N.J. 08818.
Tel (908) 225 1900 Fax (908) 417 0482

ISBN 1-55650-639-2

Typeset by Fox + Partners, Bath, and PCS Typsetting, Frome
Originated by Reprocolor International S.R.I., Milan
Printed by G. Canale & Co SpA, Turin

Contents

Introduction	6
Reporting to the guides	9
Hotel location maps	10
North-west France	18
Île-de-France	43
North-east France	71
Western France	81
Eastern France	100
South-west France	126
Massif Central	156
South of France	168
Corsica	216
Index of hotel names	217
Index of hotel locations	221

Readers' reports

Reports from readers are of enormous help to us in keeping up to date with the hotels in the guide – and other hotels that should be in it. The most helpful reporters are invited to join our Travellers' Panel, and to stay in listed hotels at little or no cost. There is more information on p9.

Introduction

This guide to French hotels – completely revised for 1994 – is part of a series also covering Italy, Spain, the British Isles, Germany, Austria and Switzerland.

The *Charming Small Hotel Guides* are different from other accommodation guides. The most fundamental difference is suggested by the title: we aim to include only those hotels and guest-houses which are in some way captivating, and which offer truly personal service, usually from the owner. In France, most of our recommendations have fewer than 20 rooms.

The guides are different in other ways, too. Our entries employ, above all, words: they contain not one symbol. They are written by people with something to say, not a bureaucracy which has long since lost the ability to distinguish the praiseworthy from the mediocre. Every entry aims to give a definite feel of what it is actually like to stay in that place. The editorial team is small and highly experienced at assessing hotels, at noticing all-important details. Although we place great emphasis on consistency, we have made use of reports from readers, and would welcome more of them (see box on page 9).

These are features which will reveal their worth only as you use your *Charming Small Hotel Guide*. Its other advantages are more obvious: it contains colour photographs of about one-third of the entries – usually the more attractive ones; the entries are presented in clear geographical groups; and each entry is categorized by the type of accommodation (for example, country inn).

Our ideal hotel has a peaceful, pretty setting; the building itself is either handsome or historic, or at least has a distinct character. The rooms are spacious, but on a human scale – not grand or intimidating. The decorations and furnishings are harmonious, comfortable and impeccably maintained, and include antique pieces that are meant to be used, not revered. The proprietors and staff are dedicated, thoughtful and sensitive in their pursuit of their guests' happiness – friendly and welcoming without being intrusive. Last but not least, the food, whether simple or ambitious, is fresh, interesting and carefully prepared. Elaborate facilities such as trouser-presses count for little, though we do generally list them.

Small French hotels
France has always been the land of the small hotel. Whereas in Britain the personally run and distinctive little hotel is a fairly recent phenomenon, in France it is a long-standing tradition. Most hotels of this kind are family-run, and handed down from one generation to the next. The owners are not burdened by huge mortgages, or by the ruinously expensive ideas of interior designers -

Introduction

so their charges can be modest. Small wonder that so many British travellers – including of course many families, so badly catered for by most British hotels – look forward eagerly to their expeditions across the Channel.

But the traditional French country hotel-restaurant is no longer the only option of those who seek a personal welcome and intimate surroundings. In recent years the French have woken up to the bed-and-breakfast concept – and the Gîtes de France organisation publishes a substantial catalogue of homes that offer it. And we detect also an increasing number of little hotels – some with, some without restaurant – being set up in the way that so many hotels were established in Britain during the 1980s: engineers, teachers or whatever, who have had enough of their particular rat-race and see the prospect of a more satisfying existence in catering for the needs of travellers.

Naturally, we welcome this broadening choice of small French hotel, which year by year is increasingly reflected in these pages.

How to find an entry
In this guide, the entries are arranged by *département*, and theses are clustered in convenient regional groups. The regions, and within them the *départements*, are arranged in a sequence starting in the north-west and working southwards and eastwards. Corsica comes last.

To find a hotel in a particular area, simply browse through headings at the top of the pages until you find that area – or use the maps following this introduction to locate the appropriate pages. To locate a specific hotel or a hotel in a specific place, use the indexes at the back.

How to read an entry
At the top of each entry is a coloured bar highlighting the name of the town or village where the establishment is located, along with a categorization which gives some clue to its character.

Fact boxes
The fact box given for each hotel follows a standard pattern which requires little explanation; but:

Under **Tel** we give the telephone number, starting with (1) if the hotel is in the Paris area; if dialling such a number within Paris, you should omit the (1). When dialling Paris from the provinces, or vice versa, you must preface the whole number with 16. When dialling a provincial number in the provinces, the eight digits we give are all you need to dial. We now also give **Fax** numbers where appropriate.

Introduction

Under **Location** we give information on the setting of the hotel and on its car parking arrangements, as well as pointers to help you find it.

Under **Meals** we list the meals available.

The basic **Prices** in this volume – unlike our volume on Britain and Ireland – are per **room**. We normally give the range of prices you can expect to pay for a room – from the cost of the cheapest single room in low season to the cost of the dearest double in high season. If the room price we give includes breakfast, we say so; otherwise, space permitting, we normally give the price of breakfast separately; where it is not given, allow 30F to 60F, according to the room price. We then give the prices of other meals, concentrating on fixed-price menus, or of prices for a room plus meals – either for dinner, bed and breakfast (DB&B), or for full board (FB) – all meals included. All these meal-inclusive prices are **per person**. Prices includes tax and service.

Wherever possible we have given prices for 1994, but for many hotels these were not available when the guide was prepared. Bear in mind also that proprietors may change their prices from one year to another by more than the rate of inflation. Always check when booking.

Under **Rooms** we summarize the number and style of bedrooms available. Our lists of facilities in bedrooms cover only mechanical gadgets, and not ornaments such as flowers or consumables such as toiletries or free drinks.

Under **Facilities** we list public rooms and then outdoor and sporting facilities which are immediately on hand; facilities in the vicinity of the hotel but not directly connected with it (for example, a nearby golf course) are not listed here, though they sometimes feature at the end of the main description in the **Nearby** section, which presents interesting things to see or do in the locality.

We use the following abbreviations for **Credit cards**:

AE American Express
DC Diners Club
MC MasterCard (Access/Eurocard)
V Visa (Barclaycard/Bank Americard/Carte Bleue etc)

The final entry in a fact box is normally the name of the proprietor(s); but where the hotel is run by a manager we give his or her name instead.

Reporting to the guides

Please write and tell us about your experiences of small hotels, guest-houses and inns, whether good or bad, whether listed in this edition or not. As well as hotels in France, we are interested in hotels in Britain and Ireland, Italy, Spain, Austria, Germany and Switzerland. We assume that reporters have no objections to our publishing their views unpaid, either verbatim or in edited form.

Readers whose reports prove particularly helpful may be invited to join our Reporters' Register; this means that you receive a free copy of the new edition of the guide in the winter, preceded by a newsletter in the autumn and followed by another in the spring. In return, we hope to receive further reports.

Register members who report regularly and reliably may be invited to join our Travellers' Panel. Members give us notice of their own travel plans; we suggest hotels that they might inspect, and contribute to the cost of accommodation.

The address to write to is:

Chris Gill,
Editor, *Charming Small Hotel Guides,*
The Old Forge,
Norton St Philip,
Bath, BA3 6LW,
England.

Checklist
Please use a separate sheet of paper for each report; include your name and address on each report.

Your reports will be received with particular pleasure if they are typed, and if they are organized under the following headings:

Name of establishment
Town or village it is in, or nearest
Full address, including post code
Date and duration of visit
The building and setting
The public rooms
The bedrooms and bathrooms
Comfort (chairs, beds, heat, light, hot water)
Standards of maintenance and housekeeping
Atmosphere, welcome and service
Food
Value for money

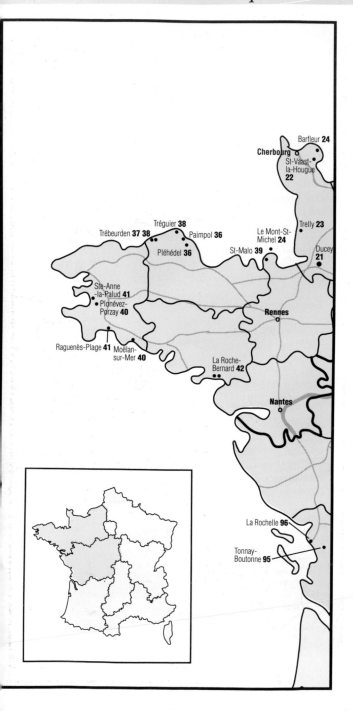

Barfleur **24**

Cherbourg

St-Vaast-
la-Hougue
22

Trelly **23**

Tréguier **38**

Trébeurden **37 38**

Paimpol **36**

Le Mont-St-
Michel **24**

Pléhédel **36**

St-Malo **39**

Ducey
21

Ste-Anne-
la-Palud **41**

Plonévez-
Porzay **40**

Rennes

Raguenès-Plage **41**

Moëlan-
sur-Mer **40**

La Roche-
Bernard **42**

Nantes

La Rochelle **96**

Tonnay-
Boutonne **95**

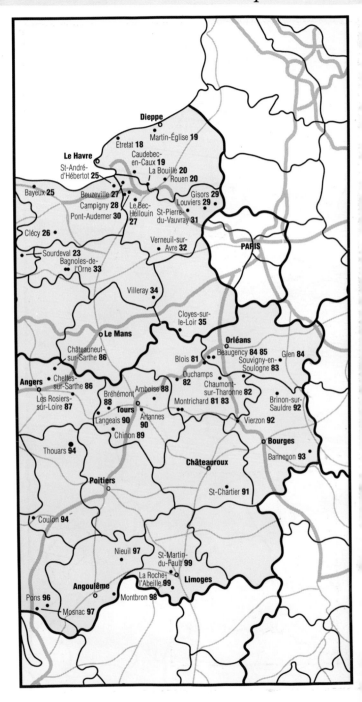

Hotel location maps

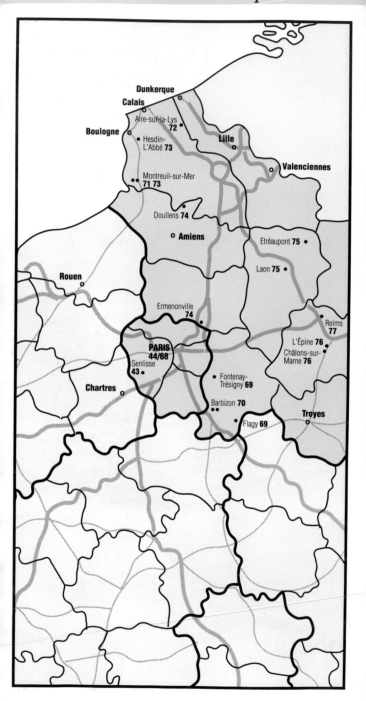

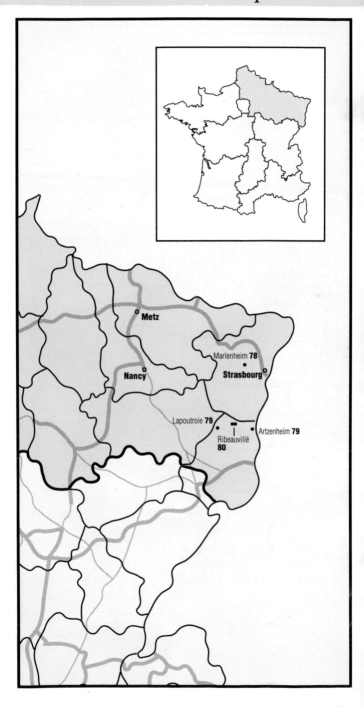

Hotel location maps

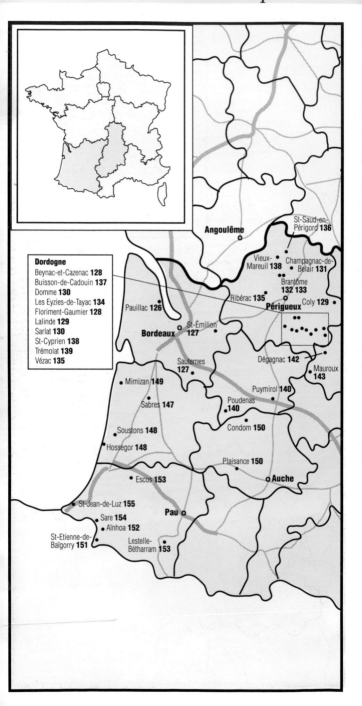

Dordogne
Beynac-et-Cazenac **128**
Buisson-de-Cadouin **137**
Domme **130**
Les Eyzies-de-Tayac **134**
Floriment-Gaumier **128**
Lalinde **129**
Sarlat **130**
St-Cyprien **138**
Trémolat **139**
Vézac **135**

Angoulême

St-Saud-en-Périgord **136**

Vieux-Mareuil **138**
Champagnac-de-Belair **131**
Brantôme **132 133**
Ribérac **135**
Périgueux
Coly **129**

Pauillac **126**

St-Émilion **127**

Bordeaux

Dégagnac **142**
Mauroux **143**

Sauternes **127**

Mimizan **149**

Puymirol **140**
Poudenas **140**

Sabres **147**

Condom **150**

Soustons **148**

Hossegor **148**

Plaisance **150**

Escos **153**

Auche

St-Jean-de-Luz **155**

Pau

Sare **154**
Aïnhoa **152**

St-Etienne-de-Baïgorry **151**

Lestelle-Bétharram **153**

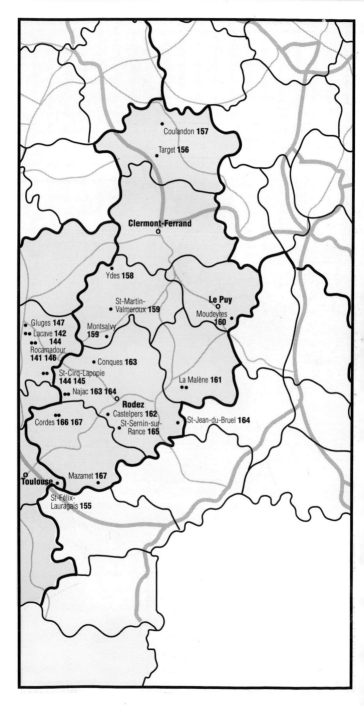

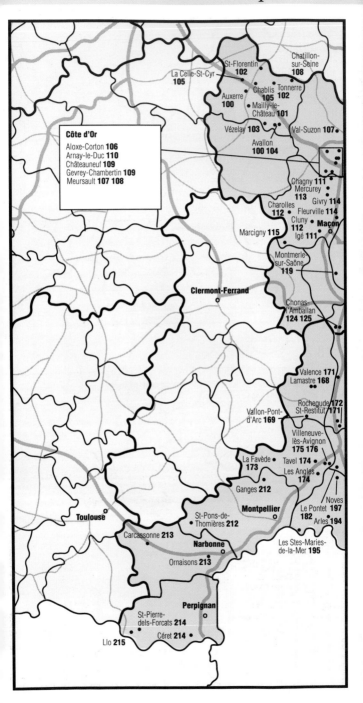

Côte d'Or

Aloxe-Corton **106**
Arnay-le-Duc **110**
Châteauneuf **109**
Gevrey-Chambertin **109**
Meursault **107 108**

St-Florentin **102**
Chatillon-sur-Saône **108**
La Celle-St-Cyr **105**
Chablis **105**
Tonnerre **102**
Auxerre **100**
Mailly-le-Château **101**
Vézelay **103**
Val-Suzon **107**
Avallon **100 104**
Chagny **111**
Mercurey **113**
Givry **114**
Charolles **112**
Fleurville **114**
Cluny **112**
Maçon
Marcigny **115**
Igé **111**
Montmerle-sur-Saône **119**
Clermont-Ferrand
Chonas-l'Amballan **124 125**
Valence **171**
Lamastre **168**
Rochegude **172**
St-Restitut **171**
Vallon-Pont-d'Arc **169**
Villeneuve-lès-Avignon **175 176**
La Favède **173**
Tavel **174**
Les Angles **174**
Ganges **212**
Noves
Le Pontet **182**
Arles **194**
Montpellier
Toulouse
St-Pons-de-Thomières **212**
Carcassonne **213**
Narbonne
Les Stes-Maries-de-la-Mer **195**
Ornaisons **213**
Perpignan
St-Pierre-dels-Forcats **214**
Llo **215**
Céret **214**

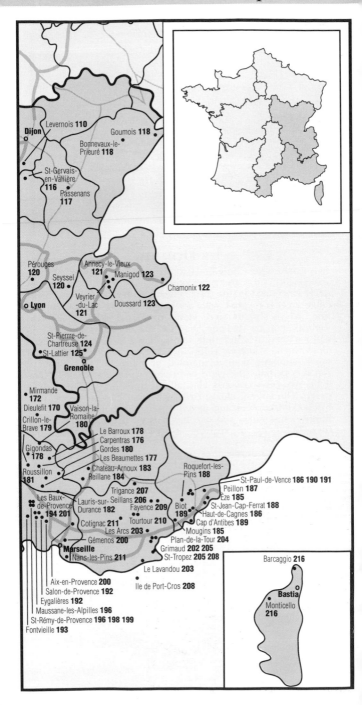

Levernois **110**

Dijon

Goumois **118**

Bonnevaux-le-
Prieuré **118**

St-Gervais-
en-Vallière
116

Passenans
117

Pérouges
120

Annecy-le-Vieux
121

Manigod **123**

Seyssel
120

Chamonix **122**

Veyrier
-du-Lac
121

Doussard **123**

Lyon

St-Pierrre-de-
Chartreuse **124**

St-Lattier **125**

Grenoble

Mirmande
172

Dieulefit **170**

Vaison-la-
Romaine
180

Crillon-le-
Brave **179**

Le Barroux **178**

Carpentras **176**

Gigondas
178

Gordes **180**

Les Beaumettes **177**

Roussillon
181

Château-Arnoux **183**

Reillane **184**

Roquefort-les-
Pins **188**

St-Paul-de-Vence **186 190 191**

Trigance **207**

Seillans **206**

Peillon **187**

Èze **185**

Les Baux-
de-Provence
194 201

Lauris-sur-
Durance **182**

Fayence **209**

Biot
189

St-Jean-Cap-Ferrat **188**

Haut-de-Cagnes **186**

Cotignac **211**

Tourtour **210**

Cap d'Antibes **189**

Les Arcs **203**

Mougins **185**

Gémenos **200**

Plan-de-la-Tour **204**

Marseille

Grimaud **202 205**

Nans-les-Pins **211**

St-Tropez **205 208**

Le Lavandou **203**

Aix-en-Provence **200**

Ile de Port-Cros **208**

Salon-de-Provence **192**

Eygalières **192**

Maussane-les-Alpilles **196**

St-Rémy-de-Provence **196 198 199**

Fontvieille **193**

Barcaggio **216**

Bastia

Monticello
216

Seine-Maritime

Le Donjon

This extraordinary little hotel, a former hilltop castle with venerable origins and secret subterranean channel to the sea, is now safely ensconced in the leafy suburbs of Etretat, and its formidable creeper-covered walls no longer appear threatening. Inside, all is bright and light, decorated with a Parisian sophistication by Madame Abo-Dib. The dining-room, candle-lit and mirrored, is wonderfully atmospheric; the cocktail bar overlooks Etretat's famous cliffs; and there is an impeccably kept small swimming pool surrounded by sunshades and loungers. But it is perhaps the eight bedrooms which best show off Madame Abo-Dib's creative skills: all are different, and immensely stylish. The largest, almost circular, has an Eastern theme, with black chintz drapes and gigantic mirror; another is in bright Impressionist hues, and one has a large fireplace for real log fires. Bathrooms are spacious and elegant in pure white; four have whirlpool baths.

The menu offers rather more possibilities for *pensionnaires* than many, with the option of choosing dishes from the carte, as well as an excellent four-course *menu du Gentleman*. This is a splendid place for a rather special short break (without the family); it is only 28 km from Le Havre.

Nearby Etretat – cliffs; Fécamp (17km) – Benedictine distillery.

Chemin de Saint Clair
76790 Etretat
Tel 35.27.08.23
Fax 35.29.92.24
Location on hill behind resort, 28 km N of Le Havre; with garden and car parking
Meals breakfast, lunch, dinner
Prices DB&B 600F-800F per person; menus 170F- 265F
Rooms 8 double, 7 with bath, one with shower (4 with whirlpool baths); all have central heating, phone, TV

Facilities dining-room, sitting-room; swimming-pool
Credit cards AE, V
Children accepted
Pets accepted
Disabled access difficult
Closed never
Proprietor Mme Abo-Dib

Seine-Maritime

Riverside hotel, Caudebec-en-Caux

Le Normandie

Caudebec was almost entirely rebuilt after the war, in a safe but uninspiring style – but it enjoys a fine setting on the Seine. The same is true of the Normandie, standing on the river promenade, looking across the road to a small garden. Its decoration and furnishing may look dated, but the atmosphere is friendly, and everything is clean and well cared for. The bedrooms are simple, but reasonably spacious and comfortable, many with river views. Food is carefully prepared and sound value, and served in a new restaurant with river views.

Nearby Church of Notre Dame; Jumièges (15 km) – abbey ruins.

19 Quai Guilbaud 76490 Caudebec-en-Caux
Tel 35.96.25.11
Fax 35.96.68.15
Location in middle of town beside river, 36 km NW of Rouen; with garden and private car parking
Meals breakfast, lunch, dinner
Prices rooms 180F-340F; meals 60F-175F
Rooms 15 double, 3 with bath, 12 with shower (one twin), one single with shower; all rooms have central heating, TV, phone
Facilities dining-room, sitting-room
Credit cards AE, DC, MC, V
Children accepted
Disabled no special facilities
Pets accepted
Closed Feb
Proprietors families Gremoud and Philippe

Village inn, Martin-Église

Auberge du Clos Normand

This simple old *auberge* epitomizes the rustic appeal of Normandy. It is set in countryside, close to a forest, and built of patterned brick and timber with a flowery garden and stream behind. Inside, ceilings are criss-crossed with beams adorned with plates and ornaments; brass pots gleam on the walls and farm noises drift through the windows; and, last but not least, M. Hauchecorne's cooking is classically Norman, involving much cholesterol and alcohol. Bedrooms (in a converted outbuilding) are attractive and comfortable, says a satisfied reporter.

Nearby Dieppe – château/museum; beaches along coast.

22 Rue Henri IV, Martin-Église 76370 Neuville-les-Dieppe
Tel 35.04.40.34
Location in countryside on D1, 5 km SE of Dieppe; with garden, ample car parking
Meals breakfast, lunch, dinner
Prices rooms 260F-460F; breakfast 32F; DB&B 340F-440F
Rooms 8 double, 5 with bath, 3 with shower (2 twin); one family room with bath; one mini-suite; all rooms have central heating, phone, TV
Facilities dining-room, sitting-room
Credit cards AE, MC, V
Children welcome **Disabled** no special facilities **Pets** welcome if well behaved (50F)
Closed mid-Nov to mid-Dec, 1st week Apr; Mon evening, Tue **Proprietor** M. Regis Hauchecorne

Seine-Maritime

Hôtel de la Cathédrale

This ancient hotel is a matter of yards from the cathedral, tucked away down a narrow pedestrian street. Behind its half-timbered façade, the building rambles around a pretty informal courtyard, with staircases and corridors wandering off in all directions. Some parts of the building are, in fact, much less ancient than the exterior suggests, and you might find yourself staying in a room built in the 1930s rather than the 1390s. Most of the chintzy, traditional-style bedrooms have been renovated satisfactorily over recent years. There is no restaurant, but a wide choice of places to eat nearby.

Nearby Cathedral, churches of St-Maclou and St-Ouen, Palais de Justice, Place du Vieux Marché.

12 Rue St-Romain 76000 Rouen **Tel** 35.71.57.95 **Fax** 35.70.15.54 **Location** in middle of old city, next to cathedral; public car parking nearby **Meals** breakfast **Prices** rooms 250F-365F; breakfast 30F **Rooms** 23 double and one	family room, all with bath or shower (3 twin); all rooms have central heating, phone, TV **Facilities** breakfast room, sitting-area **Credit cards** MC, V **Children** accepted **Disabled** access difficult **Pets** accepted **Closed** never **Proprietor** M. Olivier-Perrot

Le Saint-Pierre

Giselle and Bernard Huet's smart restaurant-with-rooms by the Seine continues to thrive, with the kitchen now under the close direction of new young chef, Joseph Prévost, and prices moderated to combat the recession. Showy modern decoration dominates, especially in the airy riverside restaurant, decorated in bright colours. The cooking is professional and inventive, with some interesting *bonnes bouches* offered at various stages of the meal. Even the cheapest menu is now available at weekends or late in the evening. The bedrooms mostly overlook the river; and there is a pleasant waterside terrace.

Nearby Rouen – cathedral, old town, museums.

La Bouille 76530 Grand Couronne **Tel** 35.18.01.01 **Fax** 35.18.12.76 **Location** on banks of the Seine, 20 km SW of Rouen; public car parking; garden **Meals** breakfast, lunch, dinner **Prices** rooms 280F-350F; menus 140F-240F **Rooms** 7 double rooms, 4 with bath, 3 with shower; all rooms	have central heating, phone, TV **Facilities** bar, sitting-room **Credit cards** AE, DC, MC, V **Children** accepted if well behaved **Disabled** no special facilities **Pets** accepted **Closed** Sun night, Mon **Proprietor** Bernard Huet

Manche

Auberge de la Sélune

Readers continue to write in endorsing our original enthusiastic description of this splendid small hotel. It offers excellent value for money and it makes a perfectly satisfactory base for touring Normandy and making excursions into Brittany. As a result, the *auberge* tends to be pretty busy in high season.

It is difficult to decide whether the housekeeping or the food earns the prize, as both are first-class. The whole place is pleasantly decorated – mainly in bright and stylish prints – and spotlessly kept; there are fluffy towels and endless hot water, crisp linen and sound beds. Jean-Pierre Girres's cooking is excellent; his fish, seafood and *pâtisserie* are particularly well regarded; crab pie is one of his noted specialities. The pretty and spacious dining-room is popular with locals, and dinner can take some time to serve – but there is not much else to occupy your time in the evening here. Breakfast is above average, too.

Josette Girres is not a chatty hostess, but her welcome is genuinely warm. The hotel fronts directly on to the street, so parking is awkward. To compensate, there is a little garden at the back beside the Sélune. We have never managed to get a satisfactory photo of this place. Can some camera-toting reader help?

Nearby Salmon fishing (river Sélune); Avranches (10 km) – museum; Le Mont-St-Michel (15 km) – fortified abbey on island.

2 Rue St-Germain 50220 Ducey
Tel 33.48.53.62
Fax 33.48.90.30
Location by river in village, on N176 11 km SE of Avranches; with small garden and some car parking
Meals breakfast, lunch, dinner
Prices rooms 255F-275F; breakfast 38F; menus 75F-190F
Rooms 19 double, all with bath (5 twin); one single; one family room with bath; all rooms have central heating, phone; TV on request
Facilities sitting-room, bar, conference room; salmon fishing
Credit cards DC, MC, V
Children accepted
Disabled no special facilities
Pets not accepted
Closed approximately mid-Jan to mid-Feb
Proprietor Jean-Pierre Girres

Photo: Le Saint-Pierre (facing page)

Manche

Seaside town hotel, St-Vaast-la-Hougue

Hotel de France et des Fuchsias

This perennially popular halt for Cherbourg ferry passengers remains resolutely French, despite the overwhelming British clientele, and wins a place here despite the large number of rooms. The emphasis is on the restaurant; and the expressions of delight at the superb seafood platters, or the wonderfully presented produce from the Brix family farm, prove that the customers are happy. The wine list offers plenty of half-bottles and good-value options, the service is friendly and efficient, the atmosphere warm – whether in the cosy dining- room or in the light conservatory, complete with very large fuschia. An added bonus is the delightful English-style garden. At the far end is the hotel's annexe, a recently converted town house, where bed-rooms are more spacious and decoration more sophisticated than in the fairly simple ones in the main part of the hotel. A 2/3-person suite has apparently been created there, and a new ground-floor bedroom is planned for this year.

It would be a shame to think of this well-run hotel only for a stop-over; it is a serious contender for a short-break holiday, in all seasons, provided that you seek little more than an idle time. **Nearby** museum, fortifications; Normandy beaches.

18 rue Marechal Foch
50550 Saint-Vaast-la-Hougue
Tel 33.54.42.26
Fax 33.43.46.79
Location in quiet street near fishing port and marina; with garden
Meals breakfast, lunch, dinner
Prices rooms 140F-410F; suite 550F; menus 72F (weekdays only)-240FF
Rooms 32 double, 27 with bath, 2 with shower; all rooms have central heating, phone; almost all have TV
Facilities dining-room, sitting-room
Credit cards AE, DC, MC, V
Children welcome; special menu available
Disabled access only to dining-room **Pets** tolerated
Closed early Jan to late Feb; Mon, except Jul, Aug and early Sep
Proprietor Mme Brix

Manche

La Maurandière

This lovely B&B enjoys one of the most idyllic settings you could hope to find. The Duparts restored their stone farmhouse to a very high standard about ten years ago and, although the precarious wooden staircase to the first floor is not to be attempted in stilettos, the spacious bedrooms are delightful. One of the rooms, with its own bathroom, is in a converted outbuilding, and you can even have a romantic private breakfast outside your own French windows. Other guests can have breakfast in the garden, too. The selection of jams and honey (and sometimes croissants and brioches) Mme Dupart provides is delicious.

Nearby Mortain (10 km); Vire (15 km); Avranches (35 km).

50150 Sourdeval
Tel 33.59.65.44
Location in rural setting, 3 km S of Sourdeval via D82, then D182, about 35 km W of Avranches; with garden and car parking
Meals breakfast, snacks
Prices rooms 180F-250F with breakfast
Rooms 2 double, 2 family rooms, one with bath, 3 with shower; all rooms have central heating
Facilities breakfast room, sitting-room with TV
Credit cards not accepted
Children welcome
Disabled one ground floor room
Pets not accepted
Closed never
Proprietor Evelyn Dupart

Verte Campagne

Verte Campagne lies deep in the countryside and is all you might expect from an 18thC Norman farmhouse. The building is covered in creepers, the garden is bursting with flowers and the interior, full of old ceramics and copper pots, is cosy and inviting. The dining-room is charming and intimate – pride of place going to a large stone fireplace, where log fires blaze in winter. Bedrooms in the main building vary considerably in size (the larger ones are very spacious) and all are delightfully decorated. There's also one less comfortable annexe suite.

Nearby Coutances (10 km); Hambye (15 km); Mont-St-Michel.

Hameau Chevallier 50660 Trelly
Tel 33.47.65.33
Location in countryside 1.5 km outside village, 12 km S of Coutances; with garden and ample car parking
Meals breakfast, lunch, dinner
Prices rooms 200F-350F; menus 140F-320F
Rooms 7 double, 5 with bath (3 twin); one single; one family room in annexe with shower; all rooms have central heating, phone
Facilities 2 dining-rooms, 2 sitting-rooms
Credit cards MC, V
Children welcome
Disabled one suitable bedroom in annexe
Pets not accepted
Closed 14 Nov to 6 Jan; restaurant Sun dinner and Mon out of season
Proprietor M & Mme Bernou

Manche

Hotel le Conquérant

In the dour and atmospheric little port/resort of Barfleur, in the north-east of the Cotentin peninsula, the fine grey-stone 17thC building now housing the Conquérant blends in well with its surroundings. A mere shell's-throw from the port, it offers a peaceful halt for travellers, and is inviting enough for a longer stay, with its spacious garden and modest but comfortable bedrooms (many suitable for families). Catherine prepares crêpes for afternoon teas or supper, served in an attractive room with a large fireplace. There are several amenable restaurants nearby.

Nearby invasion beaches; Cap de la Hague (50 km)

16-18 rue St-Thomas Becket
50760 Barfleur
Tel 33.54.00.82
Location in main street near fishing port and marina; with garden; courtyard car parking available for supplement
Meals breakfast, tea, light suppers
Prices rooms 150F-350F; breakfast 37F/41F; supper 70F-100F
Rooms 17 double, 2 with bath,

9 with shower; all rooms have phone; 5 have satellite TV
Facilities breakfast/tea room
Credit cards MC, V
Children welcome
Disabled no special facilities
Pets not accepted
Closed never
Proprietors Mme Delomenede

Hôtel Saint-Pierre

The best way to see France's premier tourist attraction is to stay there – in the few hours of relative peace after the day-trippers have left, the mount has a magic that even the daytime invasion has not managed to destroy. Of the many similar-seeming hostelries that line the main street at the foot of the rock, the Saint-Pierre is the pick. Its dining-rooms and brasserie-bar (serving food all day) are satisfyingly rustic, its recently renovated bedrooms tastefully decorated and comfortable. Happily efficient service, good plain food.

Nearby Abbey of St Michel, ramparts.

BP 16, 50116 Le
Mont-Saint-Michel
Tel 33.60.14.03
Fax 33.48.59.82
Location on the island, first hotel on right from entrance to Mont St-Michel; car parking 200m away (porters)
Meals breakfast, lunch, dinner
Prices rooms 450F-850F; breakfast 45F, dinner 120F-180F
Rooms 15 double, 5 with bath,

10 with shower; 5 family rooms, all with bath or shower; all have central heating, phone, TV, hairdrier
Facilities 3 dining-rooms, sitting-room, bar
Credit cards AE, V
Children welcome
Disabled access impossible
Pets 30F supplement
Closed Dec to Feb
Proprietors M. and Mme Gaulois

Calvados

Auberge du Prieuré

The Millets' former country rectory, pale stone beneath a steep slate roof, has made a delicious little hotel. Inside, it is all beams, stone walls, country antiques and earthy colours. There is a surprisingly big dining-room, with easy chairs before an open fire at one end; attic rooms are no less spacious than those on the first floor, but rather dark. Outside, a lush garden is surrounded by Norman orchards. Traditional food is offered – one mid-priced menu and a more expansive *carte*. The Millets have just completed their latest project – five double bedrooms in a new annexe.

Nearby Pont-l'Évêque; Honfleur (15 km); Deauville (20 km).

St-André-d'Hébertot 14130
Pont-l'Évêque
Tel 31.64.03.03
Fax 31.64.16.66
Location by church in village, S of N175 7 km E of Pont-l'Évêque; in gardens with some private car parking
Meals breakfast, lunch, dinner
Prices rooms 310F-980F; breakfast 45F, meals 145F-320F
Rooms 12 double (5 twin), 11 with bath; all rooms have central heating, phone, hairdrier, TV, radio
Facilities billiard room, library; swimming-pool
Credit cards MC, V
Children welcome; special meals **Disabled** ground-floor rooms **Pets** 30F supplement
Closed 15 Jan to 28 Feb; restaurant only Wed
Proprietors M. and Mme Millet

Hôtel d'Argouges

Even without the famous 'tapestry', the pretty and historic town of Bayeux would be worth a visit, and this simple and perfectly placed 18thC house makes an ideal base for exploring the coast, the sights of Caen and – as the hotel has no dining-room – the restaurants of the area. There is a rather formal sitting-room and a small garden. Bedrooms vary in size and are simply furnished; some are in an annexe across the courtyard, but none faces the main road.

Nearby Cathedral, Bayeux Tapestry; Caen (28 km).

21 Rue St-Patrice 14400
Bayeux
Tel 31.92.88.86
Location off busy square in middle of town; with garden and private car parking (some garages)
Meals breakfast
Prices rooms 260F-390F; suites 480F; breakfast 35F
Rooms 22 double (13 twin), 17 with bath, 5 with shower; one single and 2 suites, all with bath ; all rooms have central heating, phone, minibar
Facilities lobby, sitting-room, breakfast room
Credit cards AE, DC, MC, V
Children welcome; baby-sitting available
Disabled access difficult
Pets accepted in bedrooms
Closed never
Proprietors M. and Mme Daniel Auregan

Calvados

Converted mill, Clécy

Hostellerie du Moulin du Vey

This old, creeper-clad water-mill stands right at the heart of some of the best scenery in the region, where the river Orne has carved a majestic valley between green, rolling hills. It is within easy driving distance of the ferry port at Caen, and makes an attractive first- or last-night stop.

Both the buildings and the park-like surroundings of the mill are beautifully kept, and there is a pleasant waterside terrace for eating and drinking, with a garden beyond. Food in the half-timbered, rather barn-like restaurant, just across the courtyard from the main building, is unremarkable by exacting Norman standards but it is carefully prepared and served, and the less expensive menus are sound value. Bedrooms are comfortable, furnished simply but with touches of style, and reasonably priced by Norman standards. Some rooms are in annexes: the Manoir de Placy, 400 metres away, and the Relais de Surosne, 3 km away on the other side of the village, a peaceful, small Gothic-style house with a lush garden.

Nearby Suisse Normande region; Thury-Harcourt (10 km) – ruined château, park and garden; Falaise (30 km) – castle, William the Conqueror's birthplace; Caen (35 km) – Normandy Museum.

Le Vey 14570 Clécy
Tel 31.69.71.08
Fax 31.69.14.14
Location 2 km E of Clécy and 35 kms S of Caen; with river terrace and car parking
Meals breakfast, lunch, dinner
Prices rooms 380F-490F; menus 135F-370F
Rooms 17 double (7 twin) all with bath; 2 family rooms, one with bath, 1 with shower; all rooms have central heating, phone
Facilities dining-room, TV room, banqueting-room, conference room
Credit cards AE, DC, MC, V
Children accepted
Disabled no special facilities
Pets accepted but not in dining-room
Closed Dec
Proprietor Denise Leduc

Eure

Cochon d'Or et Petit Castel

These two small hotels on opposite sides of the main street are under the same ownership. One (the Petit Castel) offers simple and pleasant modern-style bedrooms (double-glazed on the road-side), a sitting-room and small garden. The Cochon d'Or has rather more old-fashioned bedrooms with fewer facilities, together with an extremely civilized and comfortable restaurant. The food is above average even for this well-endowed part of the country, and excellent value too. This small town is well situated both for the coast and the charming manor houses of the Pays d'Auge; it is also very near to the Caen/Paris motorway.

Nearby Deauville (28 km); Honfleur (15 km).

Place du General-de-Gaulle 27210 Beuzeville **Tel** 32.57.70.46 (Cochon) 32.57.76.08 (Petit Castel) **Fax** 32.42.25.70 **Location** in middle of small town; Petit Castel has small garden; near public car park **Meals** breakfast, lunch, dinner **Prices** rooms 160F- 310F; menus 75F-220F; breakfast 32F **Rooms** 21 double (6 twin); all with bath in Petit Castel; one with bath, 4 with shower, in Cochon d'Or; two family rooms; all rooms have central heating, phone; some have TV **Facilities** dining-room, sitting-room **Credit cards** MC, V **Children** accepted **Pets** not accepted **Disabled** no special facilities **Closed** mid-Dec to mid-Jan; restaurant Mon **Proprietor** Charles Folleau

Auberge de l'Abbaye

Le Bec-Hellouin is a great medieval Benedictine monastery, much ruined and partially restored, and one of Normandy's major sights. Despite this, the village which has grown up around the church remains small and peaceful, and the timbered *auberge*, with a terrace of sun-shaded tables overlooking the village green, seems almost too good to be true – the archetypal atmospheric Norman inn, simple and welcoming. The tiled floors, rough stone walls and gleaming furniture set the scene for typical regional meals – with apples and cider, of course, as well as quantities of cream. The rustic-style bedrooms are simple and cheerful. The lack of a sitting-room does not bother most guests.

Nearby Abbey; Pont-Audemer (20 km) – church of St-Ouen.

Le Bec-Hellouin 27800 Brionne **Tel** 32.44.86.02 **Fax** 32.46.32.23 **Location** in middle of village, 5 km N of Brionne; with ample public car parking **Meals** breakfast, lunch, dinner **Prices** rooms 350F-380F; breakfast 35F, meals 125F-250F **Rooms** 10 double, all with bath (3 twin); one family room; all rooms have central heating, phone **Facilities** bar, dining-room **Credit cards** MC, V **Children** accepted **Disabled** no special facilities **Pets** accepted **Closed** early Jan to mid-Feb; also Mon evening and Tue out of season **Proprietor** M. Sergent

Eure

Le Petit Coq aux Champs

This smart, secluded thatched house, amid rolling meadows and sweeping forests in the Risle valley, offers an intriguing mixture of the rustic, the sophisticated and the downright idiosyncratic.

The building, mostly 19thC, has two main wings – one mainly for eating, one mainly for sleeping – with a large, airy, modern extension between. The style varies considerably – modern cane furniture in the large sitting-room, while antiques predominate in the traditional-style restaurant, l'Andrien, which has a fine oak dresser at one end and a huge open fireplace at the other. A small, intimate piano bar has been squeezed into the back of the new part of the building. The bedrooms are all furnished and arranged differently, some brightly coloured, others more restrained – none of them is particularly large.

Fabienne Desmonts and Jean-Marie Huard, who took over the hotel in 1989, continue to improve and upgrade the facilities. Jean-Marie, who has returned to his Norman roots after some years in Paris, pays serious attention to detail, presentation and local tradition – with impressive results.

Nearby fishing, golf; Pont-Audemer – half-timbered houses, church of St-Ouen; Honfleur (30 km) – old port, 15thC wooden church.

Campigny 27500 Pont-Audemer **Tel** 32.41.04.19 **Fax** 32.56.06.25 **Location** in countryside, 6 km S of Pont-Audemer; in gardens with ample car parking **Meals** breakfast, lunch, dinner **Prices** rooms 420F-790F; breakfast 53F, menus 190F-310F **Rooms** 12 double (4 twin), one family room, one suite, all with bath; all rooms have central heating, phone; TV on request	**Facilities** sitting-room, 4 dining-rooms, bar; swimming-pool **Credit cards** AE, DC, MC, V **Children** very welcome **Disabled** dining-rooms and 8 bedrooms are on ground floor **Pets** welcome **Closed** 3 weeks in Jan **Proprietors** Fabienne Desmonts and Jean Marie Huard

Eure

La Haye-le-Comte

There's an energetic air about this pleasant little country house, dating from the sixteenth century: its extensive grassy grounds offer golf practice as well as tennis, and detailed maps are available suggesting local walks ranging from 3 km to 12 km in length. Rooms – as their modest prices suggest – are nothing special, but are neatly done out and airy, with big windows. Food is quite wide-ranging, with as much seafood as meat in evidence.
Nearby golf; Château Gaillard (18 km); Monet Museum (30 km); Rouen (30 km) – cathedral, old town.

4 Route de la Haye-le-Comte **27400 Louviers** **Tel** 32.40.00.40 **Fax** 32.25.03.85 **Location** in countryside, 500m SW of town on D113; in 12-acre grounds with ample private car parking **Meals** breakfast, lunch, dinner **Prices** rooms 180F-450F; breakfast 45F, menus 110F-160F, chidren's 65F; 10% reduction for 3 nights **Rooms** 13 double (6 twin), 2	single, one family room, all with bath; all have central heating, phone, satellite TV **Facilities** dining-room, sitting-room; tennis, golf driving range and practice green **Credit cards** AE, MC, V **Children** welcome **Disabled** 2 specially equipped bedrooms on ground floor **Pets** accepted except in restaurant (35F charge) **Closed** Jan to Mar **Proprietor** Pierre Granoux

Château de la Râpée

At the end of a long rutted forest track from Bazincourt lies this 19thC Gothic mansion, grandly conceived but executed on a modest scale – a perfect period piece. Inside, original features have been carefully preserved and, although rather dark in places, the house has been pleasantly furnished with antiques and reproductions. Some of the spacious, calm bedrooms are stately, with fine views, plenty of antiques and creaky wooden floors; others verge on the eccentric. The food is unremarkable – generous portions of traditional regional cooking.
Nearby Gisors – castle; Jouy-sous-Thelle (25 km) – church.

Bazincourt-sur-Epte 27140 Gisors **Tel** 32.55.11.61 **Location** in countryside 4 km NW of Gisors; in small park with ample car parking **Meals** breakfast, lunch, dinner **Prices** rooms 380F-480F; menus 150F-205F **Rooms** 13 double, 11 with bath, 2 with shower (5 twin); 2 rooms form an apartment; all rooms have central heating,	phone **Facilities** sitting-room, 2 dining-rooms, bar, banqueting-room; riding stables next door **Credit cards** AE, DC, V **Children** by arrangement **Disabled** no special facilities **Pets** small ones accepted **Closed** mid-Jan to end Feb, late Aug; restaurant Wed **Proprietors** M. and Mme Bergeron

Eure

Town inn, Pont-Audemer

Auberge du Vieux Puits

Although war-damaged Pont-Audemer still has a charming historic centre, with timbered houses and canalized streams, it is rather dwarfed by the nondescript suburbs which have grown up around it. The Vieux Puits shines out like a beacon – a wonderful, half-timbered, 17thC building (once a tannery), all crooked beams and leaded windows. The inside is a medievalist's dream, with its twisting wooden staircases and dark beams hung with shining copper and ancient pewter.

Jaques Foltz and his charming wife bring out the best in the building, by keeping the style simple and restrained. The small, intimate salon and dining-rooms are carefully furnished with antiques, and are decorated with fresh flowers. Three of the bedrooms in the old building have been recently converted into a family apartment; the other three are quite small but full of character. Across the peaceful, informal courtyard (decked out with flowers in summer, and presided over by a magnificent weeping willow) a wing has been added to provide six new bedrooms – smarter and well equipped, but in keeping.

M. Foltz sees the *auberge* very much as a restaurant with rooms, and those who want to stay are encouraged to have dinner. To do so is hardly a penance, given the kitchen's high standards and the interesting dishes on the rarely changing menus and *carte*.

Nearby Half-timbered houses, church of St-Ouen, the canalised Risle; Honfleur (25 km).

6 Rue Notre-Dame-du-Pré
27500 Pont-Audemer
Tel 32.41.01.48
Location near middle of town; with small garden and car parking
Meals breakfast, lunch, dinner
Prices rooms 240F-400F; menus 185F-290F
Rooms 12 double (4 twin), 7 with bath, 4 with shower; 11 have phone
Facilities dining-rooms,
bar/sitting-area
Credit cards MC, V
Children welome; special meals on request
Disabled 2 ground-floor rooms, specially equipped
Pets accepted in dining-room
Closed 20 Dec to 28 Jan; Mon evening, Tue in low season
Proprietors Jacques and Hélène Foltz

Eure

Riverside hotel, St-Pierre-du-Vauvray

Hostellerie St-Pierre

A bizarre concoction: a modern building, triangular in plan with a turret on one corner, dressed up with fake timbers to look like a traditional Norman manor-house – and located only a short drive from the Paris-Rouen motorway. But don't dismiss it. The St-Pierre is set on the banks of the Seine, far enough from the traffic noise to justify membership of the *Relais du Silence* consortium – and it has other attractions too.

Not the least of these is the cuisine – classical in style but inventive in approach, and of outstanding quality, with the emphasis on fish and seafood – witness the enormous tank of langoustes and other consumables dominating the heavily decorated dining-room (which has big picture windows looking on to the river). The hotel's other public areas are limited, and solid rather than elegant – the baroque/rococo decoration does not suit all tastes – but the bedrooms are comfortable and well equipped, and many have balconies overlooking the river. (For the full flavour of this eccentric establishment, opt for the top room in the turret, with exposed beams and token four-poster.) The garden, which stretches down to the water's edge, is a relaxing place to sit. The hotel is family-run; service is friendly. 'Certainly worth another stop' was a German visitor's verdict.

Nearby Louviers – church of Notre-Dame; Acquigny (10 km) – château; Gaillon (15 km) – château; Giverny (30 km).

Chemin des Amoureux 27430 St-Pierre-du-Vauvray
Tel 32.59.93.29
Fax 32.59.41.93
Location on edge of village 8 km E of Louviers, beside Seine; with gardens and car parking
Meals breakfast, lunch, dinner
Prices rooms 480F-840F; menus 145F-325F
Rooms 14 double (4 twin), all with bath; all rooms have central heating, phone, TV; most have minibar
Facilities dining-room, sitting-room
Credit cards V
Children accepted
Disabled lift/elevator
Pets accepted at extra charge
Closed mid-Nov to mid-Mar; restaurant only, Tue, and Wed lunch
Proprietors Potier family

Eure

Manor house hotel, Verneuil-sur-Avre

Le Clos

Our inspectors could hardly lavish enough praise on the Clos, which seems to embody all that is best in French château-style hotels without the all-too-common pretension and vulgarity.

The Clos is on the edge of the pleasant little country town of Verneuil, in a quiet back street – though with a busy bypass visible (and just audible) in the background. It is a rather comical turn-of-the-century building of highly patterned brick-work, with a mock-medieval tower, set in well-kept leafy grounds with lawns and creeping willows that are overlooked by a large terrace. Inside, everything is of the highest quality: smart, antique-style cane chairs, heavy linen tablecloths and huge bunches of flowers in the dining-room, neat reproduction armchairs in the salon, chintzy drapes in the bedrooms, deep pile carpets everywhere – even in the luxurious bathrooms. There is plenty of space too – although the building is not large, the bedrooms are not cramped; all of them are light and airy, and furnished in individual style. Patrick Simon masterminds the kitchen, where he produces a range of classical dishes with absolute professionalism and finesse. Desserts no longer come on a trolley, but are no less tempting.

All this comes at a price – but is well worth it if you feel like pampering yourself for a night or two.

Nearby Church of la Madeleine (flamboyant tower); Château de Pin au Haras (40 km) – stud farm; Chartres – cathedral.

98 Rue de la Ferté-Vidame
27130 Verneuil-sur-Avre
Tel 32.32.21.81
Fax 32.32.21.36
Location on edge of town, 56 km NW of Chartres and 39 km SW of Evreux; with gardens and car parking
Meals breakfast, lunch, dinner
Prices rooms 600F-780F, suites 780F-880F; apartments 950F-1,100F; DB&B 775F-925F; breakfast 80F
Rooms 6 double, 2 suites, all with bath; 3 apartments with bath/jacuzzi; all rooms have central heating, phone, TV
Facilities 2 dining-rooms, sitting-room, bar; tennis court, jacuzzi
Credit cards AE, DC, MC, V
Children welcome
Disabled 3 rooms in garden on ground floor
Pets accepted **Closed** Dec and Jan; Mon out of season
Proprietors Patrick and Colette Simon

Orne

Manoir du Lys

The Manoir du Lys is a typically Norman half-timbered hunting lodge, geraniums at its foot and dripping from its balconies. A recent harmonious extension has added 12 new bedrooms – all spacious and well equipped, with stylish furnishings. Most have balconies overlooking the gardens. Marie-France oversees the smart dining-rooms where you can enjoy her son Franck's delicious cuisine, which is rooted in local tradition but acknowledges modern preferences. There is also a cosy bar/sitting-room with a huge open fire and a grand piano (played on Friday nights).
Nearby Andaines forest – walking, riding, cycling.

La Croix Gauthier, Route de Juvigny, 61140 Bagnoles-de-l'Orne **Tel** 33.37.80.69 **Fax** 33.30.05.80
Location in middle of countryside in forest of Andaines; with car parking
Meals breakfast, lunch, dinner
Prices rooms 300F-750F; menus 130F-450F
Rooms 20 double, 19 with bath, one with shower; 3 suites; all have phone, TV, minibar
Facilities dining-room, sitting-room/bar, billiards; tennis court
Credit cards AE, DC, MC, V
Children welcome; special menu 80F **Disabled** no special facilities **Pets** dogs accepted in bedrooms only 35F
Closed 7 Jan to 28 Feb; Sun evening and Mon from Nov to Easter **Proprietor** Marie-France and Paul Quinton

Bois Joli

The Bois Joli might be an escapee from the Black Forest – a dignified, little 19thC building on three floors, partly timbered, surrounded by its own terraces and leafy gardens. The hotel is immaculately kept, and Serge and Claudine Gatti are intent on preserving the intimate, friendly atmosphere for which it is known. The centrepiece is the panelled restaurant, which serves well-prepared regional dishes – 'a cut above average' says one reader, though another disagrees. The bedrooms are notably airy and spacious, with floral wallpapers and fabrics.
Nearby Andaines Forest – walking, riding, cycling.

12 Ave P du Rozier 61140 Bagnoles-de-l'Orne
Tel 33.37.92.77
Location close to middle of resort, facing the racecourse; in gardens, with private car parking
Meals breakfast, lunch, dinner
Prices rooms 195F-495F; meals 115F-295F
Rooms 18 double (7 twin), 2 family rooms; all with bath; all have central heating, phone; TV on request
Facilities dining-room, sitting-room, lift/elevator, sauna, hammam, solarium, gym
Credit cards AE, DC, MC, V
Children welcome
Disabled no special facilities
Pets accepted, but not in dining-room
Closed never
Proprietors Serge and Claudine Gatti

Orne

Converted mill, Villeray

Moulin de Villeray

This previously derelict mill building was painstakingly transformed into a top-class hotel and restaurant by previous owners. It has now been taken over by Muriel and Christian Eelsen. It is hardly what you would call a simple rustic retreat – take a look at the prices – but the rushing stream and the mill-wheel are still there. And the setting is delectable, on the edge of a neat village of red-roofed stone houses, in rolling, wooded farmland.

Much of the tall, white-painted *moulin* has been rebuilt rather than restored, but its main focus, the restaurant, retains old beams and a huge fireplace – plus a view of the mill-wheel. Comfortable and spacious, with food more than matching up to the surroundings, the dining-room is proof that 'serious eating' need not be taken too seriously. Served with confidence and flair, specialities include salmon marinated in lemon, fillets of sole with crab sauce, curried hare, rack of lamb with basil – and even more impressive desserts. The occasional eccentricity in the dining-room – such as the cheese being served from a goat's skin – is easily forgiven.

The rest of the building – the salon where guests gather for drinks, and the very comfortable bedrooms – have recently been brightly refurbished. Outside there is a pleasant terrace where meals can be taken, beyond that a large, relaxing and informal garden bordering the river, and beyond that, countryside.

Nearby Nogent – Gothic and Renaissance buildings; Chartres (55 km) – cathedral; Alençon (55 km) – lace- making.

Villeray 61110 Condeau
Tel 33.73.30.22
Fax 33.73.38.28
Location at foot of village, 10 km NW of Nogent; with garden and car parking
Meals breakfast, lunch, dinner
Prices rooms 480F-740F; suite 1,150F; menus 130F-300F
Rooms 14 double, all with bath and shower (3 twin); one suite; all rooms have phone, minibar
Facilities sitting-room, dining-room, bar; helipad
Credit cards AE, DC, V
Children accepted
Disabled access to restaurant
Pets accepted (must be kept on lead)
Closed Jan to mid-Feb
Proprietors Christian and Muriel Eelsen

Eure-et-Loir

Country inn, Cloyes-sur-le-Loir

Hostellerie St-Jacques

An old coaching inn dating from the 16thC, the Hostellerie St-Jacques has lately enjoyed a new lease of life as an *étape gastronomique*. Eric Thureau took over from Simon and Françoise Le Bras in 1988, and has introduced many improvements.

The dining-room, looking out over the garden, is intimate and elegant – furnished with bold fabrics and antiques. But in good weather meals are served in the shade of the trees in the garden, which is a lush expanse leading down to the banks of the little Loir. The bedrooms (at the back, looking over the garden) have been smartly done out in designer fabrics and cherry-wood reproduction antiques. The food is good enough to have retained the Michelin star won by the previous owners.

Reports on the St-Jacques veer from complete satisfaction through 'unremarkable' to the downright complaining. More reports would be very welcome.

Nearby Châteaudun (10 km) – feudal château; Vendôme – la Trinité, Porte St Georges; Beaugency (45 km) – bridge, keep.

Place du Marché aux Oeufs
28220 Cloyes-sur-le-Loir
Tel 37.98.40.08
Location in village, 28 km NE of Vendôme; with garden and car parking
Meals breakfast, lunch, dinner
Prices rooms 280F-480F; menus 230F-400F
Rooms 22 double, 18 with bath, 4 with shower (5 twin); one family room; all rooms have central heating, phone, TV
Facilities dining-room, sitting-room, bar
Credit cards MC, V
Children welcome
Disabled lift/elevator
Pets accepted in room and dining-room
Closed 15 Dec to 31 Jan
Proprietor Eric Thureau

Côtes-d'Armor

Le Repaire de Kerroc'h

This beautiful 18thC house has an enviable position right on the quay of the fishing port of Paimpol and has been beautifully restored and maintained by previous owners. The bedrooms (generally rather small) are well-furnished and equipped with minibar and double-glazing; bathrooms are luxurious and spacious. There is a small dining-room, and an attractive little bar with 1930s decoration. Outside are a couple of tables for drinks or lunches. M. Broc is a recent arrival; since taking over, he has added five bedrooms – all smartly equipped and tastefully furnished – and a new dining-room. Regular visitors will be pleased to hear that he carries on the tradition of excellent breakfasts.

Nearby Arcouest Point (5 km); Tréguier (15 km).

29 Quai Morand, Port de Plaisance 22500 Paimpol
Tel 96.20.50.13
Location on quayside in middle of town; with car parking on street
Meals breakfast, lunch, dinner
Prices rooms 390F-450F; apartment 580F; breakfast 45F, menus 95F-350F
Rooms 10 double (4 twin), one single, one apartment, all with bath; all rooms have phone, minibar, TV
Facilities bar/salon, dining-room, lift/elevator
Credit cards MC, V **Children** welcome **Disabled** no special facilities **Pets** accepted (50F)
Closed 2 weeks Feb and Nov, one week Jun, Wed lunch
Proprietor J C Broc

Château de Coatguélen

This fine 19thC château, set in a large park, has a relaxed and friendly atmosphere. Families are well catered for: there is a playroom and good sports facilities, and the new manager, M. Lemée, is creating a new network of 'bush trails'. Bedrooms are large and elegantly decorated, with smart bathrooms; the attractive, formal restaurant (light, innovative cooking) opens on to a pleasant terrace. Throughout, antiques and flowers contribute to a cared-for ambience. The hotel has its own golf course.

Nearby Coast (8 km); Arcouest (20 km); La Roche-Jagu (25 km)

Pléhédel 22290 Lanvollon
Tel 96.22.31.24
Fax 96.22.37.67
Location 26 km NW of St-Brieuc; in own park with ample car parking **Meals** breakfast, lunch, dinner
Prices rooms 500F-1,200F; breakfast 55F, meals 150F-380F, children's menu 70F
Rooms 16 double, all with bath (6 twin); 2 single, both with bath; all rooms have central heating, TV
Facilities dining-room, sitting-room, 2 meeting-rooms; golf (18-hole), swimming-pool, riding, tennis
Credit cards AE, V
Children welcome
Disabled access difficult
Pets not accepted
Closed mid-Nov to end Mar; restaurant only, Mon
Proprietor M. Lemée

Côtes-d'Armor

Seaside hotel, Trébeurden

Ti Al-Lannec

Ti Al-Lannec is a handsome family house on the beautiful 'pink granite' coast of Brittany, completely renovated and opened as a hotel in 1978 by Gérard and Danielle Jouanny, and run by them with a convincing blend of charm, taste and efficiency.

Secluded in wooded grounds, the house stands high up above the sea with a path leading down to the beach; its south-facing terrace has a splendid view looking over the bay of Lannion. It is a supremely comfortable hotel, with that elusive private-house feel. Bedrooms are thoughtfully decorated to feel light and airy but cosy, with fresh flowers and books, small tables and table lamps liberally used. Some have terraces or verandas.

The dining-room has the sea view, and is crisp and fresh with its white linen, rich drapes and old stone walls. Antique and modern furnishings mix well in the comfortable sitting-room, which is dotted with pot plants. A visitor confirms that the food – Danielle's province – is excellent, the service 'five-star' and the welcome for children a genuine one – witness the swing and seesaw on the front lawn.

Nearby Perros-Guirec (15 km) – large resort; Tréguier (30 km).

Allée de Mezo-Guen, BP 3
22560 Trébeurden
Tel 96.23.57.26
Fax 96.23.62.14
Location in wooded grounds above resort, 10 km NW of Lannion; with car parking
Meals breakfast, lunch, dinner
Prices rooms 600F-960F; weekday lunch 125F, dinner menus 190F-370F, children's 85F
Rooms 20 double (8 twin), 2 single, 8 family rooms, all with bath; all rooms have TV, phone
Facilities dining-room, 2 sitting-rooms, bar, billiards room, play room, fitness centre, sauna, jacuzzi
Credit cards AE, MC, V
Children welcome; early meals, baby-sitting available
Disabled lift/elevator; some bedrooms and WCs suitable
Pets accepted in bedrooms at extra charge
Closed 15 Nov to 15 Mar
Proprietors Danielle and Gérard Jouanny

Côtes-d'Armor

Manoir de Lan-Kerellec

Trébeurden is one of the most attractive beach resorts along Brittany's north coast, though that probably matters little to visitors to what is hardly a bucket-and-spade hotel. The charming young Daubés have turned this handsome and unusual old family house into an elegant and welcoming hotel – a member of the Relais & Châteaux group, but one of the least pretentious and most captivating. It stands in trees high above the rocky shore, with splendid views from tall windows – stretch the budget and opt for one of the larger rooms which have the views.
Nearby Perros-Guirec (15 km); Tréguier (30 km).

22560 Trébeurden
Tel 96.23.50.09
Fax 96.23.66.88
Location in residential areaoverlooking the sea, 9 kmNW of Lannion; with small garden and private carparking
Meals breakfast, lunch,dinner
Prices rooms 500F-2,000F; breakfast 65F; meals 140F-350F
Rooms 18 double (12 twin), one single, 2 apartments, all with bath; 3 rooms can have extra bed; all rooms have

central heating, phone,TV
Facilities 2 sitting-rooms, 3 dining-rooms, bar
Credit cards AE, DC, MC, V
Children welcome; specialmenu available
Disabled access possible
Pets accepted
Closed 10 Nov to 15 Mar; restaurant Mon (and Tue lunch in low season)
Proprietor M. Daubé

Kastell Dinec'h

Honeysuckle sprawls over the grey stone walls of this handsome old farmhouse, tucked away down a leafy lane. There is a warm welcome for overseas visitors from Mme Pauwels and her friendly, English-speaking staff. The decoration is *style anglais* too – Laura Ashley wallpapers and a happily informal mix of antique and modern furniture. Bedrooms, some in a converted stable block, are simple, fresh and pretty. Delicious meals – a red 'Repas' from Michelin for notable value – are served in the elegantly rustic dining-room overlooking a lush courtyard.
Nearby Tréguier – cathedral; Château de la Roche-Jagu (10 km).

Rte de Lannion 22220 Tréguier
Tel 96.92.49.39
Fax 96.92.34.02
Location 1.5 km outside town, off D786 to Lannion; with garden and ample car parking
Meals breakfast, dinner
Prices rooms 390F-450F; breakfast 52F, menus 125F-300F
Rooms 14 double, 13 with bath; all rooms have central

heating, phone
Facilities dining-room, sitting-room, TV room; swimming-pool
Credit cards MC, V
Children accepted
Disabled 2 rooms with access
Pets not accepted in public rooms
Closed Jan to mid-Mar, 2 weeks end of Oct
Proprietor Bernard Pauwels

Ille-et-Vilaine

Town mansion, St-Malo

La Korrigane

This handsome, turn-of-the-century mansion near the centre of St-Servan, just south of St-Malo harbour, has been beautifully restored and is furnished throughout with antiques (the room in our picture is typical, not exceptional). The elegant bedrooms are individually decorated, and have comfortable armchairs, beautiful lamps and mirrors, and antique paintings dotted about. A reporter found her room small but 'delightful', with a luxurious bathroom. There are two sitting-rooms, all perfectly in style with the atmosphere of a fine private home. On summery days, you can have your breakfast in the small, pretty garden. There is no restaurant and no licence at present, though the new owner plans a tea room and a bar. An excellent place for a romantic short break without the children.

Nearby Emerald Coast; Château du Bosq (10 km); Dinan

39 Rue Le Pomellec 35403
St-Malo
Tel 99.81.65.85
Fax 99.82.23.89
Location in S part of town, near harbour; with gardens and car parking
Meals breakfast
Prices rooms 400F-650F
Rooms 12 double/twin, all with bath or shower; all rooms have TV, phone, central heating
Facilities 2 sitting-rooms
Credit cards AE, DC, MC, V
Children accepted
Disabled no special facilities
Pets dogs accepted (50F)
Closed never
Proprietor M Marchon

Finistère

Manoir de Moëllien

Restored from a ruin to its former glory in the 1960s, this rather stern granite manor house is now a comfortable hotel with the attraction for families of being only minutes away from some splendid Breton beaches. Its public rooms are very grand – stone walls, massive beams, open fire-places, antique Breton furniture, and ancient portraits. The baronial dining-room and vast first-floor sitting-room are off-set by a cosy rustic bar. Bedrooms are in the old stone stables just outside the courtyard. They are simply but adequately furnished, and what they lack in sophistication, they make up for in fine views of the countryside through their French windows, and their wonderfully peaceful setting.
Nearby beaches; Locronan (2 km), Quimper (20 km).

Plonévez-Porzay 29550
Tel 98.92.50.40
Fax 98.92.55.21
Location in rural setting, 1.5km S of Plonévez-Porzay; with garden and car parking
Meals breakfast, lunch, dinner
Prices rooms 350F; breakfast 40F, menus 118F-300F
Rooms 9 double, one family room, all with bath; all rooms have central heating, phone
Facilities dining-room, bar, terrace
Credit cards AE, DC, MC, V
Children welcome
Disabled access to one bedroom **Pets** accepted
Closed Jan to mid-Mar; restaurant only, Wed, and lunchtime from Oct to Jan
Proprietor M. and Mme Garet

Les Moulins du Duc

This unusual hotel is many people's idea of heaven: utterly secluded in its wooded grounds, with a large and photogenic pond complete with fat, contented ducks. The main building is a former mill, rustic and attractive, with windows overlooking the little river; there is a relaxing modern sitting-room and bar, candlelit dining-rooms (one non-smoking) and an excellent in-door swimming-pool. The accommodation is in two-storey cottages scattered around the grounds; the bedrooms are spacious and well-equipped. Breakfast can be had on the lawn. Our most recent reporter rates the food 'totally delicious.'
Nearby Concarneau (25 km) – Ville Close (walled town).

29350 Moëlan-sur-Mer
Tel 98.39.60.73
Fax 98.39.75.56
Location beside river 2 km N of village, 10 km SW of Quimperlé; in large grounds with ample private parking
Meals breakfast, lunch, dinner
Prices rooms 440F-805F; suites 1,100F- 1,300F; breakfast 55F, menus 150F-330F, children's 60F
Rooms 22 double (11 twin), 5 suites; 22 with bath, 5 with shower; all rooms have phone, TV, minibar
Facilities dining-rooms, bar sitting-room; swimming- pool
Credit cards AE, DC, MC, V
Children welcome
Disabled ground- floor rooms
Pets accepted
Closed mid-Jan to end-Feb
Proprietors Quistrebert family

Finistère

Chez Pierre

A favourite with British visitors, and for obvious reasons: a family seaside *Logis* (about 200 m inland) which is completely without pretension but offers the kind of reliably good, traditional, sea-based cooking that we hope to find in Brittany – while children can have special meals at an earlier hour. Family rooms in the attractive modern annexe next to the turn-of-the-century main house are 'superb – light and spacious', with single beds upstairs and doubles downstairs. We have been unable to extract up-to-date information from the Guillous, so don't rely on our prices.
Nearby Quimper (35 km); Pont-Aven (8 km).

Raguenès-Plage 29139 Nevez
Tel 98.06.81.06
Location in countryside 15 km SE of Concarneau; with terrace, spacious gardens and car parking
Meals breakfast, lunch, dinner
Prices rooms 172F-378F; breakfast 28F, menus 100F-245F; children's menu 75F
Rooms 31 double (13 twin), 4 family rooms, most with bath or shower; all rooms have phone
Facilities 2 dining-rooms, sitting-room, bar, TV room, playroom; garden swing
Credit cards MC, V
Children welcome
Disabled 2 specially adapted rooms
Pets dogs accepted, but not in dining-room
Closed Oct to Mar
Proprietor Xavier Guillou

Hôtel de la Plage

Strictly, the Plage (a Relais & Châteaux member) is too large for our purposes. But readers confirm that it deserves its place here. The hotel combines a splendid seaside setting – the immaculate white building stands in manicured gardens above a vast beach – with one of the best kitchens in Brittany (specialising, of course, in seafood). Mme Le Coz and her staff generate a welcoming atmosphere; service is sometimes a little slow but always friendly, and details are not overlooked. Bedrooms are comfortable, and some have stunning views (worth booking ahead).
Nearby Beach; Locronan (10 km) – town square; Quimper.

Ste-Anne-la-Palud 29127 Plonévez-Porzay
Tel 98.92.50.12
Fax 98.92.56.54
Location in countryside 4 km W of Plonévez and 25 km NW of Quimper; with garden and ample car parking
Meals breakfast, lunch, dinner
Prices rooms 465F-950F; breakfast 70F
Rooms 20 double (10 twin), 2 single, 4 family rooms, all with bath; all rooms have central heating, TV, phone, minibar
Facilities sitting-room, dining-room, bar, conference room
Credit cards AE, DC, MC, V
Children welcome
Disabled lift/elevator
Pets accepted but not in dining-room
Closed mid-Oct to Apr
Proprietor M. Le Coz

Morbihan

Auberge Bretonne

La Roche-Bernard is perched on a headland overlooking the river Vilaine; this is a small, welcoming *auberge*, set on a little square, where cooking takes pride of place. Jacques Thorel, owner and chef, is an exponent of light, natural dishes, using the best of the local ingredients. Bretons come from far afield for the six-course *menu dégustation*, and seafood specialities. The bedrooms are prettily furnished in rural Breton style; six new ones were added a couple of years ago. The public rooms are friendly rather than elegant, particularly the dining-room which is built around a vegetable garden and flowery courtyard.

Nearby Parc de Brière (15 km) – salt marshes; Guérande (25 km) – moated town; Vannes (40 km) – cathedral.

2 Place du Guesclin 56130 La Roche-Bernard
Tel 99.90.60.28
Fax 99.90.85.00
Location overlooking River Vilaine, 30 km SE of Vannes; with car parking in front
Meals breakfast, lunch, dinner
Prices rooms 250F-850F; breakfast 60F; meals 120F-450F

Rooms 11 double, all with bath and shower; all rooms have central heating
Facilities dining-room, bar
Credit cards MC, V
Children accepted
Disabled no special facilities
Pets accepted
Closed 15 Nov to 5 Dec; 5-20 Jan
Proprietor Jacques Thorel

Auberge des Deux Magots

There is a prim look to this 17thC stone house in the middle of La Roche-Bernard, but a warm welcome within. Joël Morice, chef here since 1965 and proprietor since 1981, sets the same high standards in the running of the hotel that he does in the kitchen – the furniture in the elegant dining-rooms and bedrooms may be reproduction, but it is all part of a careful, fresh decorative scheme. Improvements to facilities continue – satellite TV is the latest addition. M. Morice's good-value menus concentrate on traditional regional dishes (which of course include seafood).

Nearby Parc Régional de Brière (15 km); Guérande (25 km).

1 Place du Bouffay 56130 La Roche-Bernard
Tel 99.90.60.75
Fax 99.90.87.87
Location in the middle of town, with public parking in front
Meals breakfast, lunch, dinner
Prices rooms 280F-300F, suites/family rooms 380F-460F; breakfast 32F, menus 80F-340F
Rooms 12 double, 9 with bath, 3 with shower (4 twin); 2 family rooms with bath; all rooms have phone, satellite TV
Facilities 2 dining-rooms, TV room, bar
Credit cards MC, V
Children accepted
Disabled no special facilities
Pets not accepted
Closed restaurant only Mon; Sun eve and Mon out of season **Proprietors** M. and Mme Joël Morice

Yvelines

Village hotel, Senlisse

Auberge du Gros Marronnier

The Gros Marronnier is a rustic little inn, tucked away next door to the church (it used to be the presbytery) in an affluent residential village. When first we visited in 1990, the new owners had embarked on extensive renovations which were only partly complete, and the public areas were unimpressive. But the attic rooms we stayed in were spacious and prettily decorated (and surprisingly cool). We found the food, served on a flowery terrace overlooking the informal grassy garden, interesting, excellent and well presented, the staff smiling and helpful, though recent verdicts on the service have varied from 'slow' to 'not quick' to 'good tempo for digestion and civilised discourse'. More reports please.

Mme Trochon tells us that in 1993 she turned her attention to the garden and has built a new terrace and a glass-sided veranda from which to observe wildlife; future plans include an open fireplace and a new sitting-room.

Nearby Versailles (15 km); Paris (35 km).

3 Place de l'Église, 75720 Senlisse
Tel (1) 30.52.51.69
Fax (1) 30.52.55.91
Location in heart of village, next to church, 12 km NE of Rambouillet on D91; with garden and limited car parking
Meals breakfast, lunch, dinner
Prices rooms 280F–375F; breakfast 45F; menus 155F–295F
Rooms 15 double, 1 single, 4 family rooms, 12 with bath, 8 with shower; all rooms have central heating, phone
Facilities dining-room, TV room, bar, terrace
Credit cards AE, V
Children welcome
Disabled no special facilities
Pets accepted
Closed one week at Christmas
Proprietor Mme Trochon

Paris

Town guest-house, Paris

Hôtel Esmeralda

A small hotel of great charm and character, the Esmeralda occupies a building dating from the 16thC in the oldest quarter of the city, with good views of Nôtre-Dame. Michèle Bruel is an ex-sculptress whose collection of *objets d'art* are scattered through the hotel, mixing well with the old beams, stone walls and quarry-tiled floors. A slightly eccentric l920s style prevails in the bedrooms; most of them are small, dark and cosy, but no two are alike. One reservation: insist on a room in the main part of the hotel – those reached by a separate entrance a few paces down the street are distressingly shabby.

Nearby St Julien-de-Pauvre – oldest complete church in Paris; Ile de la Cité – Nôtre-Dame; Beaubourg (across the river).

4 Rue St-Julien-le-Pauvre
75005 Paris
Tel (1) 43.54.19.20
Fax (1) 40.51.00.68
Location left bank, near Notre Dame; public car parking close by
Meals breakfast
Prices rooms 150F-470F; breakfast 40F
Rooms 12 double, all with bath (2 twin); 7 single, 4 with shower; one family room with bath; all rooms have central heating, phone
Facilities breakfast room
Credit cards not accepted
Children welcome
Disabled no special facilities
Pets accepted
Closed never
Proprietor Michèle Bruel

Town hotel, Paris

Hôtel des Tuileries

This attractive 18thC mansion with revolutionary associations is very well placed – close to the beautiful Place Vendôme and the exclusive shops of the Rue du Faubourg St-Honoré, yet in a small quiet street. It has two small salons with velvet seats, paintings and tapestries on plain walls, and a breakfast room in the basement where there is a better-than-average buffet with cheeses and yoghurt. Bedrooms are prettily decorated, with antique, reproduction and modern furniture – front ones are the most elegant and spacious. Small but very smart bathrooms. A recent visitor commends the 'uniformly friendly and helpful' staff.

Nearby Tuileries, Louvre, Opéra, Rue de Rivoli.

10 Rue St-Hyacinthe 75001 Paris
Tel (1) 42.61.04.17
Fax (1) 49.27.91.56
Location in middle of city, N of Tuileries; with public car parking nearby Place du Marché Saint Honoré or Place Vendome
Meals breakfast
Prices rooms 690F-1,200F
Rooms 26 double (12 twin), 4 suites, all with bath; all rooms have central heating, air conditioning, phone, minibar, hairdrier, safe, satellite TV
Facilities breakfast room, bar
Credit cards AE, DC, V
Children accepted
Disabled no special facilities
Pets accepted
Closed never
Proprietors Poulle-Vidal family

Paris

L'Hôtel

The Rue des Beaux-Arts, a side street in the heart of St-Germain-des-Prés, has been the home of many artists and writers. L'Hôtel's particular claim to fame is that it was the last abode of Oscar Wilde; as the plaque on the door will tell you, he 'died here beyond his means'. Then a local hotel of no real distinction, it is now the most lavish establishment on the Left Bank, and in terms of glamour, ranks alongside the five-star hotels across the Seine. Film and pop stars and politicians figure on the guest list, along with the merely super-rich.

Bedrooms are sumptuous. All thick-pile carpets, Venetian marble bathrooms and antiques, they are the ultimate in luxury – although only the Penthouse (which takes up to five) could be described as spacious. Nostalgia value is high: you might sleep in the very bed where Oscar Wilde died, or enjoy the art deco furniture in the Mistinguett room.

Public rooms are equally extravagant. The winter garden has been converted into a glamorous piano bar/restaurant with fountain, goldfish, flowers and exotic plants. Both bar and restaurant are open until the early hours of the morning, and are popular haunts for Parisian high society.

Nearby Palais du Louvre (over the Pont des Arts); church of Saint Germain-des-Prés; Delacroix museum; Rue de Buci and Rue de Seine – one of the best food-markets in Paris.

13 Rue des Beaux Arts
75006 Paris
Tel (1) 43.25.27.22
Fax (1) 43.25.64.81
Location in Saint-Germain-des-Prés
Meals breakfast, lunch, dinner
Prices rooms 950F-2,300F; suites 2,800F-3,800F; lunch 120F-160F; dinner 170F; breakfast 90F
Rooms 23 double, 13 with bath, 10 with shower (15 twin); 3 suites; one single, with bath; all rooms have central heating, air-conditioning, minibar, phone, radio, TV, video
Facilities 2 restaurants (winter garden, cellar bar)
Credit cards AE, DC, MC, V
Children accepted
Disabled no special facilities
Pets accepted
Closed never
Manager Yves Meteignier

Photo: Hôtel des Tuileries (facing page)

Paris

Hôtel Danemark

This smart little hotel apparently takes its decorative inspiration from Henri Sauvage's turn-of-the-century ceramic-fronted gem across the Rue Vavin. Everything about it is deliberately stylish – not least the rich blue triple-arched frontage, leading to a reception/lounge which is surrounded by flowers and plants, and striking modern art on the pale stone walls. An assortment of shiny chairs, low glass tables and slick black furniture is stationed around the room. Downstairs, in the stone cellar, is a café-style breakfast-room. Bedrooms are refreshingly simple, with modern wooden furniture – oak, ash or mahogany depending on the floor – and pale walls and carpets; not a floral pattern in sight.
Nearby Luxembourg Palace and gardens, Panthéon.

21 Rue Vavin, 75006 Paris
Tel (1) 43.26.93.78
Fax (1) 46.34.66.06
Location near Luxembourg gardens, between Rue d'Assas and Bvd Montparnasse; with public car parking nearby
Meals breakfast
Prices rooms 590F-760F; breakfast 40F
Rooms 15 double, all with bath; all rooms have central heating, phone, TV, minibar, hairdrier **Facilities** breakfast room **Credit cards** AE, DC, V
Children accepted; baby-sitting possible
Disabled no special facilities
Pets well-behaved animals accepted
Closed never
Proprietor M. J Nurit

Hôtel Eber Monceau

This turn-of-the-century house is in a quiet residential area of Paris (not far from the Champs Elysées), but is well served by the metro and bus networks. It was thoroughly refurbished only a few years ago, and is now prettily furnished and decorated, and feels cared for. Breakfast is served (15 sorts of *confiture*, 3 sorts of tea) in a small patio – some of the bedrooms lead on to it – or in the rooms. There is no dining-room, but light meals can be served in the bedrooms – cheese, *charcuterie, foie gras* and so on. The small sitting-room also serves as a bar. The house rule is to 'make yourself at home' – after a hard day's sightseeing, an inviting prospect.
Nearby Parc de Monceau, Arc du Triomphe, Champs Elysées.

18 Rue Léon Jost 75017 Paris
Tel (1) 46.22.60.70
Fax (1) 47.63.01.01
Location in residential area, close to Champs Elysées; with public car parking nearby
Meals breakfast
Prices rooms 580F-650F, suites 1,000F-1,300F; breakfast 50F
Rooms 18 double (3 twin), all with bath; all rooms have central heating, cable TV, phone, minibar
Facilities some rooms have private sitting-area
Credit cards AE, DC, MC, V
Children accepted
Disabled no special facilities
Pets not accepted
Closed never
Proprietor Jean Marc Eber

Paris

Hôtel St-Germain-des-Prés

This small Left Bank hotel in a characteristic street of St-Germain-des-Prés stands out for charm and individuality, although perhaps not for notably good taste and certainly not for coherence of interior design. Its bedrooms are all furnished in different styles and colours – one with a huge canopied four-poster bed, another with exposed 18thC beams, another with pretty modern floral fabrics. There is one large salon-cum-breakfast-room with leather armchairs, flowery carpet and plenty of plants. The Rue Bonaparte is not one of the quietest in the neighbourhood but you are rarely aware of noise – and for immersion in the literary associations of the *quartier* this is a useful base.

Nearby Louvre, Conciergerie, Delacroix Museum, Café Procope.

36 Rue Bonaparte 75006 Paris
Tel (1) 43.26.00.19
Fax (1) 40.46.83.63
Location close to church of St-Germain-des-Prés; public car parking only
Meals breakfast
Prices rooms 800F-1,500F
Rooms 29 double (6 twin), one single; all with bath or shower; all rooms have central heating, phone, TV, radio, minibar; some have air-conditioning
Facilities breakfast/sitting-room
Credit cards MC, V
Children accepted
Disabled access possible; lift/elevator **Pets** not accepted
Closed never
Proprietor M. Le Boudec

Hôtel St-Louis

Of the three sister hotels on this busy street on the Ile-St-Louis, this is the simplest and cheapest. It is converted from a 17thC townhouse, and M and Mme Record look on it more as a large family-run house than a formal hotel. The welcoming atmosphere, combined with the ideal location for sightseeing and the modest prices, more than makes up for any lack of facilities (the only public room is the stone-vaulted basement salon, used for breakfast) and the small size of the recently redecorated bedrooms, which are simple and modern in style, with the addition of rustic-style furniture.

Nearby Church of Saint Louis-en-L'Ile; Ile de la Cité – Notre Dame; Boulevard Saint Germain (just over the river).

75 Rue St-Louis-en-l'Ile 75004 Paris
Tel (1) 46.34.04.80
Fax (1) 46.34.02.13
Location on island in the Seine; public car parking nearby
Meals breakfast
Prices rooms 695F-795F; breakfast 49F
Rooms 21 double, 15 with bath, 6 with shower (9 twin); all rooms have phone
Facilities breakfast cellar room
Credit cards not accepted
Children welcome if well behaved
Disabled lift/elevator
Pets accepted if small and well behaved **Closed** never
Proprietors Andrée and Guy Record

Paris

Hôtel Beaubourg

This six-storey town house dating back to the 1600s is just around the corner from the ultra-modern Pompidou Centre – itself often known as Beaubourg. Traces of the hotel's medieval past are evident throughout – the original limestone wall in the cosy beamed sitting-room, the old well in the vaulted basement breakfast room, ancient paintwork in some of the beamed front bedrooms. Nor is the hotel lacking in modern comforts; bedrooms and public rooms are pleasantly furnished and effectively lit – Mme. Morand has quite an eye for interior design. Some bedrooms overlook the delightful courtyard garden full of trailing plants. There is no restaurant.

Nearby Ile de la Cité; Pompidou Centre; Forum.

11 rue Simon Lefranc	TV, radio, minibar
Tel (1) 42.74.34.24	**Facilities** sitting-room,
Fax (1) 42.78.68.11	breakfast room; courtyard
Location near Pompidou	**Credit cards** AE, DC, MC, V
Centre; car parking nearby	**Children** accepted
Meals breakfast	**Disabled** one ground-floor
Prices rooms 480F-560F (extra	room; lift/elevator
bed 150F); breakfast 35F	**Pets** not accepted
Rooms 28 double, 24 with	**Closed** never
bath, 4 with shower; all rooms	**Proprietors** M. and Mme
have central heating, phone,	Morand

Hôtel de la Place des Vosges

The Place des Vosges, now restored to its former glory as part of the general revitalization of the formerly run-down Marais area (between Beaubourg and the Bastille), is one of the loveliest squares in Paris. The hotel is an attractive 17thC house, entirely in harmony with the style of the area, in a quiet street only 25 metres from the square. The salon Louis XIII is suitably traditional and rustic in style: exposed beams, roughcast stone walls, tapestry-covered chairs and curtains. Bedrooms are more modern in style, with less character, but they are well kept – and reasonably priced. 'We always stay there' says a recent reporter.

Nearby Place des Vosges (oldest square in Paris), Bastille, Victor Hugo museum, Hôtel de Ville, Carnavalet museum.

12 Rue de Birague 75004 Paris	rooms have central heating,
Tel and fax (1) 42.72.60.46	phone
Location off Place des Vosges,	**Facilities** sitting-area
in Marais district; with private	**Credit cards** AE, DC, MC, V
garages 300 m away	**Children** welcome
Meals breakfast	**Disabled** no special facilities
Prices rooms 300F-400F;	**Pets** accepted if well behaved
children under 2 free	**Closed** never
Rooms 15 double, 10 with	**Proprietor** M. Cros
bath, 5 with shower (4 twin);	
one family room with bath; all	

Paris

Town hotel, Paris

Hôtel le Ste-Beuve

There can be few bed-and-breakfast establishments more stylish than this turn-of-the-century hotel, in Paris or anywhere else. All is discretion and understatement: light, plain decoration; restrained patterns in the rich fabrics; beds draped in white; sparse furnishing, employing well-placed antiques mixed with modern designs; fresh flowers strategically placed. A log fire burns in the little classically-styled salon – not a place to while away evenings, but a civilized meeting-place. Cold meals are served in the bedrooms (there is no dining-room) at any time; breakfast – the best available croissants and *confitures* – arrives on a tray beautifully laid with English porcelain.

Bobette Compagnon, the arbiter of all this exquisite taste, is obviously intent on making the most of her hotel, organizing 'theme' weekends – perhaps including visits to the opera – and putting on exhibitions of contemporary artists' work in the sitting-room.

Nearby Montparnasse; Postal Museum; Jardin du Luxembourg; Blvd St-Germain within easy walking distance.

9 Rue Ste-Beuve 75006 Paris
Tel (1) 45.48.20.07
Fax (1) 45.48.67.52
Location between Blvd Montparnasse and Jardin du Luxembourg; car parking in Blvd Montparnasse
Meals breakfast; cold dishes available at all times
Prices rooms 680F-1,250F

Rooms 22 double (9 twin), all with bath; all rooms have phone, TV, minibar, safe
Facilities sitting-room
Credit cards AE, MC, V
Children accepted
Disabled no special facilities
Pets small dogs accepted
Closed never **Manager** Bobette Compagnon

Paris

Hôtel Récamier

A cheap and cheerful hotel overlooking the shady backwater of Place St-Sulpice and the church of the same name. It is one of the quieter hotels of central Paris and, although somewhat austere from the outside, it is welcoming within. One of the two small sitting-rooms doubles up as a breakfast room, and anyone worried about the absence of a bar can rest assured that there are plenty of watering-holes nearby – this is, after all, St-Germain-des-Prés. Bedrooms are small and modern, and all have been recently redecorated. All in all, a sensible choice as a quiet, central and reasonably priced base.

Nearby Luxembourg Palace and gardens; St-Germain-des-Prés – cafés, shops; church of St-Sulpice; Delacroix Museum.

3 bis Place St-Sulpice 75006 Paris
Tel (1) 43.26.04.89
Location near Luxembourg Palace and Blvd St-Germain; public car parking in square
Meals breakfast
Prices rooms 390F-520F
Rooms 30 double (13 twin), 11 with bath, 11 with shower; one single; one family room
with bath; all rooms have central heating, phone
Facilities 2 sitting-rooms
Credit cards not accepted
Children accepted by arrangement
Disabled lift/elevator
Pets not accepted
Closed never
Proprietor G Dauphin

Hôtel du Jeu de Paume

An irresistible new arrival on a desirable street already provided with desirable small hotels. It is a conversion of a 17thC real tennis-court, with what must be the greatest array of exposed beams in Paris – most notably in the atrium-style dining-room and sitting-room (complete with high-tech glass lift), but also finding their way into many of the bedrooms. These are decorated and furnished carefully and tastefully but uniformly, the building itself contributing what character they possess. Some open on to the small garden.

Nearby Church of St-Louis-en-l'Ile, Notre-Dame, Boulevard St-Germain.

54 rue St-Louis-en-l'Ile, 75004 Paris
Tel (1) 43.26.14.18
Fax (1) 40.46.02.76
Location on Ile-St-Louis; parking at Notre Dame or the Hôtel de Ville
Meals breakfast, room service
Prices rooms 795F-1,190F, breakfast 75F
Rooms 32 double, all with bath and shower; all rooms
have central heating, phone, hairdrier, TV, minibar
Facilities sitting-room, dining-room, bar; sauna, jacuzzi
Credit cards AE, DC, MC, V
Children welcome; babysitting available **Disabled** lift/elevator, some ground-floor rooms **Pets** dogs accepted (50F charge) **Closed** never
Proprietor Guy and Elyane Prache

Paris

Town hotel, Paris

Le Jardin des Plantes

Cheerful green and yellow awnings over the windows distinguish the Jardin des Plantes – directly opposite the eponymous botanical gardens – from the other town houses that line the Rue Linné. M. Amoura, who took over the hotel in 1992, aims to maintain the high standards achieved by the Bompards who thoroughly renovated the hotel in the late 1980s. Each of the five floors is decorated on a different flower theme. Bedrooms have trellised wallpaper and coordinated floral curtains and bedspreads – even the bathroom tiles have flowery patterns. Rooms on the top floor have the best views and some open on to the roof terrace. Breakfast can be served here.

Nearby Jardin des Plantes, Panthéon, church of St Médard.

5 Rue Linné, 75005 Paris **Tel** (1) 47.07.06.20 **Fax** (1) 47.07.62.74 **Location** opposite entrance to Jardin des Plantes, in Latin quarter; with public car parking nearby **Meals** breakfast, lunch **Prices** rooms 420F-640F; breakfast 40F, lunch 50F-90F **Rooms** 22 double, 7 family rooms, all with bath; 4 single, with shower; all rooms have central heating, phone, TV, minibar, hairdrier **Facilities** dining-room, sitting-room, bar, terrace; sauna **Credit cards** AE, DC, MC, V **Children** welcome **Disabled** no special facilities **Pets** accepted **Closed** restaurant only, Mon **Proprietor** M. Amoura

Town hotel, Paris

Hôtel Mayflower

Under the same ownership as the Lord Byron and right next door to it, the Mayflower shares the same refined but relaxed atmosphere and, not surprisingly, is similarly well run. It lacks the Lord Byron's attraction of a courtyard, but to some extent compensates with a sitting-room which is unusually elegant and comfortable for a Paris bed-and-breakfast, with comfy armchairs, sofas, and low tables, and a smart little breakfast room. Bedrooms, in a mix of styles, are pretty and calm, and mainly spacious – as are the bathrooms.

Nearby Arc de Triomphe, Champs Elysées, Blvd Haussmann (Jacquemart-André Museum, shopping), Ave Foch (Armenian Museum), Bois de Boulogne.

3 Rue de Chateaubriand 75008 Paris **Tel** (1) 45.62.57.46 **Fax** (1) 42.56.32.38 **Location** close to Arc de Triomphe and Champs Elysées; public car parking nearby **Meals** breakfast **Prices** rooms 650F-950F; breakfast 50F **Rooms** 18 double (5 twin), 6 single, all with bath; all rooms have central heating, phone, satellite TV, minibar **Facilities** sitting-room, breakfast area **Credit cards** MC, V **Children** accepted **Disabled** lift/elevator, but access difficult **Pets** accepted **Closed** never **Proprietor** Mme Benoit

Paris

Thoumieux

Thoumieux lies in the shadow of the Eiffel tower. It is essentially a restaurant-with-rooms, the focal point being the jolly bistro: the house-wine is drinkable, while the the country-style cooking (*andouillettes, boudin, rillettes, cassoulet au confit de canard*) is good and cheap. The fairly spacious bedrooms are modern and comfortable, with attractive fabrics and crisp, Italian-style furniture. There is a pleasant breakfast/sitting-room, decorated in shades of grey. An efficient, friendly place.

Nearby Hôtel des Invalides – military museum; Rodin museum; Palais de Chaillot and gardens.

79 Rue St-Dominique 75007 Paris	central heating, TV, phone, radio
Tel (1) 47.05.49.75	**Facilities** 2 sitting-rooms, dining-room
Fax (1) 47.05.36.96	
Location between Eiffel Tower and Les Invalides; with public car parking nearby	**Credit cards** V
	Children accepted
	Disabled no special facilities
Meals breakfast, lunch, dinner	**Pets** accepted
Prices rooms 550F-600F; breakfast 35F, meals about 150F	**Closed** never
	Proprietor Jean Bassalert
Rooms 10 double, all with bath (4 twin); all rooms have	

Hôtel Étoile Pereire

The Étoile Pereire is well placed both for motorists (take the Porte de Champerret exit from the Périphérique) and air travellers – the Air France terminal is a short taxi-ride away. The hotel has been smartly done out in a restrained modern style – plain pale walls, glass tables and low armchairs on polished floors in the little sitting-room, a slightly clubby atmosphere (dark velvet armchairs) in the little bar, delicately austere decoration in the immaculate bedrooms. Note the wide range of prices: some of the rooms are split-level, with living as well as sleeping space. Breakfast is an *à la carte* affair – something of a treat, but not cheap. There is a pretty park nearby.

Nearby Arc de Triomphe, Champs-Élysées, Bois de Boulogne.

146 Blvd Pereire 75017 Paris	with bath or shower; all rooms have central heating, phone, TV, minibar, hairdrier
Tel (1) 42.67.60.00	
Fax (1) 42.67.02.90	
Location on broad boulevard in residential area, close to Périphérique, NW of middle; with garage parking (100F for 24hr) **Meals** breakfast	**Facilities** bar, sitting-room, conference room
	Credit cards AE, DC, MC, V
	Children accepted; cots available **Disabled** no special facilities **Pets** not accepted
Prices rooms 500F-950F; breakfast 50F	**Closed** never **Manager** Ferruccio Pardi
Rooms 20 double, 6 single, all	

Paris

Town hotel, Paris

Hôtel Verneuil-St-Germain

Long established but completely renovated in recent years, the Verneuil-St-Germain – between the Blvd St-Germain and the river, not far from the marvellous Musée d'Orsay – initially makes a great impression, with its Manhattan-style reception rooms. Classical statues on a polished wooden floor are reflected in a wall of mirrored glass which contrasts with other walls of bare stone and a ceiling of exposed beams. Furnishings are imaginative, with richly striped curtains, and attractive sofas and armchairs in spotted and Paisley prints.

After all this, the bedrooms used to come as something of an anti-climax, but now they have been redecorated to fulfil the promise of the stylish ground floor, done out in floral fabrics. It pays to ask for a good-sized room when booking – they vary widely, some being very small. The marble-tiled bathrooms are well equipped – there seems to be a craze for wall-mounted hairdriers just now. In the basement there is an attractive stone-walled breakfast room, with appropriately traditional-style furniture; breakfast is copious, including fruit juice and croissants.

Nearby Musée d'Orsay, Tuileries, Louvre, Île de la Cité, Notre Dame, St-Germain-des-Prés.

8 Rue de Verneuil 75007 Paris
Tel (1) 42.60.82.14
Fax (1) 42.61.40.38
Location in middle of St-Germain-des-Prés; in quiet street with public car parking nearby
Meals breakfast
Prices rooms 700F-1,100F; breakfast 50F
Rooms 21 double (4 twin), all with bath; all rooms have central heating, TV, phone, radio, alarm
Facilities breakfast room, 2 sitting-rooms
Credit cards AE, DC, MC,V
Children welcome; baby-sitting available
Disabled no special facilities
Pets welcome if well behaved
Closed never
Proprietor M Le Boudec

Paris

Le Saint-Grégoire

This tall 18thC town house has made an exceptionally warm and sleek hotel (opened in 1988), though not a cheap one. The tone is set by the welcoming reception and sitting-room, confidently designer-decorated in neo-classical style but furnished with uncompromisingly modern chairs, bright fabrics and large mirrors. A log fire burns here in cold weather. The bedrooms are decorated with restraint, the furnishings a careful mix of modern and antique. Two of them have their own terrace/gardens. The hotel also has a tiny enclosed garden, full of ferns and flowers. Downstairs, the arched stone cellar makes a lovely breakfast room. 'Obliging staff, overpriced breakfasts,' says a visitor.
Nearby St Germain-des-Prés church, St-Germain quarter.

43 Rue de L'Abbé Gregoire, 75006 Paris
Tel (1) 45.48.23.23
Fax (1) 45.48.33.95
Location in small road off Rue de Rennes, between St-Germain and Montparnasse; car parking arranged
Meals breakfast
Prices rooms 760F-1,290F; breakfast 60F

Rooms 18 double, 2 suites, all with bath; all rooms have central heating, phone, TV, hairdrier, radio **Facilities** sitting-room **Credit cards** AE, DC, MC, V **Children** accepted; baby-sitting possible
Disabled access difficult
Pets tolerated
Closed never
Manager François de Bene

Hôtel de Lutèce

Roland Buffat has two success stories on the Ile-St-Louis – the Deux-Iles (page 57) and the Lutèce. (He was also the owner of the St-Louis until quite recently.) This is the younger of the hotels, and like its sister has been converted from one of the island's original townhouses. The foyer and salon have something of the feel of a Provençal country house, with flagstone floor, beamed ceiling (originally from a Louis XlV château), bouquets of flowers and a stone fireplace where log fires roar in winter. What bedrooms lack in space (most are decidedly small) they make up for in charming decoration and antique furnishings. Prices are relatively high, but for a combination of prime location and country-house charm Lutèce is a good choice. Note that there is no bar.
Nearby Church of St Louis-en-l'Ile, Notre-Dame, Conciergerie, Bastille, Place des Vosges, Blvd St-Germain, Hôtel de Ville.

65 Rue St-Louis-en-l'Ile 75004 Paris **Tel** (1) 43.26.23.52
Fax (1) 43.29.60.25
Location on l'Ile-St-Louis
Meals breakfast
Prices rooms 670F-770F; breakfast 40F
Rooms 23 double, 13 with

bath, 10 with shower (10 twin); all rooms have TV, phone, hairdrier **Facilities** sitting-room **Credit cards** not accepted **Children** accepted
Disabled no special facilities
Pets accepted **Closed** never
Proprietor M. Buffat

Paris

Hôtel Riboutté Lafayette

One of a chain of six, this small cheerfully furnished hotel lies close to the Rue Lafayette – convenient for nightlife and department stores. Public rooms consist of reception and a small salon, prettily furnished in rattan and bamboo, floral fabrics, plants and bouquets of flowers. Bedrooms are small, friendly and individual – some with painted-wood furnishings, others with floral fabrics and lithographs. All the rooms are quiet, whether overlooking the courtyard or the street (windows are double-glazed), and the atmosphere is almost provincial. This is not one of the most conspicuous of the city's charming small hotels, but worth considering as a reasonably priced and cheerful base.

Nearby Folies Bergères; a short walk away is the Opéra, Blvd Haussman and church of Sacré-Coeur.

5 Rue Riboutté 75009 Paris
Tel (1) 47.70.62.36
Location NE of middle of city, close to Gare du Nord; with public car parking nearby
Meals breakfast
Prices rooms 370F-460F; breakfast 30F
Rooms 18 double, 15 with bath, 3 with shower (6 twin); one single with bath; 5 family rooms, with shower; all rooms have TV, phone
Facilities 2 small sitting-rooms
Credit cards AE, V
Children accepted
Disabled no special facilities
Pets dogs accepted
Closed never **Manager** Mme Claudine Gourd

Hôtel d'Angleterre

There is a good reason why the Angleterre is so named – the 18thC building was once the British Embassy. And there is still something faintly British about it. It is in a lively area of the Left Bank, but the bedrooms are peaceful, some overlooking a delightful white courtyard with creeping ivy, camellias and a white marble fountain. You can take drinks on pretty rattan chairs in the shade of parasols, or in the bar next door. There are also a civilized, rather formal sitting-room and a charming breakfast room. Many of the bedrooms were refurbished not long ago; they are not cheap, but not bad value.

Nearby Delacroix Museum, church of St-Germain-des-Prés, Blvd St-Germain (shops, cafés), Louvre, Ile de la Cité.

44 Rue Jacob 75006 Paris
Tel (1) 42.60.34.72
Fax (1) 42.60.16.93
Location between Seine and Blvd St-Germain, near St-Germain des Prés; with garden
Meals breakfast
Prices rooms 800F-1,100F; breakfast 40F
Rooms 29 double (12 twin), with bath or shower; all rooms have central heating, phone, TV
Facilities sitting-room
Credit cards AE, DC, MC, V
Children accepted
Disabled 2 ground-floor rooms and lift/elevator
Pets not accepted
Closed never
Manager Mme Soumier

Paris

Hôtel Solférino

This is one of the few simple and modestly priced establishments in an area of high-priced hotels. The Left Bank location, on a quiet street close to the Seine and Place de la Concorde, is highly desirable. Built as a private residence 150 years ago, the Solférino today is a small and welcoming family-run hotel with a blend of classical and modern styles in its furnishings. Oil paintings, traditional furniture and carpets are features of the small, high-ceilinged salon; while the breakfast room is light and summery, with plenty of plants. Bedrooms are simple and on the small side, but quiet and prettily furnished.

Nearby Place de la Concorde, Champs Élysées, Musée d'Orsay, Hôtel des Invalides, Tuileries, Louvre.

91 Rue de Lille 75007 Paris
Tel (1) 47.05.85.54
Fax (1) 45.55.51.16
Location in middle of city, across river from Tuileries; with public car parking nearby
Meals breakfast
Prices rooms 245F-698F; breakfast 35F
Rooms 27 double, with bath (6 twin); some can take extra bed; 6 single, with shower; all rooms have phone
Facilities sitting-room, breakfast room
Credit cards MC, V
Children accepted
Disabled access difficult
Pets not accepted
Closed Christmas
Proprietors Jean-Paul Cornic and Marie Jeanne Laurent

Hôtel de l'Université

Skilfully converted from a town mansion, this middle-market hotel is in a peaceful and characteristic area of St-Germain-des-Prés. Furnishings throughout are in sober good taste. Authentic exposed beams, wooden doors, antiques and tapestries are features of the foyer, and there are period furnishings in all the rooms. Breakfast is taken at small marble tables overlooking a delightful inner courtyard with flowers and fountain. Bedrooms are well equipped but vary considerably in size and style, ranging from the plainer rooms with shower to luxury apartments with a private terrace; prices vary accordingly. A recent visitor praises the 'friendly' staff and quality and value of the breakfasts.

Nearby Louvre, Tuileries, Musée d'Orsay, Ile de la Cité.

22 Rue de l'Université
75007 Paris
Tel (1) 42.61.09.39
Location in St-Germain-des-Prés; public car parking nearby
Meals breakfast, light snacks
Prices rooms 650F-1,500F; breakfast 45F
Rooms 21 double, 17 with bath, 4 with shower (12 twin); 7 single, 3 with bath, 4 with shower; all rooms have phone, TV
Facilities sitting-room, breakfast room, bar
Credit cards V
Children accepted
Disabled access difficult
Pets not accepted
Closed never
Proprietor Mme Bergmann

Paris

Town hotel, Paris

Hôtel des Deux Iles

The enchanting Ile-St-Louis is one of the most desirable addresses in the city and has long been a popular residential area for wealthy and well-known Parisians (Pompidou among them).

The Deux Iles is one of two hotels in the same street owned and run by Roland Buffat (see also the Lutèce). Over a decade ago he converted this 17thC townhouse into what is now one of the most popular small hotels in the city – particularly among those looking for a prime location, combined with charm and individuality. Rooms need to be booked several weeks in advance – and that applies all year round.

It is a far from spacious hotel, but imaginative decoration (M. Buffat is an interior designer by trade) and the private-house atmosphere make up for the smallish size of the rooms. Reception and lounge are particularly attractive: a glassed-in area of plants and flowers gives a tropical feel. The bedrooms (and matching bathrooms) are often decorated in blue and white, and furnished with bamboo and Provençal fabrics. Breakfasts are a cut-above-average. We understand that the cellar bar, with its cosy fireplace and relaxing chairs, is now used simply as a sitting-room.

Nearby Church of St-Louis-en-L'Ile; Boulevard Saint-Germain; Ile de la Cité – Notre Dame; Rue de Rivoli.

59 Rue St-Louis-en-l'Ile 75004 Paris
Tel (1) 43.26.13.35
Fax (1) 43.29.60.25
Location on island in the Seine; car parking nearby
Meals breakfast
Prices rooms 695F-795F; breakfast 42F
Rooms 13 double, 8 with bath, 5 with shower (4 twin); 4 single, all with shower; all rooms have TV, phone
Facilities sitting-rooms
Credit cards not accepted
Children accepted
Disabled no special facilities
Pets accepted
Closed never
Proprietor Roland Buffat

Paris

Hôtel Agora

This unassuming hotel (without a restaurant) has a range of attractions. Its location in Les Halles – central and full of Parisian life – is good for sightseers and shoppers alike. With its flowery entrance (leading to reception on the first floor) and lacy curtains it is a hotel which contrives to be old-fashioned; yet in other ways it seems modern and even slightly chic. The practical necessities are looked after – all is thoroughly clean, and rooms are well sound-proofed. Furnishings are antique, and the walls are hung with old engravings. Prices are reasonable for Paris and the welcome is friendly. Hard to beat for a simple base in an ideal area.

Nearby Les Halles, Pompidou centre, Île de la Cité.

7 Rue de la Cossonerie 75001 Paris **Tel** (1) 42.33.46.02
Fax (1) 42.33.80.99
Location between Forum des Halles and Blvd Sebastopol; with public car parking nearby
Meals breakfast
Prices rooms 370F-595F; breakfast 35F
Rooms 29 double, 5 with bath, 24 with shower (12 twin); all rooms have central heating, phone, TV
Credit cards AE, MC, V
Children welcome if well behaved
Disabled access difficult: lift/elevator on first floor
Pets not accepted
Closed never
Proprietor Claude Fresnel

Hôtel Lenox

Built at the end of the last century, the Lenox started life as a pension, taking in literary figures of the time (James Joyce, for example). Today it is chic and civilized, providing comfortable rooms at reasonable prices. Decoration is in keeping: the bar has recently been redone in 'cosy English' style, furnished with chintz and marble in the salon, and English fabrics in the small but elegant bedrooms. The Rue de l'Université is a characteristic street of St-Germain-des-Prés and a particularly good location if you enjoy browsing around book shops and antique galleries.

Nearby Place St Germain-des-Prés – street performers; Rue de Buci and Rue de Seine – food-market; café Procope – haunt of Molière, Racine, Voltaire, Balzac and Anatole France.

9 Rue de l'Université 75007 Paris
Tel (1) 42.96.10.95
Fax (1) 42.61.52.83
Location in St-Germain-des-Prés
Meals breakfast
Prices rooms 580F-950F; breakfast 45F
Rooms 34 double, 26 with bath, 8 with shower (12 twin); all rooms have TV, phone, central heating
Facilities bar, sitting-room
Credit cards AE, DC, MC, V
Children accepted
Disabled no special facilities
Pets not accepted
Closed never
Manager Thierry Aiech

Paris

Le Relais Saint Germain

Christiane and Gilbert Laipsker's shared love of interior decoration is everywhere in evidence in the Relais Saint Germain, which they opened in the spring of 1987. They have filled the 17thC house with stunning antiques, period furniture, sumptuous fabrics, carefully chosen lamps and old paintings. The enormous beamed bedrooms have retained their 'olde worlde' charm, but now have every modern convenience, including large marble bathrooms. The suite on the top floor is particularly magnificent, with its striking yellow and blue striped curtains and matching sofa. Since this is about the smartest little B&B in town, prices are naturally among the highest of our Paris hotels.

Nearby St-Germain-des-Prés, St-Germain quarter.

9 Carrefour de l'Odéon, 75006 Paris
Tel (1) 43.29.12.05
Fax (1) 46.33.45.30
Location between Place de l'Odéon and Bvd St- Germain; no private car parking
Meals breakfast
Prices rooms 1,190F-1,380F with breakfast; suites 1,790F
Rooms 11 double, all with bath; all have central heating, air-conditioning, phone, TV, hairdrier, minibar, radio
Facilities breakfast room, sitting-room **Credit cards** AE, DC, V **Children** accepted; baby- sitting possible
Disabled no special facilities
Pets supplement 70F **Closed** never **Proprietors** Christiane and Gilbert Laipsker

Hôtel Bersoly's Saint Germain

On a quiet street in the administrative heart of Paris, this 17thC former convent makes an ideal sightseeing base. It has been recently renovated, to very satisfactory effect. The reception – stone-floored, heavily beamed and furnished with solid reproductions – has a small sitting area where English, German and Italian as well as French newspapers are kept. Steep stairs with iron banisters lead down to vaulted cellars (where breakfast is served and there is another small sitting-area) and up to five floors of bedrooms. These tend to be small, but have been harmoniously and thoughtfully done out – each is decorated in a favourite colour of the impressionist painter it is named after.

Nearby Musée d'Orsay, Louvre, Jardin des Tuileries.

28 Rue de Lille, 75007 Paris
Tel (1) 42.60.73.79
Fax (1) 49.27.05.55
Location near Musée d'Orsay, one street away from Seine; no private car parking
Meals breakfast, snacks
Prices rooms 550F-650F, breakfast 50F
Rooms 16 double, 9 with bath, 7 with shower; all rooms have central heating, phone, TV, hairdrier, radio, safe; some rooms have air-conditioning, minibar **Facilities** breakfast room, 2 small sitting-areas
Credit cards MC, V **Children** welcome; baby-sitting possible
Disabled no special facilities
Pets supplement 50F **Closed** 15 days in Aug
Manager M. Carbonnaux

Paris

Hôtel St-Louis Marais

This hotel in the quiet, civilized Marais district changed hands and name three years ago. Formerly the Hôtel des Célestins, it has been taken over by Andrée and Guy Record who run the St-Louis (on page 47). They have thoroughly revamped the public areas – adding a small *salon*/breakfast room and enlarging the reception – and have improved facilities in the beamed bedrooms. These are far from spacious, but the pretty decoration (antiques, tiled floors, wall hangings, fresh flowers) and friendly atmosphere make this a sound choice if you are looking for a peaceful, reasonably priced base close to the Bastille, and not far from the delightful Place des Vosges.

Nearby Bastille; Victor Hugo, Picasso and Carnavalet museums.

1 Rue Charles V 75004 Paris
Tel (1) 48.87.87.04
Fax (1) 48.87.33.26
Location between Place des Vosges and L'Ile Saint Louis; with public parking 400 metres from the hotel
Meals breakfast
Prices rooms 520F-720F; breakfast 42F
Rooms 11 double, 7 with bath, 4 with shower (2 twin); 4 single, all with shower; all rooms have central heating, phone
Facilities sitting-/breakfast room **Credit cards** MC, V
Children welcome
Disabled no special facilities
Pets small dogs accepted
Closed never **Proprietor** Andrée and Guy Record

Hôtel des Grandes Écoles

A cobbled lane reached through wooden gates leads you into the delightful courtyard-garden surrounding the main house and two annexes of this Left Bank hotel, which retains to an incredible degree the ambience of a country house. The name refers to the nearby Sorbonne and Faculté des Sciences; the hotel itself is anything but grand. Bedrooms are pleasantly simple, light and well kept, all overlooking the peaceful garden, and the reception is a cosy, welcoming area. Breakfast, if you want it, is taken in a tiny dining-room, or in the courtyard.

Nearby Boulevard Saint Germain; Ile Saint Louis; Ile de la Cité – Notre Dame; Luxembourg Palace and gardens.

75 Rue de Cardinal Lemoine 75005 Paris
Tel (1) 43.26.79.23
Fax (1) 43.25.28.15
Location in the Latin quarter; with garden and public car parking
Meals breakfast
Prices rooms 350F-650F; breakfast 40F
Rooms 39 double, 24 with bath, 7 with shower (4 twin); one single; 7 family rooms, 6 with bath, one with shower; all rooms have central heating, phone
Facilities breakfast-room, sitting-room
Credit cards MC, V
Children welcome
Disabled no special facilities
Pets welcome if well behaved
Closed never
Proprietor Mme le Floch

Paris

Hôtel de la Bretonnerie

Paris may have a great many hotels which conform to our requirements but it does not have many small hotels of distinct character. Here is one.

The Bretonnerie is a 17thC townhouse, set in the middle of the picturesque, convenient and (now) fashionable Marais district, and converted with a good deal of sympathy and style. The exposed beams in the public areas and the upper bedrooms are echoed throughout the house by the sturdy hardwood furniture (some antique, some reproduction). The small basement breakfast and sitting-rooms have a medieval feel, with pale stone vaulted ceilings, iron light fittings, richly coloured fabrics and polished tiled floors. Bedrooms are comfortable and pretty and every room is different; some are arranged with the beds on a mezzanine floor and the 'downstairs' used as a small sitting-area. All have a glossy modern bathroom or shower (most rooms have a bath) and guests will not find any lack of comfort.

Nearby Hôtel de Ville; Pompidou Centre (Beaubourg); Les Halles; Ile de la Cité – Conciergerie, Notre-Dame, Hôtel Dieu.

22 Rue Ste-Croix-de-la-Bretonnerie 75004 Paris
Tel (1) 48.87.77.63
Fax (1) 42.77.26.78
Location in Marais district, off the Rue du Temple, near Hôtel de Ville; with garage car parking nearby
Meals breakfast
Prices rooms 500F-800F; breakfast 42F
Rooms 28 double (12 twin), 4 single, all with bath or shower; all have central heating, phone, TV, minibar, safe
Facilities cellar sitting-room/breakfast room
Credit cards MC, V
Children welcome
Disabled lift/elevator but access difficult
Pets not accepted
Closed Aug
Proprietor M. P Sagot

Paris

Hôtel Prince Albert

Reasonably priced rooms of any comfort are hard to come by in the 1st *arrondissement* of Paris (the best-value hotels are nearly all on the Left Bank or in the less desirable quarters of the Right Bank). The Prince Albert, a very small hotel lying roughly half-way between the Louvre and the Opéra, is an exception. As the name suggests, this is a hotel reminiscent of Victorian England and, not surprisingly, it is popular with the British. The sitting-room is welcoming; the corridors upstairs are rather dim, but lead to bedrooms that are well cared for and comfortable – the majority with their own bathrooms.

Nearby L'Orangerie; Tuileries gardens; Place Vendôme.

5 Rue St-Hyacinthe 75001 Paris
Tel (1) 42.61.58.36
Fax (1) 42.60.04.06
Location between Rue de Rivoli and the Opéra; car parking nearby
Meals breakfast
Prices rooms 420F-550F, extra bed 165F; breakfast 38F
Rooms 21 double, 20 with bath, one with shower (6 twin); 10 single, all with bath; 2 family rooms with bath; all rooms have central heating, TV, phone, minibar, safe
Facilities sitting-room, breakfast room
Credit cards AE, MC, V
Children accepted
Disabled no special facilities
Pets not accepted
Closed never
Manager German Ross

Hôtel Gaillon Opéra

The first reason for the well established popularity of the Gaillon Opéra must be its central location – just a stone's throw from l'Opéra itself, in the heart of the Right Bank shopping district and close to many important sights. But there are other attractions as well. The salon displays the old stone walls and beams of the original 19thC building, and there is a reassuringly rustic feeling about the place as a whole. Bedrooms are neither very light nor spacious – especially at the top of the house, where rooms have been made in the roof-space – but they are warmly and tastefully furnished, many with beams and floral fabrics. Bathrooms are modern and well equipped. Although not expensive for the area, it cannot be called a cheap hotel; but it is a cut above the average in terms of comfort as well as charm.

Nearby Louvre, Opéra, Place Vendôme, Tuileries, Place de la Madeleine, Les Halles.

9 Rue Gaillon 75002 Paris
Tel (1) 47.42.47.74
Location 100 m SE of L'Opéra; with small terrace
Meals breakfast **Prices** rooms 500F-810F; breakfast 35F
Rooms 26 double, all with bath (9 twin); all have central heating, TV, phone, safe, minibar **Facilities** sitting-room
Credit cards AE, DC, MC, V
Children accepted
Disabled no special facilities
Pets accepted **Closed** never
Managers M. and Mme Wolecki

Paris

Hôtel St-Dominique

Every year, as in other big cities, various run-down Parisian hotels undergo dramatic face-lifts in the hands of new owners, many aiming more for panache than perfection. The St-Dominique, mercifully, has side-stepped the usual modern glossy design clichés in favour of freshness, simplicity and honest service. No minimalist reception desks or wall-to-wall mirrors here; instead, a couple of deep salmon-pink armchairs, a plain-carpeted floor with a Persian rug, a pine dresser, mirror, fresh flowers. Wooden stairs lead down to a little breakfast room – a white-painted vault with comfy banquette seats and Lloyd loom chairs. Even the hotel's exterior is eye-catching: a green door flanked by two large paned windows.

Bedrooms are small but well equipped, with TVs and refrigerators. In 1993 all the bedrooms and bathrooms were refurbished – not before time, we might observe – in a confidently colourful style, retaining predominantly pine furniture.

Breakfasts are generous and beautifully presented, and a reader notes that drinks can be had in the flowery little courtyard. Friendly staff.

Nearby Hôtel des Invalides (military museum), Rodin Museum, Musée d'Orsay, Blvd-St-Germain, church of St-Germain des Prés, Place de la Concorde, Tuileries.

62 Rue St-Dominique 75007 Paris
Tel (1) 47.05.51.44
Fax (1) 47.05.81.28
Location on busy street between Les Invalides and the Eiffel Tower; with patio, and car parking nearby
Meals breakfast
Prices rooms 450F-600F, extra child's bed 90F; breakfast 40F
Rooms 34 double (10 twin), 14 with bath, 20 with shower; all rooms have central heating, TV, phone, minibar
Facilities sitting-room, breakfast room
Credit cards AE, DC, MC, V
Children accepted
Disabled lift/elevator
Pets accepted
Closed never
Proprietors M. Antoine Tible and Mme Michèle Petit

Paris

La Régence Etoile

The Régence Etoile occupies a 'listed' 1875 house, and is decorated and furnished in suitably traditional style. The bedrooms are mostly spacious and comfortable (those at the front of the house being more airy but also more noisy than those at the back – the Ave Carnot is quite a thoroughfare), with smart bathrooms. And there is more space for sitting than is common in Parisian bed-and-breakfast places. The hotel has been family-run since it opened in the 1940s; Patrick Larré took over from his mother last year. The location is convenient for sights to the west of the centre.

Nearby Arc de Triomphe, Champs Elysées, Ave Foch, Bois de Boulogne – Longchamps racecourse and other attractions.

24 Ave Carnot 75017 Paris
Tel (1) 43.80.75.60
Fax (1) 47.66.78.86
Location close to Arc de Triomphe, on one of the roads radiating from it; public car parking nearby
Meals breakfast
Prices rooms 420F-700F
Rooms 33 double (8 twin), 29 with bath, 4 with shower; 5 family rooms with bath; all rooms have central heating, phone, TV, minibar, hairdrier
Facilities sitting-room, bar
Credit cards AE, MC, V
Children accepted
Disabled lift/elevator
Pets not accepted
Closed never
Proprietor Patrick Larré

Hôtel St-Merry

This former presbytery of the Church of St-Merry, next door, was converted to a private residence after the 1789 revolution, and more recently to a highly individual hotel by the charming M. Crabbe. In the past, St-Merry was distinctive for character rather than comfort, but recently some of the smaller rooms have been knocked together and refurbished. In number 9 spectacular flying buttresses form an alarmingly low canopy over the bed; numbers 12 and 17 have remarkable Gothic bedheads. Stone and dark carved wood predominate, with muted fabrics and oriental rugs. Set in a revitalised area of Paris filled with animation and interesting architecture, the St-Merry fits in well.

Nearby Ile de la Cité – Notre Dame; Pompidou centre.

78 Rue de la Verrerie 75004 Paris
Tel (1) 42.78.14.15
Fax (1) 40.29.06.82
Location in the Marais, close to Rue de Rivoli; with public car parking nearby
Meals breakfast
Prices rooms 400F-1000F; breakfast 40F
Rooms 11 double, 2 with bath, 7 with shower (4 twin); 2 family rooms, both with shower; all rooms have central heating, phone
Facilities bar beneath hotel
Credit cards not accepted
Children accepted
Disabled no special facilities
Pets accepted
Closed never
Proprietor Christian Crabbe

Paris

Résidence Lord Byron

In an area dominated by grand and impersonal hotels, the Lord Byron stands out for its personal service and (by local standards) reasonable prices. Bedrooms are modern, clean and comfortable, with a mixture of old and new furnishings; they tend to be smallish (bigger ones are described as 'small apartments') but they are pleasant, and many of them overlook the pretty tree-filled courtyard where breakfast is served on sunny days. A cool and elegant reception area, tastefully furnished with antiques, links this patio with the dignified entrance; there is also a comfortable, more modern sitting-room.

Nearby Arc de Triomphe, Champs Elysées, Blvd Haussmann.

5 Rue de Chateaubriand 75008 Paris **Tel** (1) 43.59.89.98 **Location** close to Arc de Triomphe, between Ave Friedland and Champs Elysées; with garden, and car parking in Champs Elysées **Meals** breakfast **Prices** rooms 650F-1,300F; breakfast 55F **Rooms** 23 double with bath; 1 single with shower; 7 family rooms with bath; all rooms have central heating, phone, TV, minibar **Facilities** breakfast room, sitting-room **Credit cards** MC, V **Children** accepted **Disabled** lift/elevator but access difficult **Pets** not accepted **Closed** never **Proprietor** Mme Benoit

Hôtel des Marronniers

This tall, gracious hotel, set between a courtyard and a rear garden containing the eponymous horse-chestnut trees, brings the calm of the country into the heart of bustling St-Germain. The inside is country-style too – birds and leaves decorate every available surface, and there are fresh flowers in the spacious stone-vaulted cellars which form the breakfast room and sitting-room that are cosily furnished with rugs and antiques. Bedrooms are similarly furnished, brightly decorated but variable in size. The glazed veranda, overlooking the garden, is the perfect place to laze or read or have breakfast.

Nearby Blvd St-Germain – church of St-Germain-des- Prés; Île de la Cité – Notre Dame, Conciergerie; Musée d'Orsay.

21 Rue Jacob 75006 Paris **Tel** (1) 43.25.30.60 **Fax** (1) 40.46.83.56 **Location** between the Seine and Blvd Saint-Germain; with small garden, and public car parking nearby **Meals** breakfast **Prices** rooms 450F-1,140F; breakfast 45F **Rooms** 31 double (9 twin), 3 single, 3 family rooms; all with bath or shower; all rooms have central heating, phone **Facilities** breakfast room, sitting-room **Credit cards** not accepted **Children** accepted **Disabled** no special facilities **Pets** not accepted **Closed** never **Proprietor** M. Henneveux

Paris

Hôtel Prima-Lepic

Set in bustling Montmartre, just 5 minutes' walk from Sacré-Coeur, this is a pleasant bed and breakfast place, recently taken over by Mme Renouf. The ground-floor reception and breakfast area is done out as a sort of indoor courtyard, with plenty of green plants, flowers, light walls and ceiling, white garden chairs and tables – giving an airy and peaceful effect even if it doesn't provide the greatest comfort. Bedrooms are individually and well decorated, with a mixture of modern and antique furniture – although they are not over-spacious. Front-facing rooms have recently been double-glazed to cut out street noise. Breakfast is buffet-style, with a choice of breads, croissants and cheeses.
Nearby Sacré-Coeur basilica, Place Pigalle, Moulin Rouge.

29 Rue Lepic 75018 Paris
Tel (1) 46.06.44.64
Location in Montmartre, with public car parking nearby
Meals breakfast
Prices rooms 320F-380F
Rooms 33 double (20 twin), 5 family rooms all with bath or shower; all rooms have central heating, phone
Facilities sitting-room, bar

Credit cards MC, V
Children accepted
Disabled no special facilities
Pets accepted
Closed never
Proprietor Mme Renouf

Hôtel de Banville

Finding your way from the Périphérique to the Boulevard Berthier is easy, and parking here does not pose an insoluble problem – so motorists should arrive here in good humour. Nor will this airy art deco building with flower-filled window boxes dampen your spirits. Inside, all is tastefully decorated and comfortable, bordering on the luxurious. In the bedrooms, light furniture and decorations create a spacious feel; antiques are dotted throughout, and flower arrangements add a reassuring personal touch. Peace is ensured by the efficient sound-proofing. All the public areas were renovated in 1990.
Nearby Arc de Triomphe, Champs-Élysées, Palais des Congres.

166 Blvd Berthier 75017 Paris
Tel (1) 42.67.70.16
Fax (1) 44.40.42.77
Location on service road off major boulevard, N of Arc de Triomphe; with garage and roadside car parking nearby
Meals breakfast
Prices rooms 600F-700F; breakfast 40F
Rooms 35 double, 29 with bath, 6 with shower (13 twin); 4 family rooms, 3 with bath, one with shower; all rooms have central heating, phone, TV, radio **Facilities** sitting-room, small dining- room
Credit cards AE, MC, V
Children welcome; baby-sitting available
Disabled no special facilities
Pets accepted
Closed never
Proprietor Mme Lambert

Paris

Hôtel Regent's Garden

An elegant 1820s townhouse built for Napoleon III's personal physician in a chic residential area. The outstanding asset is the shady, peaceful garden, with mature trees, lawn, lavender and tubs of flowers – and tables and chairs for breakfasts on sunny days. But the hotel has many other attractions – elegant, period-style sitting-areas, spacious bedrooms, immensely helpful and pleasant staff, private car parking (limited), and a general air of style and individuality. An otherwise enthusiastic reporter noticed signs of damp in the public rooms and felt that both the bedrooms and bathrooms needed attention.

Nearby Arc de Triomphe, Champs Elysée, Ave Foch.

6 Rue Pierre-Demours 75017 Paris
Tel (1) 45.74.07.30
Fax (1) 40.55.01.42
Location near Place Tristan Bernard on Avenue des Ternes, N of Arch de Triomphe; with garden and limited private car parking
Meals breakfast
Prices rooms 640F-930F; breakfast 38F

Rooms 39 double with bath; all rooms have central heating, TV, phone, radio, minibar, hairdrier
Facilities 1 breakfast room
Credit cards AE, DC, MC, V
Children welcome; under 12 free
Disabled lift/elevator
Pets accepted
Closed never
Proprietor M. Frot

Paris

Hôtel des Grands Hommes

Since it was built in the 18thC the Grands Hommes has always been a hotel, and was notably popular with surrealist artists and writers (perhaps the best-known among them being André Breton). The handsome building was renovated in 1982, but preserves original features such as exposed beams in some bedrooms. The best of these are very attractive, but the worst plain and 'very tired'. If you opt for a view of the Panthéon, be prepared for street noise. Stone-vaulted cellars with a tiled floor now serve as the breakfast room. The lobby is more elegant and glossy.

Nearby Panthéon (and its crypt), Luxembourg gardens and palace, Blvd St-Germain; short walk to Notre-Dame.

17 Place du Panthéon 75005 Paris **Tel** (1) 46.34.19.60
Fax (1) 43.26.67.32
Location opposite the Panthéon, in Latin quarter; with public car parking 5 minutes away
Meals breakfast
Prices rooms 600F-780F
Rooms 31 double, all with bath (9 twin); one single with shower; extra beds possible in

10 rooms ; all rooms have central heating, cable TV, radio, minibar, hairdrier
Facilities bar, breakfast room
Credit cards AE, DC, MC, V
Children very welcome; cot and baby-sitting available
Disabled no special facilities
Pets accepted if well behaved
Closed never
Proprietors M. and Mme Brethous

Hôtel Duc de St-Simon

A stylish hotel on a stylish street, just off the Blvd St-Germain. First glimpsed through two pairs of French windows which open on to a pretty courtyard, the interior looks wonderfully inviting; and so it is – there is a warm, beautifully furnished salon with the distinctly private-house feel that the proprietor seeks to maintain, and elegant yet cosy bedrooms with not a jarring note. Twin bedrooms are more spacious than those with double beds. The white-painted 19thC house backs on to a 18thC building behind, also part of the hotel, with a tiny secret garden wedged in between. Breakfasts can be had in the intimate cellar bar; service is smiling and courteous.

Nearby Hôtel des Invalides, Musée d'Orsay, church of St-Germain-des-Prés, Rodin Museum.

14 Rue de St-Simon 75007 Paris **Tel** (1) 45.48.35.66
Fax (1) 45.48.68.25
Location St-Germain-des-Prés
Meals breakfast, light meals
Prices rooms 1,000F-1,500F; suites 1,500F-2,000F
Rooms 29 double, 28 with bath, one with shower (10 twin); 5 suites, with bath; all

have central heating, phone, safe; TV on request; some rooms have air-conditioning
Facilities 2 sitting-rooms, bar
Credit cards not accepted
Children accepted
Disabled no special facilities
Pets not accepted
Closed never
Proprietor M. G Lindqvist

Seine-et-Marne

Converted mill, Flagy

Hostellerie du Moulin

In an area short on our kind of hotel, this imaginatively converted 13thC flour-mill, with gardens and stream, stands out as a gem. The mill wheels and pulleys are the focal point of the sitting-room; the bedrooms are named after cereal plants and have the requisite beams, stone walls and old prints. The food is some of the best in the region, drawing plenty of local custom. In summer you can eat outside under weeping willows; in winter there are blazing log fires. 'A real treat' enthuses a recent visitor.
Nearby Fontainbleau Château; Sens (40 km) – cathedral.

2 Rue du Moulin 77940 Flagy
Tel (1) 60.96.67.89
Fax (1) 60.96.69.51
Location in village, 23 km SE of Fontainebleau, 10 km W of Montereau; with car parking
Meals breakfast, lunch, dinner
Prices rooms 220F-450F; breakfast 40F; menus 160F-200F
Rooms 7 double, 3 family rooms, all with bath; all rooms have phone
Facilities dining-room, bar, sitting-room; fishing
Credit cards AE, DC, MC, V
Children accepted
Disabled access to dining-room, not to bedrooms
Pets accepted
Closed 11-23 Sep, 18 Dec-20 Jan; Sun evening and Mon (except Easter, Pentecost and 15 Aug: closed Mon evening and Tue)
Proprietor Claude Scheidecker

Manor-house hotel, Fontenay-Trésigny

Le Manoir

With its half-timbering, steep tiled roof and lush surrounding shrubbery, this mock-tudor turn-of-the-century mansion could be in the garden of England rather than the Ile de France, at least from the outside. Inside, the impression is emphatically corrected: the decoration and furnishings are distinctively French – rich and ornate, and occasionally gloomy. The bedrooms differ widely in style, so see a selection if the opportunity arises; the best are gloriously spacious and romantic. Fresh pink linen enlivens the grand panelled dining-room, where the increasingly ubiquitous *cuisine classique allègée* is served with due ceremony. Handily placed for both Paris airports and Eurodisney.
Nearby Vaux le Vicomte (25km) – château.

77610 Fontenay-Trésigny
Tel (1) 64.25.91.17
Location in countryside 4 km E of village; in large grounds, with ample private car parking (and airstrip)
Meals breakfast, lunch, dinner
Prices rooms 790F-1,150F; menus 240F-350F
Rooms 15 double, 5 suites, all with bath; all rooms have phone, TV, minibar
Facilities bar, sitting-room, dining-room, meeting-rooms; heated swimming-pool, tennis
Credit cards AE, DC, MC, V
Children welcome
Disabled access difficult
Pets welcome
Closed Feb
Proprietor M. Sourisseau

Seine-et-Marne

Hôtellerie du Bas-Breau

Among this handsome and luxurious inn's illustrious past guests are Emperor Hirohito and half of Europe's political grandees, which gives some clue to its reputation – and prices. Tucked away in a corner of the Fontainebleau forest, it is a black and white timbered building, decked with geraniums, around a cobbled courtyard. The best guest rooms are in the old part of the inn; but the majority are in a modern chalet set amid the beautifully tended flower gardens. All are spacious, comfortable and individually furnished with antiques and old prints. The sitting-room is cosy, the bar elegant, the dining-room suave; excellent food.
Nearby Fontainebleau; Milly (10 km).

22 Rue Grande, 77630 Barbizon
Tel (1) 60.66.40.05
Fax (1) 60.69.22.89
Location on cobbled street in heart of Barbizon, 5 km NW of Fontainebleau; with car parking
Meals breakfast, lunch, dinner
Prices rooms 950F-1,500F, suites 1,700F-2,800F; breakfast 90F, dinner from 500F

Rooms 20 double, all with bath; all rooms have central heating, phone, TV, hairdrier
Facilities dining-room, sitting-room, bar; swimming-pool, tennis
Credit cards AE, MC, V
Children welcome
Disabled ground-floor rooms
Pets supplement for dogs 75F
Closed never
Proprietor M. and Mme Fava

Hostellerie de la Clé d'Or

The key attraction of the Clé d'Or is the large, shady courtyard extending behind the hotel, where meals (well cooked, ample portions) are served in summer. There is also a delightful garden which comes into its own in the summer months. Bedrooms are in a handsome single-storey extension down one side of the courtyard; most were smartly redecorated last year. The main building has a sitting area, a small bar and a smart dining-room with an open fireplace and walls covered in daubs by local artists.
Nearby Fontainebleau (10 km) – château and forest.

73 Grande Rue 77630 Barbizon
Tel (1) 60.66.40.96
Fax (1) 60.66.42.71
Location in main street of village, off A6 autoroute; with garden and private car parking
Meals breakfast, lunch, dinner
Prices rooms 290F-480F; suite 850F; menus 200F-250F, children's 75F
Rooms 13 double (3 twin), 8 with bath, 5 with shower; 2 single with shower; one suite

with bath; all have central heating, phone, TV, minibar
Facilities dining-room, sitting-room, bar, conference room
Credit cards AE, DC, MC, V
Children welcome
Disabled 7 ground-floor bedrooms
Pets accepted
Closed never
Proprietors Philippe Gayer

Pas-de-Calais

Restaurant with rooms, Montreuil-sur-Mer

Auberge de la Grenouillère

A mere 40 km from Boulogne, tucked away in a clearing at the end of a country lane beneath the walls of the old town of Montreuil, this low Picardy-style farmhouse (known to many as the Froggery) has long been a popular gastronomic halt with the British, who appreciate its fine gravel terrace for leisurely lunches and the gleaming brass and polished wood charm of its restaurant – complete with frog-motif mural (done by an Englishman, of course). Indeed, some consider it well worth organising a ferry excursion to Boulogne just to sample Roland Gauthier's seven-course 'discovery' menu.

Now, at last, it is also worth considering the possibility of staying in this delightful place; the Gauthiers have done up four captivating bedrooms (one is particularly large, and eminently suitable for families), complete with well equipped and very attractive bathrooms.

If you are normally resolute about going native once on French soil, and feel you might be put off by all those other English voices, relax. You can safely resist the temptation to carry on driving: this is a serious French enterprise and the Gauthiers have not let their popularity make them complacent.

Nearby Ramparts, citadel; Le Touquet (15 km).

La Madelaine-sous-Montreuil, 62170 Montreuil-sur-Mer
Tel 21.06.07.22
Fax 21.86.36.36
Location by river at end of lane off D139, NW of Montreuil-sur-Mer; with ample car parking
Meals breakfast, lunch, dinner
Prices rooms 300F-500F; dinner 190F-350F
Rooms 4 double, one family room, all with bath; all rooms have central heating, phone, radio **Facilities** dining-room, small bar
Credit cards AE, DC, MC, V
Children welcome
Disabled one ground-floor room
Pets not accepted
Closed 15 Dec to 15 Jan; Tue and Wed from Sep to Jun
Proprietor M. and Mme Gauthier

Pas-de-Calais

Château hotel, Aire-sur-la-Lys

Hostellerie des 3 Mousquetaires

Since it found its way into English guidebooks some years ago, this jolly 19thC château, equidistant from the ferry ports of Boulogne, Calais and Dunkerque, has been unable to meet the demand for its few rooms – bookings have had to be made months ahead. But in 1988 the number of rooms was more than doubled by the conversion of a pavilion in the grounds. Despite the vast increase in capacity, reports confirm that the Venets continue to maintain their exceptional standards.

The hotel is a family-run *logis*, a world away from the classical château pattern. The charming and vigilant Mme Venet is in charge front of house, aided by her daughter-in-law, while husband Marcel and son Philippe prepare regionally based meals offering 'enormous portions' and 'astonishing value' in the spotless open-to-view kitchen. (The cheeseboard is 'magnificent'.) The building is an eccentric mixture of stone-and-brick stripes and pseudo-timbering beneath a steep slate roof, set in a large wooded garden with ponds and streams (ducks and swans) and comfortable chairs dotted about. The interior is traditionally grand in style, the best of the old bedrooms (eg 'Milady') huge and elegant; those in the new annexe are sumptuously decorated in various styles – one has a Japanese theme, for example.

Nearby Aire – Renaissance bailiff's court, collegiate church of St-Pierre; St Omer (20 km) – basilica, fine arts museum.

Château du Fort de la Redoute 62120 Aire-sur-la-Lys
Tel 21.39.01.11
Fax 21.39.50.10
Location in countryside off N43, 2km S of Aire; in parkland, with ample car parking
Meals breakfast, lunch, dinner
Prices rooms 250F-550F, suites 880F; breakfast 46F, menus 106F-325F, children's menu 58F **Rooms** 31 double (9 twin), 24 with bath, 2 with shower; one suite with bath; one family room with bath; all rooms have central heating, TV, phone **Facilities** 2 sitting-rooms, 2 dining-rooms, bar; golf **Credit cards** AE, MC, V **Children** welcome; cots and special menu available **Disabled** no special facilities **Pets** accepted **Closed** 15 Dec to 15 Jan; Sun evening and Mon **Proprietors** M. and Mme Philippe Venet

Pas-de-Calais

Hotel Cléry

A dignified and elegant façade dominates the fine tree-lined approach to this 18thC mansion, surrounded by parkland. If it seems at first glance a trifle intimidating, do not fear. This is not a stuffy place; there is not an antler in sight, nor are the public rooms stiff with Louis XV chairs (although there is a very fine Louis XV wrought-iron staircase), or even laden with chintz. Here, all is bright and light in harmonious pastel tones, in understated modern style. Bedrooms are well decorated, with a good modern annexe. Madame Osseland is a very welcoming but not overpowering hostess. There is no restaurant.

Nearby Hardelot, golf and beach (9km); Le Touquet (15km)

62360 Hesdin-L'Abbé
Tel 21.83.19.83
Fax 21.87.52.59
Location in tiny rural village, 9 km SE of Boulogne; with gardens and ample car parking
Meals breakfast
Prices rooms 300F-560F
Rooms 17 double, 9 with bath, 8 with shower (12 twin); all have central heating,
phone, TV
Facilities bar, sitting-room; tennis court
Credit cards AE, DC, MC, V
Pets not accepted
Disabled no special facilities
Closed mid-Dec to mid-Jan
Proprietor M. and Mme Osseland

Château de Montreuil

A substantial, luxurious country house lacking nothing except a French atmosphere (most of the resident guests are British, as is Mme Germain). The house was completely renovated in 1989: the sitting-rooms and bedrooms are immaculately decorated and furnished with taste; those on the top floor are very spacious, but the first floor rooms give better views of the beautiful English-style gardens. Christian Germain's cooking is ambitious and highly regarded (the restaurant has a loyal French following); even breakfast ('home-made everything') is unusually delicious.

Nearby Ramparts (still intact), citadel; Le Touquet (15 km).

4 Chaussée des Capucins
62170 Montreuil-sur-Mer
Tel 21.81.53.04
Fax 21.81.36.43
Location in quiet part of town, 38 km S of Boulogne, off N1; with large garden and ample car parking
Meals breakfast, lunch, dinner
Prices rooms 590F-900F, DB&B 1,550F; menus 240F-390F
Rooms 11 double, 10 with
bath (6 twin); 3 single; 2 family rooms all with bath or shower; all rooms have central heating, phone
Facilities sitting-room, dining-room, bar
Credit cards MC, V
Children welcome
Disabled 3 ground-floor bedrooms **Pets** not accepted
Closed mid-Dec to end Jan
Proprietors Christian and Lindsay Germain

Somme/Oise

Château de Remaisnil

This eighteenth-century rococo mansion in beautiful grounds was for some years the home of Bernard and Laura Ashley, whose decorative designs feature in countless British charming small hotels. The grandeur of the house may come as a surprise, but it is nevertheless a gracious home rather than a hotel, with abundant quirks and character. The most expensive rooms are extremely grand; even the simplest, in the converted coach-house, are harmonious and comfortable.

Nearby Abbeville (43 km); Amiens – cathedral (35 km)

Remaisnil 80600 Doullens
Tel 22.77.07.47
Fax 22.32.43.27
Location on edge of tiny hamlet, off D938, 8 km NW of Doullens, 35 km N of Amiens; in 35-acre grounds, with ample car parking
Meals breakfast, dinner (by arrangement)
Prices rooms 750F-1600F; breakfast 65F; dinner 395F including wine
Rooms 12 double (4 twin), 5 single, all with bath or shower; all have central heating, phone, TV, minibar
Facilities sitting-rooms, dining-room, library, billiard room; tennis, horse-riding, bicycles
Credit cards AE, MC, V
Children accepted
Disabled poor access
Pets not accepted
Closed late Feb to early Mar
Proprietors Adrian and Susan Doull

Le Prieuré

If a port of call to the north of Paris is needed, this will do nicely, provided your budget is not too tight – the rooms are not cheap by the standards of French bed-and-breakfast places, but it is an exceptionally attractive house. The creeper-covered former vicar-age, right next to the church, is beautifully furnished with antiques (Madame Treillou used to be a dealer) and decorated with unusual style. The bedrooms are well equipped, those in the roof-space on the second floor having the bonus of exposed beams. There is a neat breakfast room, and an immaculate 'English' garden. There are restaurants nearby.

Nearby Senlis; Chantilly – château (25 km); Paris (40 km).

Chevet de l'Eglise 60440 Ermenonville
Tel 44.54.00.44
Fax 44.54.02.21
Location next to church in village, on N330 9 km SE of Senlis; in garden, with private car parking
Meals breakfast
Prices rooms 450F-600F; breakfast 50F
Rooms 11 double (2 twin), all with bath or shower; all have central heating, phone, TV, minibar
Facilities 2 sitting-rooms, breakfast room
Credit cards AE, DC, MC, V
Children welcome
Disabled no special facilities
Pets accepted
Closed never
Proprietors Jean-Pierre and Marie-José Treillou

Aisne

La Bannière de France

Near Laon cathedral lies the Bannière de France, a former coaching inn dating back to the 17thC. Behind its rather plain façade, a winding staircase leads to spacious bedrooms with sloping floorboards and flowery decoration. Mme Lefèvre and her enthusiastic staff run the hotel efficiently, but visitors confirm that the highlight of a stay here is the excellent food (menus to suit all budgets), produced by chef Dominique Havot and served in the subtly lit, suitably traditional dining-room.
.**Nearby** Cathedral and narrow medieval streets; Reims (50 km).

11 Rue Franklin Roosevelt
02000 Laon
Tel 23.23.21.44
Location in centre of old town; with large garage
Meals breakfast, lunch, dinner
Prices rooms 225F-365F; menus 110F-310F, children's 48F
Rooms 11 double, 2 with bath, 9 with shower (2 twin); one single with shower; 6 family rooms, all with bath or shower; all rooms have central heating, phone, TV; most rooms have hairdrier
Facilities dining-room, breakfast room, small bar
Credit cards AE, DC, MC, V
Children accepted
Disabled no special facilities
Pets not accepted
Closed 1 May; 20 Dec to 20 Jan
Proprietors Mme Lefèvre and family

Le Clos du Montvinage

Set back from the main road in a large courtyard, the Clos du Montvinage is an imposing red-brick building. The rooms are filled with a mixture of old and new furniture. Bedrooms have every convenience, and those at the back of the house have views of the walled garden (once a vineyard) and suffer no disturbance from the busy road. Le Clos is effectively the annexe of the nearby *Auberge du Val de l'Oise*, a cosy and cheerful 19thC coaching inn, praised for its food and congenial atmosphere.
Nearby Château de Guise, Vervins (7 km); Laon (45 km).

RN 2, 02580 Etréaupont
Tel 23.97.91.10
Fax 23.97.40.18
Location set back from N2 in village, between Vervins and La Capelle; with garden and private car parking
Meals breakfast, lunch, dinner
Prices rooms 265F-410F; dinner 78F-220F
Rooms 12 double, one single, 7 family rooms, all with bath; all rooms have central heating, air-conditioning, phone, TV, hairdrier, minibar
Facilities 3 dining-rooms, sitting-room, bar (billiards); tennis, table-tennis, bicycles
Credit cards AE, DC, MC, V
Children accepted; babysitting possible **Disabled** ground-floor rooms, one specially equipped **Pets** not accepted **Closed** 9-25 Aug, 23-27 Dec; Sun night; restaurant only, Mon lunch
Proprietors Dominique and Marie-Lise Trokay

Marne

Hôtel d'Angleterre

A traditional town hotel from the outside, the Angleterre has been largely modernized inside. Subtle colour schemes predominate. Deep armchairs, low tables and fresh flowers are found in the bar and sitting-room; in the bedrooms, the flowers face some competition from the fabrics. Bathrooms are smart and modern. The dining-room has been transformed, by means of screens, plants and mirrors, into a modern and relaxing place in which to sample Jacky's innovative and successful cooking. Our inspector praises the staff: welcoming, quick to respond, yet unobtrusive.

Nearby Cathedral, church of Notre-Dame-en-Vaux.

19 Place Monseigneur Tissier
51000 Châlons-sur-Marne
Tel 26.68.21.51
Fax 26.70.51.67
Location in middle of town, with terrace and small private car park
Meals breakfast, lunch, dinner
Prices rooms 300F-540F; breakfast 50F-60F; menus 120F-400F
Rooms 16 double with bath (6 twin); 2 family rooms; all

rooms have central heating, phone, TV, minibar, hairdrier
Facilities dining-room, sitting-room, bar
Credit cards AE, DC, MC, V
Children welcome; cots available
Disabled no special facilities
Pets accepted in restaurant
Closed Sun evening; 20 Jul to 12 Aug; 2 weeks at Christmas
Proprietor Jacky Michel

Aux Armes de Champagne

The Armes de Champagne feels half its actual size; sixteen of the rooms are in an annexe 200m down the road, and Monsieur Perardel and his friendly staff welcome you as if you were their only guests. The main attractions of the hotel are its setting – opposite an enormous basilica in a village where time stands still – and its renowned cuisine and cellar; 'top-class food and an interesting wine list – but a welcome lack of pretension,' says a visitor. The busy downstairs bar has plenty of atmosphere. The modern bedrooms are comfortable and impeccable.

Nearby Basilica de Notre-Dame; Châlons-sur-Marne (10 km).

Avenue du Luxembourg,
51460 L'Épine
Tel 26.69.30.30
Fax 26.66.92.31
Location opposite basilica in heart of L'Épine village, 5·km E of Châlons; with garden and car parking
Meals breakfast, lunch, dinner
Prices rooms 380F-780F; breakfast 60F, menus 100F-480F
Rooms 35 double, 2 suites, 30

with bath, 7 with shower (16 in annexe); all rooms have central heating, TV, phone, minibar
Facilities dining-room, bar, TV room; mini-golf, tennis
Credit cards MC, V
Children accepted
Disabled no special facilities
Pets accepted
Closed 10 Jan-15 Feb; Nov-Mar; Sun night and Mon
Manager Jean-Paul Perardel

Marne

Château hotel, Reims

Château des Crayères

To stay at this wonderful place for free would be heaven itself; having to pay for the experience is only slightly less perfect. Gérard Boyer (whom almost everyone agrees is one of the finest chefs in the land) and his wife Elyane had a good starting point: a graceful turn-of-the-century mansion (built in Louis XVI style, by a member of the house of Pommery), situated in a spacious park almost at the heart of Reims, and surrounded by the *caves* of the famous champagne names. With Elyane's exquisite taste in interior decoration, and her skill in making her grand house seem more like a cherished home than a hotel, they could hardly go far wrong.

There are a wonderful grand staircase, enormous windows, marble columns and tapestries; the dining-room is wood panelled and candle-lit, the 'English-style' bar is comfortable. Bedrooms are of two kinds: '*luxe*' and '*grand luxe*'; all are large and sumptuous, individually decorated to a theme, with views over the park; two have a large balcony.

The cooking is good enough to attract businessmen from Paris. Not surprisingly, it is necessary to book well ahead for the pleasure of a night or two *Chez Boyer.*

Nearby Basilica, cathedral; Mont Chenot (10 km) – start of the Champagne Route.

64 Blvd Henry Vasnier 51100 Reims **Tel** 26.82.80.80 **Fax** 26.82.65.52 **Location** on edge of city centre, near St-Remi basilica; in own grounds with ample car parking **Meals** breakfast, lunch, dinner **Prices** rooms 990F-1,860F; meals 450F-600F **Rooms** 19 double, all with bath (15 twin); all rooms have	air-conditioning, TV, phone, radio, minibar **Facilities** dining-room, bar, function room; tennis **Credit cards** AE, DC, MC, V **Children** welcome **Disabled** access possible, lift/elevator **Pets** dogs welcome **Closed** 3 weeks at Christmas/New Year; restaurant only, Mon and Tue lunch **Proprietor** M. Boyer

Bas-Rhin

Village inn, Marlenheim

Le Cerf

Cooking is what this ancient coaching inn is all about. Owner and chef Robert Husser and son Michel are a formidable and highly acclaimed team, their inventive dishes complemented by a distinguished wine list. Bedrooms are not luxurious, but are of a fair standard in a generally rustic style. There is a cobbled courtyard for drinks and breakfast – so, when the weather is fine, the shortage of sitting space should not be a problem.

Nearby Strasbourg (20 km) – Renaissance Chamber of Commerce, cathedral, Alsatian museum, half-timbered houses.

30 Rue du Général-de-Gaulle
67520 Marlenheim
Tel 88.87.73.73
Location on main road through village, 18 km W of Strasbourg; with courtyard and car parking
Meals breakfast, lunch, dinner
Prices rooms 450F-650F; meals 390F-600F
Rooms 17 double, 8 with bath, 7 with shower (6 twin); one single with shower; 2 family rooms, both with bath; all rooms have central heating, phone
Facilities dining-room, 2 function rooms
Credit cards AE,V
Children accepted
Disabled access to dining-room; 2 ground-floor bedrooms
Pets accepted
Closed school holidays in Feb; Tue, Wed
Proprietor Robert Husser

Haut-Rhin

Auberge d'Artzenheim

This is a cosy *auberge* off the beaten wine track. It has a terrace for outdoor eating and a pleasant, small sitting area with log fire; but the focal point is the restaurant, all beams and polished wood. It is popular both with tourists and locals from Colmar – a good sign – and the chef's repertoire is not confined to Alsatian dishes; the fixed-price menus, while not exactly cheap, are good value. Bedrooms (some small) are prettily decorated with rustic furniture and jolly fabrics.

Nearby Colmar (15 km) – Unterlinden Museum, half- timbered houses; Mulhouse (55km) – museums.

30 Rue du Sponeck 68320 Artzenheim
Tel 89.71.60.51
Fax 89.71.68.21
Location in middle of village, 15 km E of Colmar; in garden, with ample car parking
Meals breakfast, lunch, dinner
Prices rooms 255F-310F; menus 110F-160F
Rooms 10 double, 6 with bath, 4 with shower (2 twin); all rooms have central heating, phone, TV
Facilities 3 dining-rooms, sitting-room, garden room
Credit cards MC, V
Children accepted
Disabled access to dining-room, but difficult to hotel
Pets not accepted
Closed Feb; restaurant only Mon dinner and Tue
Proprietor Mme Husser-Schmitt

Les Alisiers

The amiable Jacques and Ella Degouy have turned this secluded farmhouse, high in the Vosges mountains, into a simple but welcoming and reasonably-priced *Logis*. The interior is rustic and intimate, the bedrooms small but comfortable, with pale wood furnishings. There is a flowery courtyard and garden, where you can admire the mountains over breakfast or early evening drinks before enjoying Ella's Alsatian specialities – served in a pleasant, airy restaurant (no smoking) with stunning views. A beautiful, secluded spot, and good value, too.

Nearby Colmar – Unterlinden Museum, half-timbered houses.

5 Faudé 68650 Lapoutroie
Tel 89.47.52.82
Fax 89.47.22.38
Location in countryside, 20 km W of Colmar, on N415; with courtyard and parking for 30 cars
Meals breakfast, lunch, dinner
Prices rooms 250F-365F; meals 78F-149F; 30-50% reductions for children sharing parents' room
Rooms 11 double, 3 with bath, 7 with shower (3 twin); one single; one family room with shower; all rooms have phone
Facilities sitting-room, dining-room, TV room, bar
Credit cards MC, V
Children accepted
Disabled no special facilities
Pets accepted
Closed Tue; Jan
Proprietors Ella and Jacques Degouy

Haut-Rhin

Le Clos Saint-Vincent

Ribeauvillé's most elegant hotel – a chalet-style building – stands high on a hill, surrounded by vineyards, looking across to the Black Forest. The rooms are spacious and tastefully furnished: reception is a cool, tiled hall; the restaurant, renowned for its cuisine and cellar, is an airy glassed room, with a surrounding terrace. Bedrooms are quiet and comfortable, and those on the ground floor have private terraces.

Nearby Vineyards; Colmar (10 km) – Unterlinden Museum, Custom's House; Mulhouse (50 km) – museums.

Rte de Bergheim 68150 Ribeauvillé
Tel 89.73.67.65
Fax 89.73.32.20
Location in vineyards on NE outskirts of town; with garden and ample car parking
Meals breakfast, lunch, dinner
Prices rooms 680F-1,150F; meals 200F-300F
Rooms 12 double with bath (8 twin); 3 family rooms, all with bath; all rooms have central heating, phone, minibar; TV

on request
Facilities indoor swimming-pool, dining-room, bar
Credit cards V
Children accepted
Disabled no special facilities
Pets accepted
Closed mid-Nov to mid-Mar; restaurant only Tue and Wed
Proprietors Bertrand and Marie-Laure Chapotin

Les Vosges

The wine villages of Alsace are some of the most charming in France, with their streets of timbered houses, pretty fountains, and the odd stork sitting on a roof-top nest. Surprisingly, it is hard to find a hotel that matches these idyllic surroundings. Joseph Matter's establishment is clearly an exception. The building is undistinguished, but the bedrooms are perfectly satisfactory, the dining-room is restful and refined and the cooking is innovative – a recent visitor was extremely impressed, and found the service and atmosphere very pleasant.

Nearby Colmar – Unterlinden Museum, half-timbered houses; Mulhouse (50 km); Strasbourg (50 km).

2 Grande Rue 68150 Ribeauvillé
Tel 89.73.61.39
Fax 89.73.34.21
Location on main street of village, 15 km NW of Colmar
Meals breakfast, lunch, dinner
Prices rooms 255F-395F, suites 500F; breakfast 50F; menus 160F-390F
Rooms 16 double, 6 with bath, 10 with shower (13 twin); 2

suites; all rooms have phone, TV
Facilities dining-room, sitting-room
Credit cards AE, MC, V
Children accepted
Disabled no special facilities
Pets accepted
Closed Feb; restaurant only Mon
Proprietor Joseph Matter

Loir-et-Cher

Hostellerie La Malouinière

The Guide Michelin lists this captivating establishment in a Loire-side village as a restaurant with rooms. Certainly, Claude Berthon's excellent cooking is a major attraction (he gets one Michelin star), and the sitting-room is a modest affair. But the country garden and neat pool make it worth considering for more than the odd night after a blow-out dinner. The bedrooms, named after nearby châteaux, are strikingly decorated and comfortably furnished, and have splendid new bathrooms. The dining-room is elegant but inviting, with an open fire.

Nearby Blois; Chambord – château, game reserve (12 km).

1 Rue Bernard Lorjou 41000 Saint-Denis-sur-Loire
Tel 54.74.76.81
Fax 54.74.85.96
Location on edge of village, off N152, 5 km NE of Blois; in 2-acre grounds, with private car parking
Meals breakfast, lunch, dinner
Prices rooms 700F-1,200F; breakfast 75F, meals 290F-400F
Rooms 7 double (2 twin), 6 with bath, one with shower; one suite with bath; all rooms have central heating, phone, TV, minibar, safe
Facilities dining-room, sitting-room; swimming-pool
Credit cards MC, V **Children** welcome **Disabled** access easy
Pets small dogs welcome
Closed mid-Sep to mid-May; restaurant Sun dinner and Mon (Mon lunch high season)
Proprietors Denise and Claude Berthon

Château de Chissay

A small-scale fairytale château in the heart of château country, renovated in the late 1980s, with rooms ranging in price from the affordable to the rather less so – some of the most captivating being in the round turrets. Others vary widely in style, from the rather formal and high-ceilinged to the beamed medieval. At the heart of the château is a calm courtyard, complete with fountain, and the extensive grounds include a neat swimming-pool. The cooking is above average, including fish from the Loire.

Nearby vineyards and châteaux of the Loire valley – Chenonceaux (4 km), Amboise (23 km).

Chissay-en-Touraine 41400 Montrichard
Tel 54.32.32.01
Fax 54.32.43.80
Location on edge of village, on D176, 4 km W of Montrichard, 35 km E of Tours; in wooded grounds, with private car parking
Meals breakfast, lunch, dinner
Prices rooms 450F-1,500F; breakfast 60F, menus 160F-290F
Rooms 28 double (7 twin), 3 family rooms, all with bath; all have central heating, phone
Facilities dining-room, 3 sitting-rooms, TV room; swimming-pool
Credit cards AE, DC, MC, V
Children welcome
Disabled lift/elevator to all floors
Pets accepted (45F charge)
Closed mid-Nov to mid-Mar
Manager P Longet

Loir-et-Cher

Relais des Landes

This seventeenth-century mansion has more beds than we normally allow, but ample compensations: restful, spacious, well equipped bedrooms (most of them in dormer-windowed outbuildings on either side of the main house); and a splendidly peaceful setting, in neat gardens leading off to the ponds and woods that you would hope for in this area – the Sologne. The food is as traditional as the beamed, tiled dining-room in which it is served (open fire in winter). There is also a large terrace for summer dining.

Nearby tennis, bicycles; Blois – cathedral (15 km); châteaux of the Loire valley.

Ouchamps 41120 Les Montils
Tel 54.44.03.33
Fax 54.44.03.89
Location in countryside, on D7 off N764, 1 km N of Ouchamps, 15 km S of Blois; in large park with ample car parking
Meals breakfast, dinner
Prices rooms 495F-685F; DB&B 565F-855F
Rooms 26 double (10 twin), one family room, all with bath; all rooms have central heating, phone, TV, minibar
Facilities dining-room, sitting-rooms, bar; conservatory
Credit cards AE, DC, MC, V
Children welcome
Disabled easy access
Pets dogs only
Closed never
Proprietors Gérard Badenir and Andrée Rousselet

La Croix Blanche

The Goacolous took over this centuries-old auberge in 1989 from the famous Gisèle Crouzier, and by appointing one of her understudies to head the kitchen have managed to preserve the inn's 200-year-old tradition of women chefs. The style of cooking is largely Périgordian (*foie gras* and so on) but there are also local specialities and the style of the inn itself is pure Sologne – cosily traditional, with gleaming country antiques and floral-patterned fabrics and wallpapers; there are game trophies on the dining-room walls, beams and exposed brickwork in the rather prim sitting-room.

Nearby Orleans (35 km); Chambord (35 km).

41600 Chaumont-sur-Tharonne
Tel 54.88.55.12
Fax 54.88.60.40
Location in village W of N20 30km S of Orleans, with car parking
Meals breakfast, lunch, dinner
Prices rooms 290F-500F, breakfast 45F, menus 145F-350F
Rooms 12 double (5 twin), 4 family rooms, all with bath; all rooms have central heating, phone, TV, radio, minibar
Facilities reception, bar, dining-room, meeting room
Credit cards AE, DC, MC, V
Children accepted
Disabled some ground-floor rooms **Pets** dogs accepted by reservation **Closed** never
Proprietors M and Mme Michel Pierre Goacolou

Loir-et-Cher

Château de la Menaudière

A château in the heart of château country, which will not break the bank. By Loire standards it is a modest building, and its great charm is that the atmosphere is not intimidating, despite the formal furnishings. The courtyard in front of the house is a pleasant place for a drink before dinner (there is a pub-like bar in an outbuilding as an alternative) or for breakfast. There are two intimate and rather hushed dining-rooms, and a formal little sitting-room. The bedrooms are a strong point – spacious and well furnished, with smart bathrooms. Our favourites are those in a detached round tower, each occupying a floor. Excellent food, and we believe the service has improved since our last visit.

Nearby Chaumont (15 km); Amboise (13 km); Blois (35 km).

41401 Montrichard
Tel 54.32.02.44
Fax 54.71.34.58
Location in country, 2 km NW of Montrichard on D115; large grounds, ample car parking
Meals breakfast, lunch, dinner
Prices rooms 500F-650F; menus 180F-275F
Rooms 23 double, 2 single, all with bath; all have central heating, phone, TV, minibar
Facilities dining- room, sitting-room, bar, terrace; tennis
Credit cards AE, DC, MC, V
Children welcome **Disabled** access to restaurant only
Pets accepted **Closed** Dec to Feb; restaurant only, Sun night, Mon out of season
Manager Mme Moulard

Auberge de la Croix Blanche

Souvigny is a quiet, deliciously pretty little village in the middle of the Sologne – a region of woods and ponds much favoured for fishing and shooting. This family-run brick-and-timber *auberge* occupies a prime spot; within the annexe are rustic dining-rooms, all exposed beams and whitewash, and small, simple bedrooms with smartly-tiled bathrooms. M. and Mme Marois are conscientious hosts ('very warm welcome, hotel immaculate,' says a 1992 reporter) and the *cuisine traditionelle et copieuse* is highly regarded.

Nearby Sully (25 km) – château; Orléans (44 km).

Rue Eugene Labiche, Souvigny-en-Sologne 41600 Lamotte- Beuvron
Tel 54.88.40.08
Location in middle of village, 44 km SE of Orléans; with car parking
Meals breakfast, lunch, dinner
Prices rooms 120F-300F; breakfast 30F; menus 75F-230F
Rooms 8 double (5 twin), one single; all rooms have central heating, phone
Facilities 3 dining-rooms, TV room, bar
Credit cards V
Children accepted unless noisy
Disabled no special facilities
Pets accepted if well behaved
Closed mid-Jan to end-Feb; Tue dinner, Wed lunch and dinner
Proprietor M. Marois

Loiret

Hôtel de l'Abbaye

The setting of this noble building, a medieval abbey, is its main feature – on the banks of the Loire, facing the splendid old arched bridge of Beaugency. The style of the hotel retains a certain austerity – a lofty dining hall with black-and-white tiled floor and antlers over the tall fireplace, and a salon area in the similarly high-ceilinged reception hall (though here the squashy sofas are positively self-indulgent). Bedrooms (some duplex apartments) are spacious, and well decorated and equipped. Food has been reported to be above average.

Nearby golf; Tower of St-Firmin; châteaux of the Loire

2 Quai de l'Abbaye 45190 Beaugency
Tel 38.44.67.35
Fax 38.44.87.92
Location beside bridge over Loire in small town 25km SW of Orléans; with car parking
Meals breakfast, lunch, dinner
Prices rooms 420F-680F; menu 190F
Rooms 14 double (7 twin), 4 family rooms, all with bath; all rooms have central heating,
TV, phone
Facilities 2 dining-rooms, 2 sitting-rooms, bar, conference room
Credit cards AE, DC, MC, V
Children accepted
Disabled no special facilities
Pets dogs accepted
Closed never
Proprietor M. Aupetit

Hôtel du Rivage

Christian Gaillard's modern-classic cooking goes from strength to strength ('our best meal ever' enthuses one reporter), but remains only one of the attractions of this unpretentious but chic hotel facing the Loire. Lovely views over the river are shared by some of the bedrooms, the terrace of the beautiful bar/sitting-room, and the pretty dining-room, with its blue high-backed chairs. The Gaillards are ably assisted by a young staff, all anxious to please. Sadly, we have to record two complaints – of a worn-out bed, and of vegetarians being ripped off.

Nearby château (with museum); La Bussière (15 km) – château.

1 Quai de Nice 45500 Gien
Tel 38.37.79.00
Fax 38.38.10.21
Location on northern bank of Loire in town, 76 km N of Bourges; with private car parking
Meals breakfast, lunch, dinner
Prices rooms 300F-600F, suites 685F-785F; breakfast 45F; meals 155F-390F
Rooms 14 double (7 twin), all with bath; 2 single with
shower; 3 family rooms/suites with bath; all rooms have central heating, TV, phone
Facilities dining-room, sitting-room, bar
Credit cards AE, DC, MC, V
Children welcome
Disabled no special facilities
Pets welcome
Closed early Feb to Mar
Proprietor Christian Gaillard

Loiret

Village hotel, Beaugency

La Tonnellerie

A former wine merchant's house dating from around 1870, the Tonnellerie is now a charming creeper-covered hotel in the small village of Tavers, close to the Loire and not far from Beaugency, a medieval town very popular with tourists.

The hotel is set around a central courtyard-garden which is at the heart of its appeal. There is a pretty little swimming-pool, shady chestnut trees; tables for summer meals stand on the lawn and further away from the house on terrace areas. The country atmosphere extends indoors to the dining-rooms, both looking on to the garden, one in 'winter garden' style, the other handsomely rustic, with tiled floor and mellow woodwork. Cooking is *nouvelle* in style but recognizes the traditions of the region, and is above average in execution.

In the last couple of years Mme Aulagnon has steadily improved the hotel, adding four 'apartments/suites' (pastel walls, flowery drapes, polished antiques, smart tiled bathrooms) and refurbished other bedrooms.

Nearby Beaugency – Hôtel de Ville, Tour St-Firmin, church of Notre-Dame; châteaux – Chambord (25 km), Blois (30 km).

12 Rue des Eaux-Bleues, Tavers 45190 Beaugency
Tel 38.44.68.15
Fax 38.44.10.01
Location in middle of village, 3 km W of Beaugency; with garden, and private and public car parking
Meals breakfast, lunch, dinner
Prices rooms 705F-880F, apartments 880F-1,435F; breakfast 55F; menus 125F-310F
Rooms 12 double (7 twin), 3 suites, 5 apartments, all with bath; all rooms have central heating, phone, TV, hairdrier
Facilities 2 dining-rooms, sitting-room; swimming-pool, tennis, bicycle hire
Credit cards MC, V
Children welcome; cots available, special meals served in room
Disabled ground-floor rooms; lift/elevator
Pets not accepted
Closed mid-Oct to mid-Apr
Proprietor Mme Anne-Marie Aulagnon

Maine-et-Loire

Hôtel de la Sarthe

The obvious attraction of this modest *Logis* is its position, on a beautiful stretch of the river Sarthe. Grills and simple meals are served in a covered terrace beside the river, and there is a dining-room and very small bar area inside. The flowery rooms are simple but satisfactory, with plentiful towels and hot water. Food is simple and traditional, but well prepared and excellent value. The Houdebines are a handsome couple – hard-working, welcoming and tolerant, and they have a happy staff.

Nearby Anjou – châteaux; Angers – château (tapestries).

1 Rue du Port 49330
Châteauneuf-sur-Sarthe
Tel 41.69.85.29
Location near town bridge, 30 km N of Angers; with terrace and car parking
Meals breakfast, lunch, dinner
Prices rooms 190F-260F; breakfast 30F; menus 90F-200F
Rooms 7 double, 2 with bath, 5 with shower (one twin); all rooms have central heating
Facilities dining-room, sitting-room/bar

Credit cards MC, V
Children accepted
Disabled no special facilities
Pets accepted in public rooms only
Closed 3 weeks Oct, 2 weeks Feb; restaurant Sun dinner and Mon out of season
Proprietors M. and Mme Jean Pierre Houdebine

Château de Teildras

Set in acres of parkland, this aristocratic family home is a handsome creeper-clad, white-shuttered building, more approachable than many such châteaux; inside, too, it is reassuringly unpretentious, with exposed beams as well as antique furniture, pictures and tapestries. There is a large flowery terrace, with tables and comfortable chairs. Bedrooms are spacious, comfortable and reasonably stylish. Creative, but pricey, meals are served in the intimate dining-rooms.

Nearby golf; Château du Plessis-Bourré (5 km); Angers (24 km).

Cheffes 49125 Tiercé
Tel 41.42.61.08
Fax 41.42.17.01
Location in large park, N of Cheffes on minor road, 24 km N of Angers; with ample car parking
Meals breakfast, lunch, dinner
Prices rooms 620F-995F; menus 195F-320F
Rooms 11 double, with bath (4 twin); all rooms have central heating, TV, phone, minibar

Facilities 2 sitting-rooms, 2 dining-rooms; fishing, tennis
Credit cards AE, DC, MC, V
Children welcome; baby-sitting available
Disabled no special facilities
Pets accepted in bedrooms only, on lead in park
Closed restaurant only, Jan and Feb
Manager Yolaine de Bernard Smart

Maine-et-Loire

Auberge Jeanne de Laval

What brings most people here is the Michelin-starred restaurant – an elegant beamed room with a very modern glazed extension. You will not quickly forget Michel Augereau's exquisite *beurre blanc* sauce, served with fish fresh from the Loire. Only three of the bedrooms are in the *auberge* – the rest are a short walk away in the charming old Ducs d'Anjou annexe shown in our photo. They are quiet, spacious and tastefully decorated. Service in the annexe is limited to breakfast, which is served in the rooms or in the pretty garden.

Nearby Saumur (15 km); Angers (30 km) – cathedral, château.

54 Rue Nationale, Les Rosiers-sur-Loire 49350 Gennes
Tel 41.51.80.17
Location in middle of village, 15 km NW of Saumur; with flower gardens and car parking
Meals breakfast, lunch, dinner
Prices rooms 350F-550F; breakfast 50F, meals 170F-400F
Rooms 10 double, all but one with bath; all rooms have central heating, TV, minibar, phone
Facilities TV room, dining-room
Credit cards AE, DC, MC, V
Children welcome
Disabled no special facilities
Pets dogs accepted in bedrooms
Closed 11 Nov to 22 Dec; Mon (except public holidays and high season)
Proprietors Augereau family

Indre-et-Loire

Château de Pray

A 13thC château steeped in history and right in the middle of château country, in a magnificent position – high up above the Loire in its own peaceful parkland, with superb views from the windows and terraces. What is more, the formality and pretension which spoil so many château hotels are here kept within reasonable bounds. The building consists of medieval towers (complete with conical roofs) with a Renaissance house sandwiched in between; bedrooms in the towers have the advantage in terms of character, but all the rooms have been smartly redecorated since the arrival of Mme Cariou. The dining-room shares the view, and in kind weather there is service outside.
Nearby Châteaux – Amboise, Chaumont, Chenonceaux (15 km).

37400 Amboise
Tel 47.57.23.67
Fax 47.57.32.50
Location in park off D751, on S bank of Loire, 3 km NE of town; with ample car parking
Meals breakfast, lunch, dinner
Prices rooms 550F-870F; breakfast 45F, menus from 195F
Rooms 17 double, 2 suites, all with bath; all rooms have phone; 5 have TV
Facilities dining-room, sitting-room
Credit cards AE, DC, MC, V
Children accepted **Disabled** no special facilities
Pets accepted in bedrooms and garden only
Closed Jan and Feb
Proprietor Mme Cariou

Le Castel de Bray et Monts

The decoration of this elegant yet friendly establishment has a lighter touch than the French norm, and the Rochereaus are not short of ideas for keeping their rooms full – in spring and autumn they offer cookery courses with the morning spent preparing lunch under Maxime's eye and the afternoon visiting châteaux with Eliane. The 18thC manor house and converted chapel sit in their own tranquil grounds beside a stream, with shaded tables next to the house and a children's play area further away. 'The welcome is warm, the kitchen excellent.'
Nearby Châteaux – Villandry (10 km), Azay-le-Rideau (10 km).

Bréhémont, 37130 Langeais
Tel 47.96.70.47
Fax 47.96.57.36
Location in village on bank of the Loire, 5 km SW of Langeais on D16; within large park, with ample car parking
Meals breakfast, lunch, dinner
Prices rooms 295F-630F; menus 125F-260F
Rooms 9 double with bath; one family apartment with bath; all rooms have central heating, phone, TV, minibar
Facilities dining-room, sitting-room, bar
Credit cards V
Children welcome
Disabled 2 ground-floor rooms
Pets accepted
Closed mid-Nov to end-Jan
Proprietor Maxime and Eliane Rochereau

Indre-et-Loire

Town mansion, Chinon

Hôtel Diderot

Creeper-covered and white-shuttered, this handsome townhouse set in a quiet courtyard looks the epitome of 18thC elegance. And the Diderot has a faithful following of visitors who find it friendly, reliable and good value. The Cypriot proprietors are charming and unstintingly helpful, and breakfast (served on the shady terrace or in a rustic room with tiled floor and massive beams) is exceptionally tasty – thanks to Madame Kazamias's home-made preserves.

Bedrooms are very simply furnished but are spotlessly clean and some have fine views; smart new bathrooms have been recently added. Visitors confirm our recommendation.

Nearby Grand Carroi, ruined château, church of St-Maurice; châteaux – Azay-le-Rideau (20 km), Langeais (30 km); Villandry (35 km) – Renaissance gardens; Tours (48 km).

4 Rue Buffon 37500 Chinon
Tel 47.93.18.87
Location in middle of town; with courtyard and private car parking
Meals breakfast
Prices rooms 250F-380F; breakfast 36F
Rooms 28 double, 17 with bath, 11 with shower (8 twin); 3 family rooms, all with bath; all rooms have central heating, phone
Facilities bar, breakfast room
Credit cards AE, DC, MC, V
Children welcome
Disabled some ground-floor bedrooms
Pets not accepted
Closed 15 Dec to 15 Jan
Proprietor Theo Kazamias

Indre-et-Loire

Château d'Artannes

You pay a high price to stay at this historic twelfth-century castle – once the weekend retreat of the archbishops of Tours – but our instinct is that you get what you pay for. You sleep and eat in vast, high-ceilinged rooms with entirely antique furniture and Oriental rugs, and recline in panelled sitting-rooms. And you have the run of beautiful wooded grounds extending down to the pretty river Indre. The Hoffmann's 'family-style' cooking uses home-grown vegetables.

Nearby Tours – cathedral (15 km); Azay-le-Rideau – château (11 km).

Artannes 37260 Monts
Tel 47.65.70.60
Fax 47.65.72.36
Location on edge of village, 15 km SW of Tours, on D17 10 km W of Montbazon; in wooded grounds with private car parking
Meals breakfast, lunch, dinner
Prices rooms 800F-1,500F; meals 300F-500F
Rooms 6 double (3 twin), all with bath; all rooms have central heating, phone, TV on request
Facilities dining-room, sitting-rooms, function room, gym, sauna, jacuzzi, turkish bath; golf putting-green
Credit cards AE, DC, V
Children welcome; baby-sitting on request
Disabled ground floor rooms
Pets not accepted
Closed never
Proprietor M. Hoffmann

Château de Rochecotte

In the midst of châteaux country, here is an opportunity to stay and sample life in a château of the grandest style. Built at the end of the 18thC, Rochecotte was bought by the Prince de Talleyrand in 1882 and remained his favourite residence until his death. From the bedrooms to the dining-room, bright fabrics, elegant modern furniture and light decoration complement the classical proportions of the rooms. The cuisine is appropriately *gastronomique*. Formal terraces and an Italian garden are just part of the large grounds.

Nearby Châteaux – Langeais, Azay-le-Rideau (20 km).

St-Patrice 37130 Langeais
Tel 47.96.91.28
Fax 47.96.90.59
Location in extensive grounds off D35, 10 km W of Langeais; with ample car parking
Meals breakfast, lunch, dinner
Prices rooms 350F-830F, suites 1,100F; menu 190F-280F
Rooms 28 double (2 twin), 2 suites, all with bath; all rooms have central heating, phone, TV
Facilities sitting-room, library, dining-room
Credit cards AE, DC, MC, V
Children accepted; special meals available
Disabled no special facilities
Pets accepted
Closed Feb
Proprietor M. Pasquier

Indre

Château hotel, St-Chartier

Château de la Vallée Bleue

The young Gasquets took over this handsome château in 1985, and have been assiduously improving it ever since. Having tended to the drive, the grounds and the exterior paintwork, they have built a swimming-pool behind the château and have thoroughly refurbished the bathrooms.

Inside, the atmosphere of the house is, as always, warm and easy. Fresh flowers and a cosy log fire in the spacious entrance hall set the tone, and personal touches are in evidence in every room. The château overlooks gardens front and back, giving all the bedrooms – big, and comfortably furnished with antiques – a pleasant outlook; just visible, beyond cows grazing in the fields, are the terracotta roof-tops of the village. Public rooms are gracious and charming, furnished with solid antiques and looking on to the garden.

Cooking is regionally based but *nouvelle*-oriented and way above average in execution. A recent visitor staying on half-board terms was distressed to find no choice of dishes, but nevertheless judged the food 'beautifully cooked and presented'.

Nearby Tour de la Prison (Museum of George Sand and Vallée Noire); Sarzay (10 km) – château; Nohant (5 km) – château.

Rte de Verneuil, St-Chartier
36400 La Châtre
Tel 54.31.01.91
Fax 54.31.04.48
Location just outside hamlet, on D69 9 km N of La Châtre, 26 km SE of Châteauroux; in large grounds with ample car parking
Meals breakfast, lunch, dinner
Prices rooms 390F-490F; breakfast 48F; menus 120F-250F; children 60F
Rooms 11 double (3 twin), 5 with bath 6 with shower; one single with shower; 2 family rooms with bath; all rooms have central heating, TV, phone, minibar, hairdrier
Facilities 2 dining-rooms, sitting-room; swimming-pool
Credit cards MC, V
Children welcome; special menus available
Disabled 3 ground-floor rooms
Pets accepted at extra charge
Closed Feb
Proprietors Brigitte and Gérard Gasquet

Cher

Auberge de la Solognote

In a peaceful, typical Sologne village, at the edge of the forest that signals Alain-Fournier country, the attractions of this rather dull-looking townhouse are revealed only as you go through the door. The furnishings are elegantly rustic, the decor restrained. A welcoming atmosphere in the dining-room does justice to M. Girard's excellent Sologne game. All the bedrooms face the garden; they are furnished with care and style, and were awarded top marks for comfort at our last inspection.

Nearby châteaux at Sully and Gien; Route Jacques Coeur.

18410 Brinon-sur-Sauldre
Tel 48.58.50.29
Fax 48.58.56.00
Location on main street of hamlet on D923, 4 km W of Argent-sur- Sauldre; in garden, with car parking
Meals breakfast, lunch, dinner
Prices rooms 290F-380F; menus 160F-320F
Rooms 11 double, 6 with bath, 5 with shower (4 twin); 2 family rooms, one with bath, one with shower; all rooms have central heating, phone, TV
Facilities dining-room, sitting-room, bar
Credit cards MC, V
Children accepted
Disabled some ground-floor rooms
Pets not accepted
Closed Feb, 10 days in May, 10 days in Sep
Proprietors André and Dominique Girard

Château de la Beuvrière

A beautifully restored medieval château with 11thC origins – complete with conical slate roofs atop its round towers. Inside, the scale is more domestic than in many such châteaux, and the atmosphere more welcoming – though the plain walls, beneath heavily beamed ceilings, do accommodate massive paintings. Bedrooms may lack style but they do not lack comfort, and they are moderately priced. And outside, the vast and beautiful grounds are waiting to be explored.

Nearby fishing, horse-riding; Bourges (35 km).

Saint-Hilaire-de-Court 18100 Vierzon
Tel 48.75.14.63
Fax 48.75.47.62
Location in countryside, on D90 off N20, 7 km SW of Vierzon, 35 km NW of Bourges; in huge grounds with ample private car parking
Meals breakfast, lunch, dinner
Prices rooms 330F-460F, suite 570F; menus 130F-196F
Rooms 11 double (3 twin), 8 with bath, 3 with shower; one single; 3 suites, 2 with bath, one with shower; all rooms have central heating, phone
Facilities dining-room, 2 sitting-rooms, function rooms; swimming-pool, tennis
Credit cards AE, DC, V
Children accepted
Disabled no special facilities
Pets accepted
Closed Sun evening and Mon
Proprietors Arnaud and Chantal de Brach

Cher

Converted mill, Bannegon

Auberge du Moulin de Chaméron

Jacques and Annie Candoré converted this ancient water-mill into a restaurant in 1972, later adding bedrooms in a garden annexe; the food is still a great attraction, but no longer the only one. The dining-room is romantic and intimate, with old beams and fireplace; there is also a terrace beside the stream. Bedrooms differ in size and style; all are modest, but calm and comfortable. A visitor pronounces the food 'expensive, but worth it'.
Nearby Meillant castle (25 km); Noirlac abbey (30 km).

Bannegon 18210
Charenton-du-Cher
Tel 48.61.83.80
Fax 48.61.84.92
Location in countryside between Bannegon and Neuilly, 40 km SE of Bourges; with garden and ample car parking
Meals breakfast, lunch, dinner
Prices rooms 320F-580F; menus 150F-220F, children's 60F
Rooms 13 double, 8 with bath, 5 with shower (5 twin); one family room with bath; all rooms have central heating, phone, TV
Facilities 2 dining-rooms, bar, 2 sitting-rooms; swimming-pool, fishing
Credit cards AE, MC, V
Children welcome
Disabled no special facilities
Pets accepted in bedrooms; charge
Closed 15 Nov to 4 Mar; Tue in low season
Proprietors M. Candoré and M. Merilleau

Deux Sèvres

Au Marais

The Marais in question is the Poitevin – a huge area of salt marshes west of Niort, reclaimed from the sea since the 17thC. The part of the area between Niort and Damvix, known as La Venise Verte, is laced with shady canals, once the main form of local transport but now a tourist curiosity. Coulon is the main point of departure for boat trips, and this friendly little inn on the banks of the Sèvre-Niort river makes a peaceful and pleasant stop-over. The rooms, decorated in bright pastel tones and immaculately kept, are accommodated in a separate building from the restaurant, where Alain Nerrière's inventive but regional-based cooking attracts a steady trade. Martine Nerrière-Mathé serves with a smile.

Nearby Boat trips; Fontenay-le-Comte (26 km).

46-48 Quai Louis-Tardy 79510 Coulon
Tel 49.35.90.43
Fax 49.35.81.98
Location in village 6 km W of Niort
Meals breakfast, lunch, dinner
Prices rooms 360F; breakfast 50F; lunch 90F, dinner 150F
Rooms 11 double, all with bath; all rooms have central heating, phone, TV **Facilities** dining-room **Credit cards** MC, V **Children** accepted **Disabled** no special facilities **Pets** accepted at extra charge **Closed** 15 Nov to 15 Mar; restaurant only Sun dinner and Mon **Proprietor** Martine and Alain Nerrière-Mathé

Le Clos St-Médard

Thouars is a pleasant medieval town surrounded by vineyards and orchards. Pierre and Yanelle Aracil's stylishly simple restaurant with rooms is a fine half-timbered 13thC building in the old part of town, and retains some ancient features – a spiral staircase leading to the four smart, pastel bedrooms, huge stone fireplaces. The bedrooms and the refined dining-rooms dotted with antiques have panoramic views over the Thouet valley. Cooking is ambitious and competent – 'delicate and imaginative combinations of taste and smell' enthuses a recent visitor.

Nearby church, medieval houses, vineyards; Loire (30 km).

14 Place St Médard 79100 Thouars
Tel 49.66.66.00
Fax 49.96.15.01
Location on square in heart of village; with garden and car parking nearby
Meals breakfast, lunch, dinner
Prices rooms 240F-320F, DB&B 300F
Rooms 4 double, all with bath (2 twin); all rooms have central heating, phone, TV
Facilities 2 dining-rooms
Credit cards AE, MC, V
Children welcome
Disabled no special facilities
Pets accepted
Closed one week in Feb
Proprietors Yanelle and Pierre Aracil

Charente-Maritime

Village hotel, Tonnay-Boutonne

Le Prieuré

Tonnay-Boutonne is a small, rather dull village lying between the old military town of Rochefort and St-Jean-d'Angély, a former wine port. Set slightly back from the (not very busy) main road, Le Prieuré is a typical Charentaise building: handsome, symmetrical, with white shuttered windows. It was the family home of the proprietors before they opened it as a hotel, and retains a friendly atmosphere.

The bedrooms and bathrooms have been recently revamped and are comfortable. The Vernoux's next project is a heated swimming-pool, and a terrace extension to the dining-room, in order to benefit more fully from the large garden.

Nearby Rochefort – 17thC Corderie Royale, Navy Museum; La Roche Courbon (25 km) – château; Saintes (30 km).

17380 Tonnay-Boutonne
Tel 46.33.20.18
Location in village 21 km E of Rochefort; with large garden and ample car parking
Meals breakfast, lunch, dinner
Prices rooms 250F-450F, breakfast 45F per person, menu 140F
Rooms 16 double (6 twin), 2 family rooms; 15 with bath, 3 with shower; all rooms have phone, TV
Facilities reception/sitting-area, TV/sitting-room, 2 dining-rooms
Credit cards MC, V
Children welcome
Disabled no special facilities
Pets accepted
Closed Christmas/New Year
Proprietors M. and Mme Paul Vernoux

Charente-Maritime

Auberge Pontoise

Most travellers who have a choice would prefer to stay in a village or in the countryside rather than in a town hotel like this, but Philippe Chat has the answer that keeps the customers coming: ambitious and competent cooking, recognized with the award of a Michelin star. The hotel remains simple and unpretentious, relying heavily on the honest virtue of good housekeeping for its appeal – though the rooms (some facing the garden) are of a fair size and attractively decorated, and there is a pleasant court-yard where meals are served in summer.

Nearby Castle (12thC keep); Saintes (22 km).

23 Ave Gambetta 17800 Pons
Tel 46.94.00.99
Fax 46.91.33.40
Location on narrow through-road in middle of town; with limited private car parking
Meals breakfast, lunch, dinner
Prices rooms 240F-400F; menus 160F-300F
Rooms 21 double, all with bath or shower (some twin); one suite; all rooms have

central heating, phone, TV
Facilities sitting-room/bar, 2 dining-rooms, small conference room
Credit cards AE, MC, V
Children accepted
Disabled access difficult, outside steps
Pets not accepted
Closed 5 weeks Dec to Jan; Sun dinner and Mon out of season
Proprietor Philippe Chat

33 Rue Thiers

33 Rue Thiers is a renovated 18thC town house in the heart of La Rochelle. Its welcoming owner and renovator is a half-Ameri-can/half-French cook-book author, Maybelle Iribe. She opened for business in 1987, and the word spread like wildfire; she already has a faithful band of enthusiastic guests who return year after year. She has filled the public rooms with antiques and (mainly) stylish modern furniture, and decorated each of the huge bedrooms individually, from her own collection of art and ornaments. Sumptuous breakfasts and dinner can be eaten on the patio in the walled garden. Maybelle also runs a cookery school which guests are welcome to attend.

Nearby old quarter and port, lantern tower; Ile de Ré.

33 Rue Thiers 17000 La Rochelle **Tel** 46.41.62.23
Fax 46.41.10.76
Location in street next to central market; with small walled garden and car parking
Meals breakfast, dinner, picnics
Prices rooms 480F-550F with breakfast; dinner 120F
Rooms 5 double, one family

room, all with bath; all rooms have central heating
Facilities dining-room, sitting-room, TV room
Credit cards not accepted
Children welcome; special meals, baby-sitting available
Disabled no special facilities
Pets dogs accepted
Closed never
Proprietor Maybelle Iribe

Charente

Moulin de Marcouze

The food is the main draw of this smartly converted mill beside the Seugne – Dominique Bouchet is a graduate of the Tour d'Argent in Paris, and earns two stars from Michelin for dishes such as his famous *gigot d'agneau de sept heures*. The modern bedrooms, like the dining-room, employ a light, simple style, with antique and reproduction furniture on plain quarry-tiled floors. Some overlook the river, like the dining-room and terrace.
Nearby Saintes – Roman baths, amphitheatre, arch, cathedral (30 km); Cognac – cellar visits, châteaux (35 km).

Mosnac 17240
Saint-Genis-de-Saintonge
Tel 46.70.46.16
Fax 46.70.48.14
Location in countryside, on D134 off N137, 1 km SE of Mosnac, 30 km S of Saintes; with garden and car parking
Meals breakfast, lunch, dinner
Prices rooms 525F-1,100F; breakfast 70F, menus 190F-420F **Rooms** 8 double (3 twin), all with bath; one suite with bath; all rooms have central heating, phone, TV, minibar, safe, air-conditioning, hairdrier
Facilities dining-room, sitting-room; swimming-pool **Credit cards** AE, MC, V **Children** no special facilities **Disabled** all rooms on ground floor **Pets** welcome (50F charge) **Closed** mid-Nov to Feb; restaurant only, Tue and Wed lunch except Jul, Aug and public holidays **Proprietor** Dominique Bouchet

Château de Nieuil

This fairy-tale Renaissance château – steep-roofed, turreted, and surrounded by parkland – has been in the Bodinaud family for over a hundred years. It could be embarrassingly pretentious, but it is not – it is run along family lines; Mme Bodinaud (an ex-design-lecturer) does all the interior decoration and earns a Michelin star for her imaginative food. Her husband has set up a gallery in the stables. Rooms are furnished with exquisite antiques, porcelain and tapestries. 'Extremely comfortable and one of the best value rooms of our holiday' comments a guest.
Nearby Limoges (65 km).

Rte de Fontafie, 16270 Nieuil
Tel 45.71.36.38
Fax 45.71.46.45
Location in wooded park, 2 km E of Nieuil; with extensive grounds, car parking and garage for 8 cars
Meals breakfast, lunch, dinner
Prices rooms 700F-1,300F; menus 235F-310F
Rooms 11 double, 3 apartments, all with bath; all rooms have central heating, phone, TV, minibar; 5 have air-conditioning
Facilities dining-room, sitting-room, bar; swimming-pool, tennis court
Credit cards AE, DC, MC, V
Children accepted **Disabled** access possible to one bedroom and apartment **Pets** welcome
Closed Nov to Apr **Proprietor** Jean-Michel and Luce Bodinaud

Charente

Hostellerie Ste-Catherine

The stately approach to the Hostellerie Ste-Catherine – through a stone archway and along a winding drive – is imposing and grand. The house, too – built in a pale, irregular stone, dating back to the 17th century, and once a residence of the Empress Joséphine – looks handsome but austere, and exudes an aura of formality. But inside it is a different story: despite fine furnishings and immaculate housekeeping, there is none of the expected pretension, but a relaxed and easy atmosphere, which the new proprietor, Mme Rey, seems intent on preserving.

Rooms are decorated and furnished with proper regard for both style and comfort: the dining-rooms (one leads in to the other) have tapestries on the walls, and a carved wooden mantlepiece stands over an old fireplace; the two sitting-rooms are inviting and relaxing (one has board games, the other an open fireplace and a TV). Most of the individually furnished and thoroughly comfortable bedrooms have views of the surrounding parkland; they do vary in size, and the prices reflect this. A choice of interesting fare is offered – one menu and an 'intersting' *carte* – and the reassuring sound of satisfied lunchtime guests lingers well into the afternoon.

The eight hectares of parkland and walled garden are beautiful to explore, and there is the river Tardoire, and its attendant boats, nearby.

Nearby Angoulême (30 km) – cathedral, walk along ramparts; châteaux – de Brie (40 km); Rochechouart (40 km).

Route de Marthon 16220 Montbron
Tel 45.23.60.03
Fax 45.70.72.00
Location in park off D16, 4 km SW of Montbron, 28 km E of Angoulême; with ample car parking
Meals breakfast, lunch, dinner
Prices rooms 450F-800F; breakfast 49F; menu 170F
Rooms 14 double and 4 family rooms, most with bath or shower; all rooms have central heating, phone, TV
Facilities 2 dining-rooms, 2 sitting-rooms, bar; swimming-pool
Credit cards AE, DC, MC, V
Children accepted
Disabled no special facilities
Pets accepted
Closed never
Proprietor Marie-Michelle Rey

Haute-Vienne

La Chapelle Saint-Martin

This suave country house – a mini-château, in effect – may be rather too formal for the travel-weary family *en route* for the south-west, but it has clear attractions. It is a neat, shuttered house in lovely manicured grounds that include ornamental lakes. The interior is designer-decorated and luxuriously furnished, mixing antiques, modern conveniences and rich fabrics in the best of taste. Bedrooms, particularly the recently renovated 'luxe' first-floor ones, are equally impressive. The Michelin-starred food of Dudognon *fils* makes this a natural haunt of the beau monde of Limoges; naturally, the crockery is rather smart.
Nearby Limoges.

St-Martin-du-Fault 87510 Nieul
Tel 55.75.80.17
Fax 55.75.89.50
Location in countryside 12 km NW of Limoges; in parkland with ample car parking
Meals breakfast, lunch, dinner
Prices rooms 680F-980F, suites 1,350F-1,500F; DB&B 800F-1,100F
Rooms 10 double (3 twin), all with bath; 3 suites; all have central heating, phone, TV
Facilities dining-rooms, sitting-room, bar; swimming-pool, tennis-court
Credit cards AE, MC, V
Children accepted
Disabled three ground-floor rooms **Pets** not accepted in restaurant **Closed** Jan and Feb; restaurant only, Mon
Proprietors Jacques and Viviane Dudognon

Moulin de la Gorce

A tranquil setting and renowned cooking (2 stars from Michelin, 2 *toques* from Gault-Millau) are the primary attractions of this 16thC mill – a neat, low-lying, white-painted building beside a lake in the middle of wooded grounds. Within are two dining-rooms (one delicately decorated, the other more rustic) and a comfortable, unassuming salon. The bedrooms – some richly furnished, some more bland – are split between the main building and a nearby annexe. Reproduction tapestries are a recurring feature. Mme Bertranet greets guests warmly.
Nearby St-Yrieix (10km); Coussac-Bonneval (10 km) – château.

La Roche l'Abeille 87800
Tel 55.00.70.66
Fax 55.00.76.57
Location in countryside 2 km S of village, 35 km S of Limoges; with large grounds and ample car parking
Meals breakfast, lunch, dinner
Prices rooms 350F-700F; apartment 1,300F; breakfast 65F, menus 160F-450F
Rooms 9 double (2 twin), one apartment, all with bath; all rooms have phone, TV
Facilities 2 dining-rooms, sitting-room/bar
Credit cards AE, DC, MC, V
Children welcome; special meals available
Disabled 2 ground-floor rooms
Pets accepted if kept on leash
Closed Jan; Sun dinner and Mon, Oct to Apr
Proprietors Jean and Annie Bertranet

Yonne

Town mansion, Auxerre

Parc des Maréchaux

This substantial 1850s house was restored from near-dereliction by Espérance Hervé and her doctor husband, and is now run with great enthusiasm by her. They have cut no corners: the welcoming ambience, confident style and solid comfort of the house would do credit to any professional hotelier. For a bed-and-breakfast establishment, the public rooms are exceptionally comfortable, and the large bedrooms are beautifully done out in restrained colours, and handsomely furnished. A German reader warns against those on the noisy road side and advises booking one that overlooks the garden – the secluded, leafy park from which the hotel takes its name. Breakfast is had there in summer.

Nearby cathedral, abbey church of St-Germain; Chablis (20 km).

6 Ave Foch 89000 Auxerre
Tel 86.51.43.77
Fax 86.51.31.72
Location close to middle of town; with gardens and car parking
Meals breakfast
Prices rooms 285F-490F (under 7s free); breakfast 45F
Rooms 19 double (7 twin), 2 single, 3 family rooms; all with bath; all rooms have central heating, phone, TV
Facilities sitting-room, bar, breakfast room
Credit cards AE, V
Children welcome
Disabled 3 ground-floor bedrooms; lift/elevator
Pets accepted (50F)
Closed never
Proprietor Espérance Hervé

Converted mill, Avallon

Moulin des Templiers

The little River Cousin burbling merrily past is virtually the only sound to disturb the peace of this pretty old mill, yet it is close enough to the motorway to make a splendid stop-over on the way through Burgundy. Breakfast is served on the shady riverside terrace on fine days, otherwise in a tiny room – there may be a queue. The bedrooms are freshly decorated and well kept, but most are small and the smallest is minute. If planning to stay more than a night or two, book well ahead and ask for a larger room. Note that no food (other than breakfast) and no alcohol is available in the hotel – but there are good restaurants in Avallon, and nearer to hand in Pontaubert; the courteous Mme Hilmoine will make reservations.

Nearby Avallon – ramparts, St-Lazare; Vézelay (10 km).

Vallée du Cousin, Pontaubert 89200 Avallon
Tel 86.34.10.80
Location in secluded valley, 4 km SW of Avallon on D427; with garden and separate car park
Meals breakfast
Prices rooms 240F-340F; breakfast 34F
Rooms 12 double (3 twin), 2 single; all with shower; all rooms have phone
Facilities breakfast room
Credit cards not accepted
Children accepted
Disabled no special facilities
Pets accepted at extra charge
Closed Nov to mid-Mar
Proprietor Mme Hilmoine

Yonne

Village mansion, Mailly-le-Château

Le Castel

This charming old *maison bourgeoise* makes an excellent base for a touring holiday, or a welcoming stopover. Built at the end of the last century, it is a large shuttered house lying in the shadow of the village church, with a well-kept garden and a flowery terrace shaded by lime trees, where you can have breakfast.

Since 1979 the hotel has been run by the exceptionally friendly and courteous Breerettes. Michel speaks English (he worked at Gleneagles Hotel in Scotland and spent 15 years as a chef on ocean-going liners) and is in charge of the kitchen. Food is taken seriously here, and is both excellent and inexpensive – though one visitor found the choice limited. There are two dining-rooms, separated by a small salon with Empire-style furnishings and a handsome fireplace. Bedrooms vary widely – from spacious ones with touches of grandeur, such as chandeliers and drapes over bedheads, to much smaller and simpler rooms. Some much needed refurbishment was undertaken in 1993, and prices remain modest.

Visitors have found Le Castel a very friendly, unpretentious place. There is plenty to do in the surrounding countryside, such as walks through the forest and fishing and sailing nearby.

Nearby Vézelay (30 km) – Romanesque buildings; Avallon (30 km) – ramparts; Chablis (45 km) – vineyards.

Place de l'Église 89660 Mailly-le-Château
Tel 86.81.43.06
Fax 86.81.49.26
Location in church square of village, 30 km S of Auxerre; with garden, terrace and car parking
Meals breakfast, lunch, dinner
Prices rooms 155F-330F; meals 73F-170F
Rooms 10 double (5 twin), 7 with bath, 2 with shower; 2 family rooms with bath ; all rooms have central heating, phone
Facilities 2 dining-rooms, sitting-room
Credit cards MC, V
Children accepted
Disabled no special facilities
Pets accepted **Closed** Wed
Proprietors M. and Mme Breerette

Yonne

Converted abbey, Tonnerre

L'Abbaye St-Michel

Not everyone likes the way Daniel Cussac has elevated this ancient abbey to Relais & Châteaux status – using plate glass or stainless steel as readily as stone and wood. But there is no disputing the achievements of son Christophe, whose innovative cooking has earned countless *toques* and stars from the gastronomic guides. One dining-room is a stone vault dating from the 12th century, the other gives views of the countryside. There are several sitting areas decorated in a mix of styles, and bedrooms also blend old and new successfully.

Nearby Tonnerre – Fosse Dionne (spring), museum.

Montée de St-Michel 89700 Tonnerre
Tel 86.55.05.99
Fax 86.55.00.10
Location in countryside on edge of village, 35 km E of Auxerre; in large garden with ample car parking
Meals breakfast, lunch, dinner
Prices rooms 700F-1,600F; suites 1,800F-2,000F; meals 300F-590F; breakfast 85F
Rooms 14 double (9 twin), all with bath; all rooms have central heating, phone, TV, minibar
Facilities 2 dining-rooms, 3 sitting-rooms, bar; tennis court
Credit cards AE, DC, MC, V
Children welcome
Disabled no special facilities
Pets accepted
Closed Jan
Proprietor Daniel Cussac

Town hotel, St-Florentin

La Grande Chaumière

The small town of St-Florentin makes a pleasant stop-over if you are touring northern Burgundy or making your way south through France, and La Grande Chaumière is an attractive pink turn-of-the-century building close to the middle and set in a pretty garden. The Bonvalots have steadily improved the place since their arrival in 1975; They have entirely redecorated the bedrooms in an essentially modern style, and recently revamped the restaurant (light, smartly furnished) and the *salon*. Jean-Pierre cooks, while Madame manages the front of house with enthusiasm. 'From all aspects, very good,' says a visitor.

Nearby Chablis (30 km) – wine; Auxerre (30 km) – cathedral.

3 Rue des Capucins 89600 St-Florentin
Tel 86.35.15.12
Fax 86.35.33.14
Location on quiet road in middle of town; with gardens and ample car parking
Meals breakfast, lunch, dinner
Prices rooms 320F-450F, suites 650F-850F; meals 130F-480F
Rooms 11 double, (3 twin), 10 with bath, one with shower; all rooms have central heating, phone, TV
Facilities dining-room, bar, sitting-area, breakfast room
Credit cards AE, DC, MC, V
Children welcome; special meals, extra beds available
Disabled no special facilities
Pets accepted if well behaved
Closed first week Sep, mid- Dec to mid-Jan; Wed out of season
Proprietor J-P Bonvalot

Yonne

Town mansion, Vézelay

Le Pontot

There is only one hotel inside the walls of the old town of Vézelay, and that is Le Pontot. Just a short walk from the famous basilica, it is a fine fortified mansion, thought to have been rebuilt on 11thC cellars after the Hundred Years War, and added to in the 18th century.

It has existed as a hotel only since 1984. The American owner, architect Charles Thum, and manager Christian Abadie have skilfully converted the building into a rather special bed-and-breakfast. (Who needs a restaurant when the famous l'Espérance lies just down the road?) The bedrooms include a large Louis XVI apartment, with canopied beds, fireplace and private dressing room; and another with stone paving, 16thC beamed ceiling and antique, country-style, furnishings.

Breakfast is quite a sumptuous affair, served as it is on gold-encrusted, royal blue Limoges porcelain. On cool days, it is eaten in front of a blazing fire in the handsome, panelled, Louis XVI salon; but in summer you sit outside in the delightful walled garden.

Among the amusements offered by this rather exclusive hotel are cruises on the Canal du Nivernais, and hot-air balloon rides over the rolling Burgundian hills.

Nearby St-Père-sous-Vézelay (2 km) – church; Avallon (15 km); Auxerre (50 km); Chablis and Sancerre (50 km) – vineyards.

Place du Pontot 89450 Vézelay
Tel 86.33.24.40
Location in middle of town; with small walled garden and car parking
Meals breakfast
Prices rooms 550F-900F (child sharing room 100F); breakfast 60F
Rooms 9 double, 1 single, all with bath and shower (4 twin); all rooms have phone, radio
Facilities sitting-room, bar, breakfast room; boat on canal
Credit cards DC, MC, V
Children accepted
Disabled not suitable for wheelchairs
Pets accepted; 50F charge
Closed Nov to Easter
Manager Christian Abadie

Yonne

Château de Vault-de-Lugny

Only a couple of miles from the dear little Moulin des Templiers (page 100), west of Avallon, but as sharp a contrast as you will find: an impressive and expensive château, of plain medieval rather than fancy Renaissance origin, with exceptionally grand bedrooms.

The house was restored and opened as a hotel in the mid-1980s, and has been in the hands of Elisabeth Audan throughout that time. Some of the rooms retain their aristocratic style, with period decoration and sparse antique furnishings that contribute more to atmosphere than comfort; others have something of a modern designer feel, with subtly coloured fabrics, and comfortable furniture that looks suspiciously like reproduction rather than the real thing. Bathrooms are ritzy, as they should be at these prices.

The extensive, well-wooded grounds include a well-used kitchen garden, contributing to the proprietors' *cuisine traditionelle*, and a fair stretch of trout fishing, as well as a tennis-court. Hot-air balloon flights can be arranged.

Nearby Avallon – ramparts; Vézelay (10 km).

89200 Avallon
Tel 86.34.07.86
Fax 86.34.16.36
Location 4 km W of Avallon, 1 km N of Pontaubert, on D427 outside village of Vault-de-Lugny, in large grounds with ample car parking
Meals breakfast, lunch, dinner, snacks
Prices rooms 700F-2,200F with breakfast, dinner 290F; reductions for 5 nights or more
Rooms 11 double (4 twin), all with bath; all rooms have central heating, phone, TV, minibar; most rooms have hairdrier
Facilities sitting-room/bar, sitting-room, restaurant; tennis, fishing
Credit cards AE, MC, V
Children welcome; babysitting available
Disabled easy access, room on ground floor
Pets welcome (50F charge)
Closed mid-Nov to early Apr
Proprietor Elisabeth Audan

Yonne

La Fontaine aux Muses

This creeper-covered rural *auberge* five minutes from the *autoroute* has more to offer than most of its kind: a six-hole golf course with sweeping views, a tennis-court and swimming-pool nestling among immaculate lawns, a sunny tree-bordered terrace for summer dining, and – most important of all – a music room. The family are devoted to music and often play for their guests, outside in summer or by the fireside in winter. M. and Mme Langevin rescued the house from ruin in the 1960s and created pretty rustic bedrooms, a cosy beamed sitting-room and smart restaurant which opens out on to the terrace. Their son Vincent does the cooking – good simple dishes with an emphasis on fish.
Nearby fishing, horse-riding; Joigny (10 km).

Route de la Fontaine 89116 La Celle-St-Cyr **Tel** 86.73.40.22 **Fax** 86.73.48.66 **Location** on edge of village, 10 km W of Joigny, off D943; with garden and car parking **Meals** breakfast, lunch, dinner **Prices** rooms 330F-385F; suites 550F-650F; breakfast 35F, menu 185F **Rooms** 13 double, 12 with bath, 2 with shower; 4 suites; all rooms have central heat- ing, phone **Facilities** sitting- room, dining-room; terrace, golf, swimming-pool, tennis- court **Credit cards** MC, V **Children** welcome **Disabled** access difficult **Pets** not accepted **Closed** Mon, Tue lunch **Proprietors** Pointeau- Langevin family

Hostellerie des Clos

This reconstructed hospice, opened only since 1986, is bigger than most establishments that we categorize as restaurants with rooms, but the label simply reflects the Vignauds' priorities: you go here for the food, and the 26 modern, tasteful but unremark-able rooms are a bonus. The designer-decorated dining-room is light and stylish, with conservatory-style windows looking on to the garden. Michel Vignaud's light, innovative cooking (Michelin star, two toques from Gault-Millau) makes full use of the famous local white wines, and of course there is an impressive (and not entirely high-priced) wine-list.
Nearby vineyards; Tonnerre (15 km); Auxerre (20 km).

Rue Jules Rathier, 89800 Chablis **Tel** 86.42.10.63 **Fax** 86.42.17.11 **Location** in centre of old town 20 km SE of Auxerre **Meals** breakfast, lunch, dinner **Prices** rooms 250F-570F; breakfast 50F; menus 160F-420F **Rooms** 25 double (9 twin), all with bath; one family room; all rooms have central heating, radio, phone, TV, **Facilities** dining-room, sitting-rooms, bar; play area **Credit cards** MC, V **Children** accepted **Disabled** access easy, lift **Pets** dogs accepted **Closed** 2 weeks Christmas and New Year; Wed and Thu lunch from Oct to Apr **Proprietors** M and Mme Michel Vignaud

Côte-d'Or

Hôtel Clarion

The tiny village of Aloxe-Corton is a place of pilgrimage for lovers of great white wine. Its symbol is the château of Corton-André, a picturesque building of gleaming coloured tiles and tidy tunnels full of *premiers crus*. Next to it lies the Hôtel Clarion, a 17thC mansion which has been cleverly converted into a small and exclusive hotel.

The style is a mix of modern and old, namely art deco furnishings set against old timberwork and beamed ceilings. Bedrooms are stylish and well co-ordinated, mainly in matching fabrics of pastel shades. Although varied in size and price, all are thoroughly comfortable and well-equipped (leave yours for an hour or two, and you may well come back to fresh fruit or gateaux). Bathrooms, in marble, are large and luxurious.

Other merits of the hotel are the comfortable salon (beams, open fireplace) opening out on to the park and vineyards, the free wine-tasting for guests in the impressive 18thC vaulted cellars, the large garden and the excellent breakfasts, which include eggs, cheese and fresh fruit in addition to the usual coffee and croissants.

Nearby Vineyards; Beaune – infirmary, wine museum; Le Rochepot (25 km) – château; Dijon (35 km).

21420 Aloxe-Corton
Tel 80.26.46.70
Fax 80.26.47.16
Location in middle of village, 3.5 km N of Beaune on N74; in large garden with ample car parking
Meals breakfast
Prices rooms 485F-790F
Rooms 10 double (7 twin), all with bath; one family room with bath ; all rooms have central heating, phone, TV, minibar
Facilities sitting-room; bicycles
Credit cards MC, V
Children welcome; cots, special meals, baby-sitting available
Disabled one ground-floor bedroom specially equipped
Pets accepted
Closed never
Proprietor Christian Voarick

Côte-d'Or

Les Magnolias

In a pleasantly quiet location in the famous Burgundy wine village of Meursault, Les Magnolias is a polished and unusually stylish place – a group of old houses around a small courtyard, with spacious bedrooms that have been individually decorated with panache. Breakfast is served in the rooms, but there is a sitting-room as well as a little terrace. Dinner probably means a drive – the best local restaurant is a mile or two away, and there are lots of tempting places further afield. M. Delarue apparently has English blood, and speaks both English and German.

Nearby tennis, swimming-pool; Beaune – wine museum (6 km); Nolay – covered market (18 km); Château Rochepot (18 km); vineyards of Burgundy.

8 Rue Pierre Joigneaux 21190 Meursault
Tel 80.21.23.23
Fax 80.21.29.10
Location on N edge of village, 6 km SW of Beaune, off N74 on D23; private car parking
Meals breakfast
Prices rooms 350F-700F; breakfast 45F
Rooms 11 double (5 twin), 9 with bath, 2 with shower; one suite with bath; all rooms have central heating, phone; TV on request
Facilities sitting-room
Credit cards DC, MC, V
Children accepted
Disabled access possible
Pets not accepted
Closed Dec to mid-Mar
Proprietor M. A M Delarue

Hostellerie du Val-Suzon

The Hostellerie du Val-Suzon, a country inn situated in a large flower-filled park, was originally an 18thC mill. It is now a charming little hotel, with beams and flowery prints in the bedrooms and cuisine which a recent guest praises as 'nouvelle orientated with excellent fish dishes – a memorable experience'. The modern annexe, known as the Chalet de la Fontaine aux Geais, is a short walk up the hillside. It is the more peaceful of the two buildings, but the less charming.

Nearby Route des Grands Crus.

RN 71, Val-Suzon 21121 Fontaine-lès-Dijon
Tel 80.35.60.15
Location in countryside 15 km NW of Dijon; with large gardens and ample car parking
Meals breakfast, lunch, dinner
Prices rooms 350F-500F; suite 600F-800F; menus 180F-380F
Rooms 15 double, 12 with bath, 3 with shower; one single with bath; one suite with bath and shower, TV, radio; all have central heating, phone, alarm; 9 have TV, radio
Facilities 2 dining-rooms, bar, sitting-room
Credit cards AE, DC, MC, V
Children accepted; special meals available
Disabled no special facilities
Pets accepted in bedrooms; 35F charge
Closed Jan; Wed and Thu lunch, except Jun to Sep
Proprietors Yves and Chantal Perreau

Côte-d'Or

Hotel les Charmes

Danielle Flamant opened the doors of her 18thC *maison bourgeoise* in 1988, having renovated it with care and style. It sits peacefully, close to the centre of the wine-village of Meursault, in a park-like garden with mature trees. Breakfast can be had here in fine weather. A refined private-house atmosphere prevails: in the sitting-room, there are rugs and upright armchairs on a polished wooden floor; in the bedrooms (named after the wines of Burgundy), the furniture is antique and elegant, the decorative schemes individual and harmonious. The best rooms are spacious, retaining their stone fireplaces.
Nearby Route du Vin; Beaune; Dijon (40 km).

10 Place du Murger 21190 Meursault
Tel 80.21.63.53
Fax 80.21.62.89
Location near centre of village, 6km S of Beaune, in gardens with garages and private parking
Meals breakfast, snacks
Prices rooms 370F-500F; breakfast 45F
Rooms 14 double (4 twin), 10 single, 3 family rooms, all with bath; all rooms have central heating, phone, TV
Facilities sitting-room, breakfast room, bar; terrace, swimming-pool
Credit cards MC, V
Children welcome; babysitting
Disabled one ground-floor room **Pets** not accepted
Closed early Feb **Proprietor** Mme Danielle Flamant

La Côte-d'Or

With Champagne to the north and Burgundy to the south, the valley of the upper Seine tends to be neglected, but it has plenty of scenic and historic interest, and Châtillon makes a good base or stopover. This creeper-covered family-run *auberge* in a leafy garden offers prettily decorated rooms at modest prices, friendly but proper service and food that is interesting and competently cooked (and served on the terrace when weather permits).
Nearby swimming-pool, tennis, horse-riding, fishing; Celtic museum; Fontenay Abbey (35 km); château at Tanlay (40 km).

Rue Charles-Ronot 21400 Châtillon-sur-Seine
Tel 80.91.13.29
Fax 80.91.29.15
Location in middle of town near river, 85 km NW of Dijon, on N71, 60 km SW of Chaumont; with car parking and shady garden
Meals breakfast, lunch, dinner
Prices rooms 200F-560F; DB&B 230F-280F; menus 95F-340F
Rooms 11 double (4 twin), 7 with bath, 2 with shower; all rooms have central heating, phone, TV
Facilities sitting-room, bar, dining-room
Credit cards AE, DC, MC, V
Children accepted
Disabled no special facilities
Pets accepted
Closed Jan to mid-Mar; restaurant Tues except Jul, Aug and public holidays
Propreitor M. Chalut-Natal

Côte-d'Or

Hostellerie du Château

From the A6 you can see the medieval village of Châteauneuf-en-Auxois perched on a hilltop, but once you are there you feel a million miles from any modern motorway. The picturesque Hostellerie, cleverly converted from a 15thC presbytery close to the château, is almost entirely in keeping with the village around it: old stone walls, quiet rustic rooms, a delightful beamed restaurant (where wholesome Burgundian dishes are the order of the day) and charming terraced gardens.

Nearby Castle; Commarin (10 km) – château; Beaune (35 km).

Châteauneuf 21320
Pouilly-en-Auxois
Tel 80.49.22.00
Fax 80.49.21.27
Location overlooking château in hill village, 42 km SW of Dijon and 35 km NW of Beaune; with small garden
Meals breakfast, lunch, dinner
Prices rooms 200F-450F; menu 140F-300F
Rooms 14 double, 2 single, all with bath or shower; all rooms have central heating, phone

Facilities 2 dining-rooms, sitting-room, bar
Credit cards AE, MC, V
Children welcome
Disabled no special facilities
Pets accepted
Closed 30 Nov to 10 Feb
Managers M. and Mme Poirier

Les Grands Crus

Quarry-tiled floors, old beams, lime-washed walls, tapestry fabrics and a carved-stone fireplace all add to the illusion that this handsome Burgundian house was built far less recently than 1977; it combines the charm of the old with the comfort of the new – with perhaps too much emphasis on the latter in the small salon. The bedrooms, too, lack style in decoration, but they are peaceful, spacious and thoughtfully furnished, and look out over the famous Gevrey-Chambertin vineyards. Breakfast is served in the small flowery garden in fine weather. There are plenty of good restaurants nearby for other meals. 'Truly relaxing' and 'friendly and hospitable' say recent visitors.

Nearby Dijon – Grand Duke's palace, Place de la Libération.

Rte des Grands Crus 21220
Gevrey-Chambertin
Tel 80.34.34.15
Fax 80.51.89.07
Location in middle of village, 10 km SW of Dijon; with garden and ample car parking
Meals breakfast
Prices rooms 330F-410F; breakfast 42F; children under 4 free

Rooms 24 double (8 twin) all with bath; all rooms have phone
Facilities sitting-room
Credit cards MC, V
Children welcome **Disabled** no special facilities **Pets** accepted but not to be left in rooms **Closed** Dec to Feb
Proprietors Mme Marie-Paule Farnier

Côte-d'Or

Chez Camille

Armand Poinsot's excellent cooking (traditional but light, Michelin-starred) is only one attraction of this captivating little hotel. The bedrooms (the best of them quite spacious) are tastefully decorated and cluttered with antiques, and effectively double-glazed against noise from the RN6. Downstairs there is a cosy little salon with an enormous open fireplace, as well as the focus of the hotel – the conservatory-style dining-room. Created in an inner courtyard with stone walls and floor, wicker chairs, trellis and plants, it has an outdoor feel. Monique works front-of-house with charm and good humour.

Nearby Châteaux: Sully-sur-Loire (20 km), Le Rochepot (25 km).

1 Place Édouard-Herriot
21230 Arnay-le-Duc
Tel 80.90.01.38
Fax 80.90.04.64
Location in middle of town on RN6, 28km SE of Saulieu; with car parking and garage
Meals breakfast, lunch, dinner
Prices rooms 400F-600F; menus 130F-250F
Rooms 12 double (6 twin), all with bath; 2 family rooms with bath; all rooms have central heating, phone, TV
Facilities dining-room, sitting-room
Credit cards AE, DC, V
Children welcome; special menu available
Disabled no special facilities
Pets welcome
Closed never
Proprietors Monique and Armand Poinsot

Le Parc

As the centre of Burgundy's wine trade, Beaune is liberally endowed with wine-tasting cellars, and is also a fine town in its own right. Its only drawback as a stopping-off spot for motorists is the dearth of reasonably priced accommodation – at least in the middle of the town. But for those prepared to stay 5 km away, the Parc at Levernois offers excellent value and a pleasant rural setting. It is a simple hotel, converted from an old farmhouse, larger than many in this book but retaining the atmosphere of a small *auberge*. Christiane Oudot, who took over the Parc three years ago, assures us that it is run rather like a private home. Breakfast is served in the courtyard in summer.

Nearby Beaune; Archéodrome (5 km); Dijon (45 km).

Levernois 21200 Beaune
Tel 80.24.63.00
Fax 80.24.21.19
Location on edge of village 5 km SE of Beaune; with garden and ample car parking
Meals breakfast
Prices rooms 180F-440F
Rooms 25 double (6 twin), 6 with bath, 18 with shower; all rooms have central heating, phone, TV
Facilities bar, breakfast room; ping pong
Credit cards MC, V
Children accepted
Disabled several ground-floor bedrooms
Pets accepted
Closed 2 weeks late Nov
Proprietor Christiane Oudot

Saône-et-Loire

Château d'Igé

This turreted, creeper-covered castle was rescued from ruin and converted into a luxurious hotel about twenty years ago. M. Jadot has taken great care to retain its medieval atmosphere; the circular turret bedrooms are reached up well-worn stone stairs and through heavy wooden doors. They are spacious and comfortable (particularly the apartments), and furnished with antiques. Dinner is served in front of a huge open hearth in the massively beamed dining-room, and the cuisine is increasingly well regarded. There are several acres of enclosed gardens.

Nearby Cluny (10 km); Mâcon (15 km).

71960 Igé
Tel 85.33.33.99
Fax 85.33.41.41
Location in quiet village surrounded by vineyards; with garden and car parking
Meals breakfast, lunch, dinner
Prices rooms 480F-710F, apartments 875F-1,100F; breakfast 60F, dinner 190F-360F
Rooms 6 double, 6 suites, all with bath; all rooms have central heating, phone, TV, hair-drier
Facilities dining-room, sitting-room
Credit cards AE, DC, V
Children welcome; baby-sitting possible
Disabled no special facilities
Pets supplement of 55F for dogs
Closed Dec to Feb
Proprietor Henri Jadot

Hôtel Lameloise

In an ancient whitewashed house, in the rather dull heart of Chagny, Jacques Lameloise carries on his father Jean's reputation for excellent cooking. The house lacks the public rooms to be considered a proper hotel – apart from the elegant restaurant, there is only a small bar and a pleasant little sitting-area by reception – and has no garden or terrace. But there are compensations: all is beautifully decorated and serene, and the bedrooms (reached by stair or lift/elevator) are thoroughly comfortable, all with well-equipped bathrooms and some with private terraces. And of course the food is the thing – about the best in a region noted for its excellent cuisine.

Nearby Beaune (15 km) – medieval infirmary, wine tasting.

36 Place d'Armes 71150 Chagny
Tel 85.87.08.85
Location in middle of town
Meals breakfast, lunch, dinner
Prices rooms 600F-1,500F; menus 360F-570F
Rooms 19 double (7 twin), all with bath; all rooms have TV, phone; some rooms have air-conditioning
Facilities sitting-room, dining-room, bar, lift/elevator
Credit cards AE, MC, V
Children accepted
Disabled lift/elevator
Pets accepted
Closed 20 Dec to 25 Jan and 1st May; Wed, and Thu until 5 pm
Proprietors Lameloise family

Saône-et-Loire

Hôtel de la Poste

A prime example of an unassuming provincial hotel in the heart of beef-cattle country, doing a sound job. Flowers and shrubs crowd the pavement outside; the white-painted building is immaculately maintained, as is the smart bar-salon; and the dining-room has been made positively ritzy by small-town standards, so as not to undermine Daniel Doucet's culinary amibitions – though they remain firmly rooted in *cuisine bourgeoise*. (Naturally, *entrecôte charolaise* is among his specialities.) Bedrooms are unremarkable but comfortable.

Nearby Paray-le-Monial (15 km); Cluny (40 km).

2 Ave de la Libération 71120
Charolles
Tel 85.24.11.32
Fax 85.24.05.74
Location in middle of small town, 55 km W of Mâcon; with garage and car parking opposite
Meals breakfast, lunch, dinner
Prices rooms 220F-340F; suite 500F-600F; menus 140F-380F; breakfast 40F
Rooms 9 double (4 twin), 6

with bath, 3 with shower; 3 family rooms; one suite; all rooms have central heating, TV, phone
Facilities sitting-room, dining-room
Credit cards AE, MC, V
Children very welcome
Disabled no special facilities
Pets very welcome
Closed Nov; Sun evening, Mon
Proprietors M. and Mme Daniel Doucet

Hôtel de Bourgogne

Run by the Gosse family for over three decades, the Hôtel de Bourgogne is the most comfortable and central hotel in Cluny. An attractive stone mansion, dating from 1817, it is built around a garden and courtyard. Most of the bedrooms look out on to the remains of the abbey, or over surrounding green hills, and the elegant setting and Burgundian specialities of the restaurant draw many non-residents despite losing its Michelin star this year.

Nearby Abbey ruins; Azé caves (10 km); St-Point château and church (15 km); Cormatin château (15 km).

Place de l'Abbaye 71250
Cluny
Tel 85.59.00.58
Fax 85.59.03.73
Location in middle of town, 24 km NW of Mâcon; with small courtyard and garage for 15 cars
Meals breakfast, lunch, dinner
Prices rooms 420F-510F, suites 920F-995F; breakfast 55F; meals 210F-450F
Rooms 12 double (9 twin), all with bath; 3 suites; all rooms

have phone, central heating, TV
Facilities dining-room, sitting-room, bar/breakfast room
Credit cards AE, DC, MC, V
Children welcome; special meals available
Disabled access difficult
Pets accepted in bedrooms (40F), not in restaurant
Closed mid-Nov to Feb; Tue lunch
Proprietor J-C Gosse

Saône-et-Loire

Village inn, Mercurey

Hôtellerie du Val d'Or

This early 19thC coaching inn, on the main street of the rather dull wine village of Mercurey, continues to delight visitors. It is easy to see why: in a region of culinary excellence and exorbitant prices, many are daunted by the formal (or even pretentious) style of most hotels in the area, and long to find some village-inn simplicity. The Val d'Or obliges, and combines this with excellent cooking and comfortable, neatly decorated bedrooms – though some are rather small.

Nearby Château de Germolles (10 km); Buxy (20 km).

Grande-Rue 71640 Mercurey
Tel 85.45.13.70
Fax 85.45.18.45
Location in middle of village, 9 km S of Chagny; with garden
Meals breakfast, lunch, dinner
Prices rooms 320F-550F; meals 160F-370F, children's meals 85F
Rooms 10 double (3 twin), one single, 2 family rooms; all with bath or shower; all rooms have central heating, TV,

phone
Facilities 2 dining-rooms, lounge/bar
Credit cards MC, V
Children accepted
Disabled no special facilities
Pets not accepted
Closed Mon and Tue lunch
Proprietor Jean Claude Cogny

Saône-et-Loire

Château de Fleurville

Unlike so many châteaux hotels, this is not a formal, luxury establishment – the atmosphere is pleasantly relaxed (you can feel at ease here with children) and it is reasonably priced. It is well placed for touring, or for a stop-over on the way south (close to the A6 and N6, though in a large, quiet park). Dating from the 16th century, it retains many of the original features – old stone fireplaces, timbered ceilings, quarry-tiled floors – and despite various modernizations there is still a medieval atmosphere. Bedrooms are simply furnished with a variety of antiques. There are mixed reports about the food, though one reporter was 'extremely satisfied'.

Nearby Azé caves (10 km); Tournus – abbey (15 km).

71260 Fleurville
Tel 85.33.12.17
Location 17 km N of Mâcon, off N6; with gardens and ample car parking
Meals breakfast, lunch, dinner
Prices rooms 420F; breakfast 40F, meals 150F-260F
Rooms 14 double, all with bath (7 twin); one family room with bath; all rooms have central heating, phone
Facilities sitting-room, bar, 2 dining-rooms; tennis, swimming-pool
Credit cards AE, MC, V
Children welcome
Disabled no special facilities
Pets accepted
Closed 15 Nov to 25 Dec
Proprietors Naudin family

Hotel de la Halle

The façade of La Halle is undistinguished – with its slightly grubby white-shuttered windows and glass-fronted bar – and furniture and decoration in both the dining-room and the bedrooms are distinctly basic. What captivates a steady stream of British visitors – as well as the large band of local regulars in the restaurant – is the scrupulous housekeeping, Christian Renard's excellent traditional Burgundian cuisine, the exceptionally low prices for both rooms and meals and (most of all) the Renards' good-hearted welcome. The one notable feature of the building is a splendid 12thC spiral staircase.

Nearby Chalon (10 km) – photography museum; Beaune (35 km).

Place de la Halle 71640 Givry
Tel 85.44.32.45
Fax 85.44.45.45
Location in middle of village, 10 km W of Chalon-sur-Saône; with car parking
Meals breakfast, lunch, dinner
Prices rooms 220F-250F; breakfast 25F, menus 90F-200F
Rooms 10 double (3 twin), 3 with bath, 7 with shower; all rooms have central heating, phone
Facilities sitting-room, dining-room, bar
Credit cards AE, DC, MC, V
Children accepted
Disabled access to restaurant only
Pets accepted if clean
Closed mid-Nov to early Dec
Proprietor Christian Renard

Saône-et-Loire

Converted convent, Marcigny

Les Récollets

The Brionnais is a rural region, with gently rolling hills and lush meadows where Charollais cattle graze. It is a part of Burgundy that few French, let alone foreigners, are really familiar with, and even in summer months you can drive for miles without meeting another tourist.

The small market town of Marcigny provides an excellent base for touring – it is close to the Loire, and not far from the famous cattle market of St-Christophe-en-Brionnais. It is also the location of one of the most delightful hotels in the region, and one which has (up to now) escaped the notice of any guidebook. Converted from an ancient convent, Les Récollets is an ideal combination of French chic and home comforts. There are log fires, home-made *brioches* for breakfast, hand-made chocolates by the bedside (along with sleeping tablets, indigestion pills and painkillers). Indeed, every need is catered for, and the only house-rule is 'do as you please'.

Josette Badin, who runs the place with Burgundian *bonhomie*, has furnished the rooms superbly, from the dining-room with its hand-painted cupboards to the antique-laden bedrooms. Officially, only breakfast is served, but ask in advance and Josette will be happy to prepare a simple meal: soup or omelette – even *foie gras*, followed by Charollais beef.

Nearby Mill Tower Museum; La Clayette (25 km); Charlieu Abbey (30 km); Château Drée (30 km).

Place du Champ de Foire
71110 Marcigny
Tel 85.25.05.16
Fax 85.25.06.91
Location on edge of small town 22 km S of Paray; in grounds with ample car parking
Meals breakfast; lunch and dinner on request
Prices rooms 320F-550F with breakfast; menu 170F-200F
Rooms 6 double (2 twin), all with bath; 3 family rooms, all with bath; all rooms have central heating, phone
Facilities TV room, library, breakfast/dining-room
Credit cards AE, V
Children accepted
Disabled one ground-floor bedroom
Pets accepted
Closed never
Proprietor Mme Josette Badin

Saône-et-Loire

Converted mill, St-Gervais-en-Vallière

Moulin d'Hauterive

The wheels of this ancient watermill were still turning less than 30 years ago; only for the last decade or so has it been enjoying a new lease of life as a country hotel – offering an unusual blend of rural seclusion (it used to be a *Relais du Silence*), good living and sporting activities.

It is a handsome creeper-clad building, three storeys high, surrounded by lower outbuildings. The interior is the epitome of rustic chic. The building contributes beams, smooth stone-flagged floors, whitewashed or rough pale stone walls. Against this backdrop are placed bright fabrics, delicate mellow antiques, gleaming ornaments, and vivid bowls of flowers. Bedrooms are romantically done out – beds are often draped or canopied with lacy fabrics.

The Moilles are a young couple who were new to hotel keeping when they set up the Moulin. Madame came new to professional cooking, too, but has gained a formidable reputation for her essentially simple but inventive dishes.

The swimming-pool has a lift-off cover/roof which is doubtless a great aid to child safety and energy conservation when the pool is not in use, but diminishes the pleasure of swimming.

Nearby Archéodrome (10 km) – archeological centre; Beaune (15 km) – medieval infirmary, wine museum.

Chaublanc 71350
St-Gervais-en-Vallière
Tel 85.91.55.56
Fax 85.91.89.65
Location in countryside beside river, 16 km SE of Beaune, off D970; in grounds with ample car parking
Meals breakfast, lunch, dinner
Prices rooms 530F-650F, suites 850F; DB&B 580F-730F; menus 160F-380F
Rooms 11 double, 11 family rooms, all with bath or shower; all rooms have central heating, TV, phone, minibar
Facilities 2 dining-rooms, bar, 4 seminar rooms; swimming-pool, tennis, spa, billiards, heliport, sauna, solarium, fitness room
Credit cards AE, DC, V
Children accepted
Disabled one room
Pets dogs accepted in bedrooms at extra charge
Closed over Christmas, Jan
Proprietors Christiane and Michel Moille

Jura

Country inn, Passenans

Auberge du Rostaing

This is a completely peaceful and relaxed *auberge* on the edge of the sleepy village of Passenans in an unspoiled area west of the Jura hills – great for getting away from it all, with lovely walks (or bicycle rides) for the active.

It is a simple place, but well run by a charming Franco-Swiss couple, the Eckerts. It also has more to offer than most similarly simple competitors: an inviting sitting-room with music, games and books (and emphatically no TV), a shady courtyard garden where meals and drinks are served in summer, a large airy dining-room with an open fireplace and rustic furniture, and nine fresh, spacious and simple bedrooms – some of them in an adjacent building, reached by an outside staircase and a balcony decked with climbing vines and geraniums.

Madame Eckert does the cooking, and by all accounts it is good and wholesome, with lots of Swiss influences; *fondue* and *raclette* sometimes crop up. Many of the guests come back year after year and it is easy to see why – just look at the prices. 'Helpful, smiling service, pleasantly relaxed atmosphere.'

Nearby forest walks, bicycle rides, vineyards; Château-Chalon (5 km); Cirque de Ladoye (10 km); Poligny (10 km)

39230 Passenans
Tel 84.85.23.70
Fax 84.44.66.87
Location on outskirts of village, 11 km SW of Poligny on D57; follow Route des Vins
Meals breakfast, lunch, dinner
Prices rooms 105F-215F; breakfast 22F, menus 63F-156F
Rooms 7 double (2 twin), 5 with shower; 2 family rooms with bath; all rooms have central heating
Facilities dining-room, sitting-room; bicycles for hire; garden; walk and ride
Credit cards DC, MC, V
Children accepted; reductions by arrangement
Disabled no special facilities
Pets accepted
Closed Mon evenings except high season; Dec, Jan
Proprietor Félix Eckert

Doubs

Converted mill, Bonnevaux-le-Prieuré

Moulin du Prieuré

A widely travelled reader brings this little hotel to our attention. The converted watermill comprises the highly regarded restaurant and adjacent sitting-room, complete with bits of the original mechanism; the bedrooms are located (in pairs) in little modern chalets in the garden, with sound insulation that is apparently getting much-needed improvement. You prepare your own breakfast in your room, an arrangement justified by the unreasonable hours kept by the trout fishermen who come here. For the rest of us, the attractions are the complete peace, the scenery of the winding valleys hereabouts, and Marc Gatez's thoroughly competent cooking (including trout, of course).
Nearby Loue valley; Besançon (25 km).

25620 Bonnevaux-le-Prieuré
Tel 81.59.28.79
Fax 81.59.21.47
Location in countryside N of Ornans, on D280, with garden and car parking
Meals breakfast, lunch, dinner
Prices rooms 350F, breakfast 30F; meals (at least one obligatory) 280F-350F
Rooms 8 double (4 twin), all with bath or shower; all rooms have phone, TV, minibar
Facilities dining-room, sitting-room
Credit cards AE, DC, MC, V
Children accepted
Disabled one adapted room
Pets accepted
Closed mid-Nov to early Mar, Sun evening and Mon
Proprietors M. and Mme Gatez

Chalet hotel, Goumois

Hôtel Taillard

The wooded Doubs valley is a paradise for fishermen, and this fine traditional chalet hotel is where to come and eat trout or salmon (and much else besides – the restaurant earns a Michelin star), and then to linger over the peaceful view towards Switzerland. With its wide picture windows, the chalet is light and airy; there is a comfortable sitting-room, and for fine days a splendid terrace. Bedrooms are immaculate and comfortable; some have balconies. Guests in this remote spot are generally regulars or guidebook-led; few are disappointed. The Taillard family are excellent hosts. 'Definitely good value' says a recent guest.
Nearby Doubs valley, mountains, forests, walking, fishing

25470 Goumois
Tel 81.44.20.75
Fax 81.44.26.15
Location in fields above village, 18 km E of Maîche, on Swiss frontier; with ample car parking and garage
Meals breakfast, lunch, dinner
Prices rooms 265F-410F; menus 130F-320F
Rooms 17 double with bath or shower; all rooms have central heating, TV, phone
Facilities bar, sitting-room, 2 dining-rooms; swimming-pool
Credit cards AE, DC, MC, V
Children accepted; special meals available
Disabled access easy to dining-room
Pets accepted
Closed Nov to Mar
Proprietor M. Taillard

Ain

Restaurant with rooms, Montmerle-sur-Saône

Castel de Valrose

The Castel de Valrose is only 6.5 km from the A6, but the peaceful setting, just 100 metres from the River Saône, seems far removed from the hurly-burly of the *autoroute*. What is more, it is a friendly, comfortable place to stay and is now in the capable hands of Chantal Moschetto. This is no castle: it is a large 1930s house, with modern decoration, and bedrooms are mostly spacious but ordinary. The food alone is usually worth a detour; sadly, on our last inspection visit we found the fish (a house speciality) very good, but the rest of the meal rather dreary.

Nearby Villefranche-sur-Saône – wine centre; Trévoux (20 km).

360 Blvd de la République
01090 Montmerle-sur-Saône
Tel 74.69.30.52
Location S of village, close to river Saône, 30 km S of Mâcon; in garden, with car parking
Meals breakfast, lunch, dinner
Prices rooms 220F-350F; menus 140F-320F
Rooms 4 double, 3 family rooms, all with bath; all rooms have central heating, phone
Facilities 2 dining-rooms, banquet room
Credit cards MC, V
Children accepted
Disabled no special facilities
Pets dogs welcome if well behaved
Closed never
Proprietor Chantal Moschetto

Ain

Ostellerie du Vieux Pérouges

Pérouges is a perfectly preserved medieval village and at its heart, on the main square, is the Ostellerie du Vieux Pérouges, an irresistible timbered building. Both village and hotel have, not surprisingly, an eye to the tourist, but not offensively so. In the restaurant, the theme is medieval: meals on copper dishes, aperitifs in pewter goblets. Food is essentially regional and a speciality is the *galette Pérougienne*, a sort of sweet tart, served with plenty of thick cream. The bedrooms (some are in two nearby annexes) are mostly furnished with handsome antiques, including four-poster beds, and a few have small terraces.

Nearby Rue des Rondes; Villars-les-Dombes (30 km) – bird sanctuary; Lyons (35 km); Bourg (45 km).

Place du Tilleul, Pérouges
01800 Meximieux
Tel 74.61.00.88
Fax 74.34.77.90
Location in middle of medieval town; with car parking and garage
Meals breakfast, lunch, dinner
Prices rooms 390F-900F; meals 170F-390F
Rooms 25 double (14 twin), all with bath; 4 family rooms, all with bath; all rooms have phone
Facilities dining-room, sitting-rooms, bar
Credit cards V
Children accepted
Disabled no special facilities
Pets accepted
Closed Wed out of season
Proprietor Georges Thibaut

Hôtel du Rhône

Seyssel is a small town split in two by the upper Rhône; the main part is on the left bank, in Haute-Savoie, the minor part across the river in Ain – which is where the Hôtel du Rhône is found, separated from the river bank only by its sunny elevated dining terrace and a minor road (reportedly busy in the mornings). The setting apart, the hotel is a modest place, with no pretensions to luxury or style, offering basic, but perfectly comfortable accommodation. Anne-Marie, M. Vion's wife, is an 'absolute delight' front of house. Food is good and wholesome but not the main attraction.

Nearby Le Grand-Colombier (20 km); Abbaye de Hautecombe (30 km).

Quai de Gaulle 01420 Seyssel
Tel 50.59.20.30
Location outside town beside Rhône, 37 km W of Annecy; with garage and car parking
Meals breakfast, lunch, dinner
Prices rooms 150F-260F; meals from 90F
Rooms 11 double, all with bath or shower; all rooms have central heating
Facilities dining-room, sitting-room
Credit cards DC, MC, V
Children welcome
Disabled no special facilities
Pets welcome
Closed Jan; Sun dinner and Mon out of season
Manager Jacques Vion

Haute-Savoie

La Demeure de Chavoire

Opened at the end of 1989, the Demeure de Chavoire is a glowing example of an elegant modern hotel. It is an attractive white building with red-tiled roofs and gabled windows, set in a pretty garden on the shores of lovely Lake Annecy. Every room has been thoughtfully and richly furnished. The lounge and breakfast room are decorated in pink and pastel shades with floral curtains; walls are wood-panelled and floors inlaid. The bedrooms are all individually furnished in romantic style, and named after local beauty spots and Annecy's famous writers; the Jean-Jacques Rousseau suite accommodates (just) a modern four-poster bed.

Nearby Lake Annecy, Annecy.

71 Route d'Annecy-Chavoire, 74290 Veyrier-du-Lac
Tel 50.60.04.38 **Fax** 50.60.05.36
Location on shores of Lake Annecy close to village; with garden, parking for 15 cars
Meals breakfast, snacks
Prices rooms 600F-1,000F, suites 1,100F-1,500F; breakfast 60F
Rooms 10 double, 3 suites, all with bath; all rooms have central heating, phone, TV, hairdrier, minibar, radio; suites have jacuzzis **Facilities** sitting-room; verandah
Credit cards AE, DC, MC, V
Children welcome; baby-sitting possible **Disabled** 3 ground-floor rooms **Pets** small dogs accepted **Closed** never
Proprietor M. and Mme Brun

L'Abbaye

Annecy-le-Vieux is not the lovely medieval heart of Annecy, but a sprawling residential area north of the lake. But this suave little hotel was indeed an ancient abbey. A stone archway leads into a cobbled courtyard surrounded by a wooden balcony. The dining-room is a splendid, vaulted room sporting a motley array of decoration: gold mythological masks, chandeliers, Renaissance fresco, Indian print napkins – not to mention the waiter in surfer T-shirt when our inspector visited. In summer, tables are set up in the shade of horse-chestnut trees. The bedrooms have been beautifully furnished again in a variety of styles, and with every modern convenience.

Nearby lake; Annecy (old town, churches, château).

15, Chemin de l'Abbaye, 74940 Annecy-le-Vieux
Tel 50.23.61.08 **Fax** 50.27.77.65
Location in rural setting, 2 km NE of Annecy; with garden and car parking
Meals breakfast, dinner
Prices rooms 400F-650F; breakfast 45F, meals 200F-330F
Rooms 15 double, 2 suites, one apart- ment, all with bath; all have central heating, phone, TV, minibar
Facilities dining-room, bar, piano bar, terrace **Credit cards** AE, DC, MC, V **Children** welcome **Disabled** no special facilities **Pets** accepted
Closed restaurant only, Mon
Proprietor M. Menges and M. Burnet

Haute-Savoie

Auberge du Bois Prin

The Auberge du Bois Prin is a superior chalet-style hotel close to the foot of the Brévent cable-car, with a magnificent panorama of the snow-capped dome of Mont Blanc. The friendly Carriers have run the hotel since it was built in 1976; Denis's brother also runs a hotel in Chamonix, whose facilities can be used by guests at the Bois Prin. Bedrooms are luxuriously furnished, with flowery fabrics and carved woodwork (much of it Denis's own work); nine have a private terrace.

Nearby Mt Blanc and Le Brévent – walking, rock climbing.

69 Chemin de l'Hermine, Les Moussoux 74400 Chamonix
Tel 50.53.33.51
Fax 50.53.48.75
Location on hillside, NW of town; with garden and ample car parking and garages
Meals breakfast, lunch, dinner
Prices rooms 760F-1,030F with breakfast; meals 160F-400F
Rooms 9 double (5 twin), all with bath; 2 family rooms, with bath; all rooms have TV, phone, minibar

Facilities dining-room, seminar room
Credit cards AE, DC, MC, V
Children welcome; special meals, high-chair available
Disabled no special facilities
Pets accepted
Closed 18 Apr to 5 May, 24 Oct to 1 Dec
Proprietors Monique and Denis Carrier

Haute-Savoie

Marceau Hôtel

The Marceau has the best of both worlds; it is within easy reach of touristy Lake Annecy (and has spectacular views of the valley and mountains), yet is far enough away to ensure complete peace. Originally built as a private house, it was converted into a hotel over sixty years ago and has been run by the same family ever since. The views are not the only attraction; bedrooms are spacious and dotted with antiques, there is a cosy sitting-room with leather chairs, a rambling garden with a tennis court, and a spectacular terrace where meals are served in summer.

Nearby Lake Annecy – swimming; Albertville – Savoie ski resorts.

Bout du Lac 74210 Doussard
Tel 50.44.30.11
Fax 50.44.39.44
Location in countryside, at S end of Lake Annecy; with large garden and car parking
Meals breakfast, lunch, dinner
Prices rooms 440F-660F; breakfast 50F, menus 130F-330F
Rooms 16 double, 14 with bath, 2 with shower; all rooms have central heating, phone, TV, radio
Facilities sitting-room, dining-room; terrace, tennis court
Credit cards AE, DC, MC, V
Children welcome
Disabled 2 ground-floor rooms
Pets accepted
Closed Oct to Jan
Proprietor Mme Sallaz

Chalet Hôtel de la Croix-Fry

Mountain chalets come in many styles, but the pretty-as-a-cuckoo-clock variety is all too rare in France. This cosy modern hotel is about as close as you get; it has kept a rustic style even in its modern annexe-chalets, which offer flexible and comfortable accommodation (with kitchenettes) for all sizes of family. Style apart, the peaceful setting is the attraction, with superb views across the valley from the flowery terrace. The tennis court and swimming-pool are further pluses; and the welcoming owners have prepared detailed information about things to do.

Nearby skiing; Vallée de Manigod, Thônes (10 km); Annecy.

Rte du Col de la Croix-Fry, Manigod 74230 Thônes
Tel 50.44.90.16
Location at the col, 5 km NE of Manigod, on D16 6 km S of La Clusaz; in countryside, with garden and ample car parking
Meals breakfast, lunch, dinner
Prices rooms 850F-1,500F; breakfast 60F; DB&B 550F-750F; menu 130F-320F
Rooms 12 double with bath; all rooms have central heating, phone
Facilities dining-room, sitting-room, bar; heated swimming-pool, tennis, ski bus
Credit cards MC, V
Children accepted
Disabled no special facilities
Pets not accepted in dining-room
Closed mid-Sep to mid-Dec, mid-Apr to mid-Jun
Proprietor Mme Marie-Ange Guelpa-Veyrat

Isère

Le Cucheron

This roadside chalet occupies a beautiful spot, on the summit of the Col du Cucheron, surrounded by firs and Alpine meadows, ideal for mountain hikes and skiing – the *pistes* are only 20 metres away. Don't expect too much from the hotel. It is no more than a simple, family-run restaurant, with basic rooms and a cosy sitting-room. The food complements the setting: mountain hams, fresh trout, local cheeses and Savoie wines; finishing, inevitably, with a glass (or two) of the famous local liqueur – rather an acquired taste.

Nearby Grande Chartreuse monastery (7km); Grenoble (25 km) – art museum, Fort de la Bastille (by cable-car).

St-Pierre-de-Chartreuse 38380 St-Laurent-du-Pont
Tel 76.88.62.06
Fax 76.88.65.43
Location on roadside 3 km N of St-Pierre-de-Chartreuse; with ample car parking
Meals breakfast, lunch, dinner
Prices rooms 130F-192F; breakfast 26F, meals 90F-170F
Rooms 6 double (2 twin), 3 with bath; one family room with bath; all have central heating **Facilities** dining-room, bar, games/TV room
Credit cards AE, DC, MC, V
Children welcome; special meals available **Disabled** no special facilities **Pets** dogs accepted in bedrooms only
Closed mid-Oct to 20 Dec, 2 weeks mid-Jan; Tue, except in school holidays
Proprietor André Mahaut

Le Marais St-Jean

The plain exterior of this country hotel gives precious little indication that it has been converted from an ancient farmhouse. But inside all is attractive and inviting – modern comforts blending with the timbered ceilings, beams and quarry tiles of the original building. Recent improvements include a shady terrace, with views over the gardens. The Girardon family run their *hostellerie* more like a private house than a hotel. The cooking is among the best you will come across in the area. The location is quiet and rural – yet conveniently close to the A7 autoroute at Vienne.

Nearby Condrieu (5 km); Malleval (10 km).

Chonas-l'Amballan 38121 Reventin-Vaugris
Tel 74.58.83.28
Fax 74.58.81.96
Location just outside village, 10 km S of Vienne; with garden and car parking
Meals breakfast, lunch, dinner
Prices rooms 550F; menus 165F-300F
Rooms 10 double, all with bath and shower (5 twin); all have phone, minibar, satellite TV
Facilities 2 sitting-rooms, bar, dining-room, conference room
Credit cards AE, DC, MC, V
Children welcome; extra bed and special menu available
Disabled one ground-floor bedroom **Pets** welcome
Closed Feb; Wed evening and Thu morning
Proprietors Girardon family

Isère

Country inn, St-Lattier

Le Lièvre Amoureux

An old hunting lodge that has made an exceptionally appealing staging post between the Alps and the Rhône valley, in a peaceful position despite the proximity of the *route nationale* and parallel railway. The main building is creeper-clad, with shutters and flowers at the windows; rooms here are perfectly satisfactory, with pretty decoration and tasteful furnishings, while those in the modern annexe are larger and more sophisticated, with direct access to the attractive swimming-pool and the rest of the flowery garden. Food is reportedly wholesome, served on the terrace in summer (candle-lit at night), in winter before an open fire.
Nearby Vercors massif.

La Gare, 38840 St-Lattier
Tel 76.64.50.67
Fax 76.64.31.21
Location set back from N92 between St-Marcellin and Romans, 30 km NE of Valence, with car parking
Meals breakfast, lunch, dinner
Prices rooms 320F-430F; breakfast 50F, menus 175F-275F, children's 65F
Rooms 14 double (5 twin), all with bath; all rooms have central heating, phone, hairdrier, TV
Facilities dining-room, sitting-room; tennis nearby
Credit cards DC, MC, V
Children welcome; babysitting available
Disabled ground floor rooms
Pets accepted (40F charge)
Closed Nov to mid-Feb
Manager Gisele Carmet

Country mansion, Chonas-l'Amballan

Domaine de Clairefontaine

A species of hotel virtually unknown outside France – a handsome old house in splendid park-like grounds, family-run and completely without pretention, offering entirely comfortable rooms at modest prices and serving sophisticated food – earning a star from Michelin and a *toque* from Gault-Millau – in an elegant dining-room. Although it is close to the N7, the setting is utterly peaceful, making this an excellent overnight stop; but it merits consideration for longer stays if you are happy with a traditional French atmosphere. Rooms in the main house are more spacious than those in the converted outbuilding.
Nearby Condrieu (vineyards) (5 km); Malleval (15 km).

Chonas-l'Amballan, 38121 Reventin-Vaugris
Tel 74.58.81.52
Fax 74.58.80.93
Location in countryside 9 km S of Vienne, just off N7; in grounds with ample parking
Meals breakfast, lunch, dinner
Prices rooms 180F-370F, breakfast 40F, menus 130F-350F
Rooms 14 double, all with bath or shower; 2 suites; all have central heating, phone
Facilities sitting-room, 2 dining-rooms; tennis courts
Credit cards AE, MC, V
Children accepted
Disabled ground-floor rooms
Pets accepted, but not in dining-room **Closed** 20 Dec to 31 Jan; restaurant only, Sun in low season
Proprietor Mme Girardon

Gironde

Château hotel, Pauillac

Château Cordeillan-Bages

In the short time since Château Cordeillan-Bages opened its doors (in spring 1989) it has established a formidable reputation for comfort, character, fine food and great wine.

This is a château in the Bordeaux manner – not a Loire-style extravagance, but a harmoniously proportioned, single-storey stone mansion dating from the 17thC, with an associated expanse of vineyard (once a great one, and gradually gaining in stature again). Pierre and Danielle Paillardon were closely involved in the château's renovation and decoration, and are justifiably proud of the result, which is stylish and restful. There is something of the feel of an English country house about the intimate sitting-rooms and elegant dining-room, though the illusion disappears when you go out on to the terrace to be confronted by vines. The bedrooms are very comfortable, with the sure hand of the interior designer given full rein.

Chef Pascal Charreyras is young, but has an impressive track record and does not lack imagination or confidence in his *nouvelle*-style cooking. Not surprisingly, the wine-list is encyclopaedic.

Nearby Château Mouton-Rothschild (museum) (2 km).

Route des Châteaux, 33250 Pauillac
Tel 56.59.24.24
Fax 56.59.01.89
Location in wine village on D2, 20 km N of Bordeaux; in own grounds, with ample car parking
Meals breakfast, lunch, dinner
Prices rooms 560F-770F, breakfast 60F-90F, menus 175F-280F
Rooms 18 double, all with bath; all rooms have central

heating, phone, hairdrier, TV, minibar, radio
Facilities sitting-rooms, bar, dining-room, breakfast room
Credit cards AE, DC, V
Children welcome; babysitting available **Disabled**
lift/elevator, access ramp, ground-floor rooms, toilets
Pets small ones accepted
Closed Christmas to end Jan; restaurant only, Mon and Sun evening **Manager** Pierre Paillardon

Gironde

Town hotel, St-Émilion

Hostellerie de Plaisance

The Plaisance is a converted monastery in the heart of medieval St-Émilion, 'capital' of the Bordeaux wine region. Its position is superb – in the centre, but on top of a small cliff (which contains a cave-church), with captivating views of the town, castle and vineyards. The dining-room is another big attraction; ask for a table by the window, so you can digest the view along with your excellent three-course menu – 'particularly good value' says a recent visitor – or the four-course 'gastronomic' one at twice the price. Most bedrooms are smart and comfortable.

Nearby Various sights in St-Émilion; Bordeaux vineyards.

Place du Clocher 33330 St-Émilion **Tel** 57.24.72.32 **Fax** 57.74.41.11 **Location** next to medieval bell-tower in heart of town; with car parking on street opposite **Meals** breakfast, lunch, dinner **Prices** rooms 495F-790F, suites 1,300F; breakfast 52F; menus 136F-270F **Rooms** 9 double, one single, 2	suites, all with bath; all rooms have central heating, phone; most rooms have air-conditioning **Facilities** dining-room, bar, TV room **Credit cards** AE, DC, MC, V **Children** accepted **Disabled** 3 ground-floor rooms **Pets** welcome **Closed** Jan **Proprietor** Louis Quilain

Country hotel, Sauternes

Château de Commarque

Since they took over this solid house in 1986, Nigel and Georgea Reay-Jones, an English couple, have restored the neglected Sauternes vineyards, and converted the stables into simple self-contained apartments. A reporter complained of paper-thin walls, but others have found the rooms satisfactory, particularly for families – and the 3 rooms added in 1993 have thick walls. On the other side of the courtyard is a rustic dining-room in the old winery; Georgea's regional dishes are highly praised.

Nearby Trips to vineyards; Bordeaux (40 km).

33210 Sauternes, Langon **Tel** 56.76.65.94 **Fax** 56.76.64.30 **Location** surrounded by its own vineyards overlooking undulating valleys; with car parking **Meals** breakfast, lunch, dinner **Prices** rooms 190F-325F; dinner from 75F **Rooms** 9 double (2 twin), one family room, 2 with bath, all with shower; all rooms have central heating; most have	sitting-room (some with sofa-bed) **Facilities** dining-room, terrace; swimming-pool **Credit cards** MC, V **Children** welcome **Disabled** one ground-floor room; easy access to dining-room **Pets** dogs must be kept on leads **Closed** Feb; restaurant only, Wed out of season **Proprietor** Nigel and Georgea Reay-Jones

Dordogne

Hôtel Bonnet

Beynac-et-Cazenac is one of Dordogne's showpiece villages – a cluster of honey-coloured stone houses lying in the shadow of a castle and with glorious views over the valley. The Bonnet (named after the family who have run it for almost a century) has been a favourite with foreign visitors for years. They are attracted by the setting, the friendly welcome and the reasonably priced bedrooms – simple, airy and in traditional style.

One of the great assets is the delightful terrace, where on warm days you can admire the views while enjoying competent regional cuisine under an arbour of vines (though dinner is served only indoors).

Nearby Sarlat; Domme (10 km) – *bastide*; Les Eyzies (25 km).

Beynac-et-Cazenac 24220 Beynac	120F-280F
Tel 53.29.50.01	**Rooms** 21 double, one single; all with bath or shower
Fax 53.29.83.74	**Facilities** dining-room; sitting-room
Location on main road beside Dordogne, on edge of village, 11 km SW of Sarlat; with terrace and small garden	**Credit cards** MC, V
	Children accepted
	Disabled no special facilities
Meals breakfast, lunch, dinner	**Pets** not accepted in bedrooms
Prices rooms 240F-310F; breakfast 32F, menus	**Closed** mid-Oct to Easter
	Proprietors Bonnet family

La Daille

British *emigrés* Barbara and Derek Brown have been running this unusual establishment just south of the Dordogne for nearly 20 years now – and have built up a regular local clientele for their afternoon teas and set dinners. It is a small-scale *pension* (half board obligatory, minimum stay three days) catering for no more than 7 residents and 14 non-resident diners. The bedrooms are in a modern single-storey building – thoroughly comfortable, with big bathrooms – and each with a terrace overlooking the neat, flowery garden from the original farmhouse, which contains the cool, rustic dining-room.

Nearby golf, canoeing; Domme (15 km) – *bastide*; Sarlat (25 km).

Florimont-Gaumiers 24250 Domme	all rooms have central heating
Tel 53.28.40.71	**Facilities** dining-room
	Credit cards not accepted
Location in countryside, 2 km S of Gaumiers (signposted from village); in large grounds with ample car parking	**Children** accepted over 7
	Disabled access difficult
	Pets not accepted
Meals breakfast, afternoon tea, dinner	**Closed** Nov to 1 May
	Proprietors Mr and Mrs Derek Vaughan Brown
Prices DB&B (with wine) 420F	
Rooms 3 double (2 twin), one single, all with bath or shower;	

Dordogne

Hotel du Château

Guy Gensou is rapidly making a name for himself in his extraordinary little turreted chateau perched above the water's edge in the heart of the small market town of Lalinde. Having established a very solid reputation for excellent cooking, he is now turning to the building itself – hitherto a charming but decidedly modest establishment. There is already a tiny swimming-pool on the attractive dining-terrace; bedrooms have been refurbished and a new sitting area designed. Monsieur Gensou is tackling the building with taste and flair. But it is unlikely to distract him from his main passion – cooking.

Nearby Monpazier (30 km), Les Eyzies-de-Tayac (40 km).

Rue de Verdun
24150 Lalinde-en-Pergord
Tel 53.61.01.82
Fax 53.24.74.60
Location in quiet street and on water's edge
Meals breakfast, lunch, dinner
Prices 350F-850F; breakfast 60F; menus 160F-230F
Rooms 7 double, 4 with bath, 3 with shower; all with phone, TV

Facilities dining-room, sitting-room, terrace with swimming-pool
Credit cards MC, V
Children accepted
Disabled access difficult
Pets accepted
Closed mid-Dec to Mar; restaurant only, Fri out of season
Proprietor Guy Gensou

Manoir d'Hautegente

This creeper-clad manor house set in beautiful wooded grounds has been in the Hamelin family for about 300 years, and is now run by Edith Hamelin and her son Patrick. It was built as a forge in the 13th century, later became a mill (using the stream that runs beside it), was then embellished and turned into a family residence and was finally converted into a hotel. Public rooms and the spacious, comfortable bedrooms are imaginatively decorated with family antiques and paintings. Dinner in the pretty vaulted dining-room is a five-course affair – good home-cooking which inevitably includes home-produced *foie gras*, another of the Hamelin's commercial successes.

Nearby châteaux, old Dordogne villages; Lascaux (15 km).

Coly 24120 Terrasson
Tel (53.51.68.03
Location in countryside, 6 km SE of Le Lardin on the D62; with grounds and car parking
Meals breakfast, dinner
Prices rooms 500F-850F; breakfast 50F, menus 180F-230F
Rooms 10 double, all with bath (2 twin); all rooms have

central heating, phone; hairdrier, TV on request
Facilities dining-room, sitting-room; swimming pool
Credit cards MC, V
Children welcome
Disabled one ground-floor room
Pets accepted if well behaved
Closed Nov to Mar
Proprietor Edith Hamelin

Dordogne

Village hotel, Domme

Hôtel de l'Esplanade

Like many other busy tourist villages, Domme is best enjoyed in the evening and early morning; if that is your aim, the place to stay is the Esplanade, with the splendid view over the Dordogne that is one of the village's chief attractions. The hotel is beautifully furnished with taste and flair, and well run. The housekeeping is immaculate, and service (under the uncompromising eye of the charming Mme Gillard) is efficient and pleasant. Some bedrooms are in annexes, some have private terraces; all are comfortable and the best are very spacious. René Gillard is the chef, and has earned a Michelin star. DB&B is encouraged.
Nearby Beynac (10 km); Les Eyzies-de-Tayac (40 km).

24250 Domme	heating, phone, hairdrier, TV
Tel 53.28.31.41	**Facilities** dining-room,
Fax 53.28.49.92	sitting-room, bar
Location in heart of village 12	**Credit cards** AE, MC, V
km S of Sarlat; with terrace	**Children** accepted
Meals breakfast, lunch, dinner	**Disabled** access difficult
Prices rooms 350F-550F,	**Pets** accepted
apartment 800F; breakfast	**Closed** Nov to mid-Feb; Mon
45F, menus 150F-300F	and Sun evening out of season
Rooms 25 double (13 twin),	restaurant only
17 with bath, 8 with shower;	**Proprietor** M. and Mme René
all rooms have central	Gillard

Country hotel, Sarlat-en-Périgord

Hostellerie de Meysset

'Splendid room, very good food, pleasant owners, good views,' goes the telegraphic report from a reader alerting us to this creeper-covered, typically Perigordian country house. The position is rather unusual, with views in two different directions – and a degree of seclusion that is very welcome, given the proximity to bustling Sarlat. The style inside is traditional and unpretentious, though without floral excesses. As you might expect, the food also leans towards the traditional regional elements such as *confit* and *cèpes*.
Nearby Sarlat; Beynac – château (12 km); Les-Eyzies-de-Tayac – prehistoric paintings, Prehistoric Museum (30 km).

Route des Eyzies 24200	bath or shower; 4 suites; all
Sarlat-en-Périgord	room have phone
Tel 53.59.08.29	**Facilities** sitting-room,
Fax 53.28.47.61	dining-room
Location in countryside, 3 km	**Credit cards** AE, DC, MC, V
NW of town off D47; in 3-acre	**Children** welcome
grounds, with private parking	**Disabled** some ground-floor
Meals breakfast, lunch, dinner	rooms
Prices rooms 375F-450F, suites	**Pets** accepted
560F-750F; breakfast 50F;	**Closed** mid-Oct to Apr
menus 165F, 250F	**Proprietors** M. and Mme
Rooms 22 double, all with	Brottier

Dordogne

Converted mill, Champagnac-de-Belair

Hostellerie Moulin du Roc

The perfect upmarket French hotel? Not far from it, in the view of many visitors to this delectable old walnut-oil mill, described by one guest as 'overflowing with character, and verging on the delightfully eccentric'. Its setting on the banks of the Dronne (a few miles upstream of Brantôme) is wonderfully romantic and rural; the waterside gardens are lush, secluded, shady and bursting with colour – and, with the addition of a brand-new heated swimming-pool, more difficult than ever to leave.

Inside the rough-stone 17thC building, old beams, fireplaces, mill machinery, fine old carved furniture and massive oil paintings – together with plenty of ornaments and flower arrangements – create a style far removed from the designer-decorated pastel look that is creeping into French luxury hotels. Some may find it rather heavy. The same cannot be said of the food: in an area dominated by *foie gras* and *confit*, Solange Gardillou manages to build on culinary traditions to produce remarkably light and inventive dishes which earn high praise from the gastronomic guides. Breakfasts are a treat, with home-made rolls and jams, beautifully served. 'Excellent' value.

Nearby Brantôme; Bourdeilles (15 km) – château.

24530 Champagnac-de-Belair	TV, minibar
Tel 53.54.80.36	**Facilities** sitting-room,
Fax 53.54.21.31	dining-room; heated
Location in hamlet, on D82	swimming-pool, tennis court,
and D83, 6 km NE of	terrace
Brantôme; with large garden	**Credit cards** AE, DC, MC, V
and ample car parking	**Children** welcome
Meals breakfast, lunch, dinner	**Disabled** two ground-floor
Prices rooms 380F-680F;	rooms **Pets** accepted
breakfast 55F, menus	**Closed** mid-Nov to mid-Dec,
200F-280F, children's 100F	mid-Jan to mid-Feb; restaurant
Rooms 10 double (2 twin), 4	Tue
suites; all with bath; all rooms	**Proprietors** M. and Mme
have central heating, phone,	Gardillou

Dordogne

Manor house hotel, Brantôme

Le Chatenet

Brantôme is one of the most popular tourist towns in Périgord, so Le Chatenet comes as a pleasant surprise – 'quite a find', to quote both our captivated inspector and a visitor. It is only a short drive outside the town, down a country track off the busy riverside road, but blissfully far removed from the tourist bustle.

The appeal of this well restored 17thC manor house stems not only from its rural surroundings but also from its informal atmosphere: despite evidently heavy investment in rich furnishings, the Laxtons attach importance to maintaining the family-home feel, and it shows. Inside there are vases of freshly cut flowers on low tables, deep armchairs, and country antiques in both the sitting-room and breakfast room, which form part of the Laxton's home. Bedrooms are spacious, with elegant decoration. In the cosy clubhouse there's an 'honesty' bar and room for wet-weather activities. Outside, deckchairs are scattered invitingly around the garden beneath shady trees, and there is plenty of space for children.

Breakfasts (Magdeleine has a repertoire of 10 sorts of home-made *confiture*) are served on a covered terrace in fine weather, and guests may have the use of an outdoor barbecue. If do-it-yourself doesn't appeal, there are several excellent restaurants nearby. The welcome is 'very cordial'.

Nearby Brantôme – monks' garden, belfry, troglodyte caves; Bourdeilles (10 km) – château; Chancelade (30 km) – abbey.

24310 Brantôme
Tel 53.05.81.08
Location 1.5 km SW of town, off D78; in large grounds with ample car parking
Meals breakfast
Prices rooms 350F-550F, suites 750F
Rooms 8 double, all with bath (6 twin); 2 suites; one cottage with 2 double rooms; all rooms have central heating, phone; TV on request
Facilities sitting-room, breakfast room, clubhouse with billiards; heated swimming-pool, tennis
Credit cards MC, V
Children welcome if well behaved
Disabled access easy; 2 ground-floor bedrooms, one specially equipped
Pets welcome if well behaved
Closed at times Nov to Apr – phone to check
Proprietors Philippe and Magdeleine Laxton

Dordogne

Converted mill, Brantôme

Moulin de l'Abbaye

It used to be possible to grumble about the parking arrangements at this exquisite little mill; but the excavation of a cave across the road has dealt with that problem, leaving nothing to deter the visitor except the Relais & Châteaux prices and the muted roar of the adjacent river Dronne tumbling over the nearby weir.

The setting is the thing. The shady riverside terrace, illuminated in the evening, is an idyllic place for a drink or a meal while admiring Brantôme's unusual angled bridge, the tower of the eponymous abbey or the swans gliding by. Wonderful views over the river and the old houses of one of the prettiest villages in France are also to be had from many of the bedrooms – all beautifully decorated and comfortably furnished (some have four-poster beds and antiques, others are more modern).

Traditional Périgord dishes with a *nouvelle* touch earn the restaurant 3 *toques* from Gault-Millau and a star from Michelin. The dining-room is as pleasant a place to enjoy this excellent cuisine as the terrace it leads to, though we can raise no enthusiasm for the 'Monet-style' colour scheme.

There are fresh flowers, sparkling glass and silverware, and soft lighting in the evening. Staff are correct and courteous; service is efficient.

Nearby Monk's garden, belfry; Antonne-et-Trigonant (3 km) – 15thC Périgord manor; Bourdeilles (10 km) – château.

1 Rte de Bourdeilles 24310 Brantôme
Tel 53.05.80.22
Location on edge of town, 20 km N of Périgueux; with garden, and ample car parking across road
Meals breakfast, lunch, dinner
Prices rooms 650F-900F, apartments 900F-1,350F; breakfast 65F, menus 240F-350F
Rooms 16 double, 4

apartments, all with bath; all rooms have central heating, TV, radio, minibar
Facilities dining-room, sitting-room
Credit cards AE, DC, MC, V
Children welcome; special meals available
Disabled no special facilities
Pets dogs accepted
Closed Nov to May; restaurant Mon lunch
Manager M. Dessum

Dordogne

Don't miss

Les Glycines

The name means wisteria, and that lovely flower is to be found in abundance behind this handsome 19thC house, close to the station on the edge of Les Eyzies, in the lush and beautiful gardens that are the hotel's chief attraction. There is also a swimming-pool and a terrace for drinks. Les Glycines is larger than most of our hotels, but appealing none the less. There are plenty of sitting-areas, well supplied with reading material. The dining-room and covered terrace are very attractive, and all the bedrooms are comfortable; those at the back are superior and less affected by daytime road noise.

Nearby Château de Fages (15 km); Sarlat (21 km); Lascaux caves (25 km); Beynac (30 km) – village and castle.

24620 Les Eyzies-de-Tayac
Tel 53.06.97.07
Fax 53.06.92.19
Location on edge of town, on main road; with large gardens and ample car parking
Meals breakfast, lunch, dinner
Prices rooms 350F-402F; menus 140F-280F
Rooms 25 double, all with bath or shower (12 twin); all rooms have central heating, phone
Facilities 2 sitting-rooms, dining-room, bar; swimming-pool **Credit cards** AE, MC, V
Children accepted **Disabled** access possible **Pets** accepted
Closed Nov to Easter; restaurant Sat lunch out of season **Proprietors** M. and Mme Henri Mercat

Moulin de la Beune

This little mill lies in the heart of Les Eyzies, down on the bank of the river Beune – making it a peaceful place to stay, despite the business of the town. The bedrooms are all excellent, decorated with bright co-ordinating fabrics and colour schemes, the majority with a view over the river. The large fireplace in the sitting-room is turned to good use at the slightest excuse. There's a simple breakfast room and an inviting restaurant in another mill building in the garden.

Nearby Caves, here and further afield – Lascaux (25 km).

24620 Les Eyzies-de-Tayac
Tel 53.06.94.33
Fax 53.06.98.06
Location in middle of town, next to river; with small garden and car parking
Meals breakfast, lunch, dinner
Prices rooms 265F-400F; breakfast 42F, menus 85F-315F
Rooms 20 double, 14 with bath, 6 with shower; 4 family rooms with bath; all have central heating, phone
Facilities sitting-room, breakfast room, dining-room
Credit cards AE, MC, V
Children accepted
Disabled 4 ground-floor bedrooms
Pets accepted
Closed Nov to Mar; restaurant Tue lunch out of season
Proprietors M. and Mme Soulié

Dordogne

Manor house, Vézac

Manoir de Rochecourbe

This 15thC manor house, in the same family for over 100 years and open as a guest-house since 1978, offers an unusual and entirely peaceful place to stay in the popular Dordogne valley. Outside, it is informal and rural, partly creeper-covered, with the air of an old farmhouse, though a grander note is added by the single round tower housing the spiral staircase which you climb to reach the bedrooms. Inside there is space in plenty, and solid antique furnishings in harmony with the massive carved stone chimneypieces, great old beams and bare-board ceilings. Bedrooms are comfortable and have fine views across the valley. There is no restaurant but Mme Roger's breakfasts are reportedly excellent.

Nearby Beynac (2 km) – village and castle; Sarlat (7 km).

Vézac 24220 St-Cyprien
Tel 53.29.50.79
Location in countryside, off D57 6 km SW of Sarlat; with garden and car parking
Meals breakfast
Prices rooms 330-420F; breakfast 34F
Rooms 5 double, all with bath, one with shower (3 twin); all have central heating, phone
Facilities sitting-room, breakfast room
Credit cards MC, V
Children welcome
Disabled no special facilities
Pets accepted by arrangement
Closed Oct to May
Proprietors M. and Mme Roger

Town hotel, Ribérac

Hôtel de France

This is just the sort of French hotel you conjure up in your mind when planning a drive through France – an old flower-decked inn at the heart of a bustling market town, with a pretty and warmly inviting restaurant, and tables laid outside for leisurely dinners under clear skies, modest but spacious bedrooms which can accommodate families, and excellent value. If the emphasis is on the restaurant, that's no bad thing; neither is the fact that the France has long been discovered by the area's colony of British residents – it ensures that the restaurant remains full and the standards remain high.

Nearby Brantôme (25 km), Périgueux (30 km).

3 rue Marc Dufraisse 24600 Ribérac
Tel 53.90.00.61
Fax 53.91.06.05
Location in side street just off market square; with small garden (full of tables and chairs)
Meals breakfast, lunch, dinner
Prices 190F-205F (family rooms 240F-250F); breakfast 25F; menus 68F-270F
Rooms 20 double, 10 with bath, 10 with shower; all have phone
Facilities dining-room, breakfast room, sitting-room
Credit cards MC, V
Children welcome
Disabled access only to dining-room
Pets accepted
Closed 15 days in Jan
Proprietors M and Mme Jauvin

Dordogne

Hostellerie St-Jacques

The front of the creeper-clad 18thC building on the main road through the hamlet of St-Saud gives little clue to what lies within – or, more to the point, what lies behind: the Babayou's 'summer sitting-room', which consists of lovely sloping gardens, with masses of colourful flowers, a fair-sized pool, tennis court and plenty of shade and space for children.

Inside there is an unusually spacious dining-room/bar – now redecorated, we are told, in fresh summer colours – with big windows which open on to the terrace above the garden. All the bedrooms are comfortable, spacious and attractively decorated; several can accommodate families.

The food is rich and varied, with Périgord specialities in abundance – even the basic menu is probably enough to satisfy most appetites. A buffet breakfast/brunch is served in the garden under the shade of the trees, or by the pool. Occasionally there are lively evenings with dancing and games.

In general, we get good reports on this friendly hotel, particularly from satisfied families. If there are lapses in housekeeping standards, we're sure they are occasional and short-lived: the Babayou family does a thoroughly good job, and are justifiably proud of what they have to offer.

Nearby Montbrun (15 km) – fortress; Brantôme (30 km) – monks' garden, château de Richemont; Rochechouart (45 km).

24470 Saint-Saud-en-Périgord
Tel 53.56.97.21
Fax 53.56.91.33
Location in quiet village, 30 km N of Brantôme; with garden and car parking
Meals breakfast/brunch, lunch, dinner
Prices rooms 300F-515F, suites 860F; DB&B 255F-285F; breakfast 45F; menus 115F-250F
Rooms 22 double (7 twin), 2 suites, all with bath or shower; all rooms have central heating, phone; 10 have TV and minibar
Facilities 2 dining-rooms, bar, TV room; swimming-pool, tennis **Credit cards** MC, V
Children very welcome
Disabled no special facilities
Pets accepted
Closed mid-Oct to Mar; restaurant closed to non-residents Sun dinner and Mon
Proprietor Jean-Pierre Babayou

Dordogne

Manor house hotel, Le Buisson-de-Cadouin

Manoir de Bellerive

An impressive restoration project has turned this fine Napoléon III manor house into a sixteen-room hotel. For three months of the year (mid-March to mid-June and mid-September to mid-November), it is also used as a conference centre. Don't let this put you off; for most of the year there is no evidence of boardroom furniture and the hotel has a very peaceful atmosphere.

It is set in lovely grounds which stretch down to the banks of the Dordogne. Sun beds and tables are liberally scattered over the lawns, and there is a swimming-pool and tennis court tucked away between the pine trees and flower borders. If you prefer to watch the world – and the slow-moving river – go by from a more elevated position, you can sit out on the balustraded first-floor terrace. Once you step inside the lofty entrance hall, you will be tnsported back in time. The elegant staircase sweeps up to spacious and very comfortable designer-decorated bedrooms. Breakfast can be taken on the terrace or in a room with murals on the pale walls. There is now a restaurant offering a light, simple menu featuring regional delicacies (foie gras, for example), and snacks are available throughout the day. 'Magnificent rooms, very helpful staff,' comments a recent visitor.

Nearby walking, golf; Lascaux – caves; Les Eyzies; Sarlat (35 km).

Route de Siorac 24480 Le Buisson-de-Cadouin
Tel 53.27.16.19
Fax 53.22.09.05
Location in countryside, 800 m SE of Le Buisson-de-Cadouin on D25; with grounds and ample car parking
Meals breakfast
Prices rooms 400F-750F; breakfast 50F-60F; menu 145F
Rooms 16 double, 8 with bath, 8 with shower (6 twin); all rooms have central heating, phone, satellite TV, minibar
Facilities sitting-room, breakfast room, sauna, jacuzzi, conference facilities; swimming-pool, tennis court
Credit cards AE, DC, MC, V
Children accepted
Disabled access difficult
Pets not accepted
Closed Nov to mid-Apr
Proprietor Mme Huin

Dordogne

Village hotel, St-Cyprien

L'Abbaye

There is a captivating atmosphere about this friendly, constantly improving hotel, particularly since the refurbishment of the lobby, with its colourful fabrics and solid antiques set against large quarry tiles and warm stone walls. In the rustic, stone-flagged sitting-room you can see the old pastry oven and *potager*. The best bedrooms (first floor of newer annexe) are spacious and very attractive. The cooking is supervised by Yvette Schaller and is based on local and regional produce; meals are served in the elegant dining-room or on the terrace in summer.

Nearby Château de Fages (1 km); Les Eyzies (15 km).

24220 St-Cyprien **Tel** 53.29.20.48 **Fax** 53.29.15.85 **Location** near middle of village; with gardens and car parking **Meals** breakfast, lunch, dinner **Prices** rooms 360F-680F; menus 140F-320F **Rooms** 23 double, 13 with bath, 10 with shower; one suite with bath; all rooms have phone	**Facilities** sitting-room, dining-room; swimming-pool **Credit cards** AE, DC, MC, V **Children** welcome **Disabled** no special facilities **Pets** dogs accepted in bedrooms **Closed** mid-Oct to Apr **Proprietors** Yvette and Marcel Schaller

Château hotel, Vieux-Mareuil

Château de Vieux Mareuil

Since Jean-Pierre and Annie Lefranc took over this 15thC fortified house five years ago, its reputation – like that of its imaginative young chef – has gone from strength to strength. The British flock here, and it is easy to see why. Behind the thick, ivy-clad stone walls lies a stylish little hotel, prettily decorated with lots of attention to detail. The spacious bedrooms are well coordinated and have some sitting space, but most guests linger in the home-like sitting-room, the pastel dining-room or by the swimming-pool, tucked into a courtyard below the crenellated tower. There are acres of parkland to explore.

Nearby Villars (5 km) – prehistoric caves; Dronne valley (20 km).

Route Angoulême-Périgueux 24340 Vieux Mareuil **Tel** 53.60.77.15 **Fax** 53.56.49.33 **Location** in countryside 15 km NW of Brantôme; in grounds with parking **Meals** breakfast, lunch, dinner **Prices** rooms 600F-1,000F; breakfast 60F, menus 120F-300F **Rooms** 14 double with bath (6	twin); all have central heating, phone, hairdrier, TV **Facilities** sitting-room, dining-room; swimming-pool **Credit cards** AE, DC, MC, V **Children** not accepted **Disabled** one adapted room **Pets** accepted on night stays only **Closed** 15 Jan to 1 Mar; Sun dinner, Mon in winter only **Proprietor** Jean-Pierre and Annie Lefranc

Dordogne

Village hotel, Trémolat

Le Vieux Logis

The Giraudel-Destords, an old Perigordian family, have lived in this complex of farm and village houses for nearly 400 years. The part which is now the dining-room was a barn for tobacco drying, pigs and wine barrels; upstairs they kept fodder.

None of this can be detected now, of course, in what has for decades been one of the region's most civilized country hotels, now in the hands of Bernard Giraudel, a natural host. All has been designer-decorated to produce comfort of a high degree. The bedrooms are particularly delightful, individually furnished and very cosy in a sophisticated rustic style, with fine materials and furniture; some have four-poster beds. Public rooms are elegant and comfortable, and there are plenty of nooks where you can enjoy after-dinner chess or a quiet read; the small salon has an open fire, and there are fine antiques throughout. The galleried dining-room is very attractive, and looks out on to the green and flowery garden, where you can choose to take breakfast. The classic and modern cooking of Pierre-Jean Duribreux is excellent (two *toques* from Gault-Millau) and the wine list extensive. All of which makes for a very pleasant stay indeed.

Nearby Les Eyzies-de-Tayac (25 km) – National Prehistoric Museum; Monpazier (30 km) – *bastide* ; Beynac (30 km).

24510 Trémolat
Tel 53.22.80.06
Fax 53.22.84.89
Location in village 15 km SW of Le Bugue; with garden and private car parking
Meals breakfast, lunch, dinner
Prices rooms 700F-1,260F; breakfast 72F; menus 180F-370F, children's 85F
Rooms 24 double (13 twin), all with bath; all rooms have central heating, phone, TV, minibar
Facilities 2 dining-rooms, 3 sitting-rooms, bar, conference room, swimming-pool
Credit cards AE, DC, MC, V
Children welcome
Disabled one adapted room; easy access to dining-room
Pets welcome
Closed never
Proprietors M. Bernard Giraudel

Lot-et-Garonne

Les Loges de l'Aubergade

The Agenais is not noted for its gastronomic highlights; but Michel Trama's cooking – and especially his patisserie – is among the best in France. Since the spring of 1989, visitors have had further cause for rejoicing: 10 luxurious bedrooms in a dignified, pale-stone, 13thC building next door to the restaurant have been created with the help of a prestigious designer. They are spacious and highly individual, in a modern Italian style. In the enclosed courtyard is a Roman-style spa bath. The self-taught Michel produces *'cuisine creative à base de produits du terroir'*; the results are inspiring. Maryse oversees the service (on a pretty terrace or in the stone-walled dining-room) with grace.

Nearby Auvillar (15 km); Agen (17 km); Moissac (30 km).

52 Rue Royale, 47270 Puymirol
Tel 53.95.31.46
Location in heart of village, 17 km E of Agen on D16; with garden and car parking
Meals breakfast, lunch, dinner
Prices rooms 750F-1,450F; dinner from 270F
Rooms 10 double, all with bath or shower; all rooms have central heating, air-conditioning, phone, TV
Facilities dining-room, sitting-room, bar, patio
Credit cards AE, DC, V
Children welcome **Disabled** 2 rooms with easy access
Pets supplement **Closed** 2 weeks school holidays in Feb; restaurant only, Mon out of season **Proprietors** Michel and Maryse Trama

Auberge à la Belle Gasconne

A detour to the pretty little village of Poudenas in the heart of Gascony is highly recommended – not only to visit its Roman monuments and château of Henry IV, but also to sample Marie-Claude Gracia's splendid cooking, served in her charming miller's house, and to stay in the lovingly converted 14thC watermill next door, jutting out into the Gélise river. The bedrooms are delightfully cosy, with thick whitewashed walls and wood-beamed ceilings; bathrooms are smart and tiled. Stone floors, arched doorways and original grinding stones complete the picture and there is a wonderfully romantic terrace and large garden.

Nearby Château of Henry IV, Roman bridge and chapels.

47170 Poudenas
Tel 53.65.71.58 **Fax** 53.65.87.39
Location on an islet in Gélise river, in Poudenas, 20 km SW of Herac on D656; with car parking
Meals breakfast, lunch, dinner
Prices rooms 490F-620F; breakfast 45F, dinner 165F-260F
Rooms 6 double, 5 with bath, one with shower; one suite
with bath; all rooms have central heating, phone
Facilities dining-room, sitting-room; swimming-pool
Credit cards AE, DC, MC, V
Children accepted
Disabled no special facilities
Pets accepted
Closed last 2 weeks of Dec and Jan
Proprietor Richard and Marie-Claude Gracia

Lot

Converted stables, Rocamadour

Domaine de la Rhue

It is hard to believe that this peaceful little hotel, set amid rolling countryside out of sight of any other building, is only a few kilometres away from bustling Rocamadour. It is run by a charming young couple, Eric and Christine Jooris, who go out of their way to please their guests. They are only too happy to give advice on which of the pretty nearby villages are worth visiting and – since the hotel has no restaurant – the best local places to dine (and the ones to avoid).

You might be somewhat disappointed to discover that the hotel does not occupy the magnificent family-owned château, but the adjoining stable block. But your disappointment would be short-lived; this superb 19thC stone building has been carefully and imaginatively converted into eleven pretty, spacious bedrooms – 'wonderfully comfortable,' says an enthusiastic visitor. Several are suitable for families. (Plans for 1993 include the addition of a kitcheneette to three large ground floor rooms.) Breakfast is served in a pleasant *salon*, and the Joorises are happy to make snack lunches, which can be eaten beside the glorious swimming-pool in front of the hotel.

You might also want to take advantage of Eric's other passion; he is a qualified hot-air balloon pilot and offers his guests the chance to see Rocamadour from the air – 'an experience not to be missed,' says a reporter.

Nearby hot-air ballooning; Rocamadour (7 km); Padirac (10 km), Loubressac (20 km); Carennac (20 km).

La Rhue 46500 Rocamadour
Tel 65.33.71.50
Fax 65.33.72.48
Location in countryside, 7 km N of Rocamadour on N140; with grounds and ample car parking **Meals** breakfast **Prices** rooms 370F-570F; breakfast 42F-65F
Rooms 11 double, one suite, several suitable for families, all with bath; all rooms have phone **Facilities** sitting-room; swimming-pool
Credit cards MC, V
Children accepted
Disabled access easy **Pets** accepted **Closed** Nov to Easter
Proprietors Eric and Christine Jooris

Lot

Auberge sans Frontière

This simple little *auberge* is an integral part of the life of sleepy Dégagnac. It is a little old-fashioned, but friendly, and decorated in a pretty style, with antiques in evidence. Bedrooms are smallish – there are four attic rooms – but comfortable and inviting. The dining-rooms serve also as bar and sitting-room. Our most recent visit yielded very positive conclusions: 'Jolly atmosphere, excellent food, unbeatable value'. But last year a new *patronne* arrived; reports on the new regime welcome.

Nearby Domme (20 km) – *bastide*; Sarlat (25 km).

Dégagnac 46340 Salviac
Tel 65.41.52.88
Location in village on D6, 10 km SW of Gourdon; with ample public car parking
Meals breakfast, lunch, dinner
Prices rooms 110F-175F; lunch 55F, dinner 85F-125F
Rooms 7 double, one with bath, 5 with shower (4 twin); one single; one family room with shower; all rooms have central heating

Facilities 2 bar/dining-rooms
Credit cards DC, MC, V
Children accepted
Disabled access to restaurant only
Pets accepted if well behaved
Closed never
Proprietor Isabelle Planche-Cazard

Château de la Treyne

Michèle Gombert-Devals' house has made a splendid small hotel. It starts with the advantage of a beautiful position, in woods on a low cliff cut by the meandering river Dordogne. But the compelling attraction of the château is the near-ideal balance struck between the impressiveness of a fortified manor-house and the intimacy of a genuine home. The building dates from the early 14th century, but was substantially rebuilt in the 1600s; it is now tastefully equipped with a happy mix of furnishings – comfy sofas as well as grand antiques. There are long walks to enjoy in the grounds. Excellent regional food is served – on the delightful river terrace in good weather.

Nearby Souillac – abbey church; Rocamadour, Sarlat.

Lacave 46200 Souillac
Tel 65.32.66.66
Fax 65.37.06.57
Location 3 km W of village on D43, 6 km SE of Souillac; in large grounds beside river, with ample private car parking
Meals breakfast, lunch, dinner
Prices rooms 900F-1,800F; DB&B 350F; breakfast 70F, menus 180F-280F **Rooms** 14 double, all with bath; all

rooms have central heating, phone, TV **Facilities** 3 sitting-rooms, dining-room, bar, billiard room, meeting-room; sauna, swimming-pool, tennis **Credit cards** AE, DC, MC, V **Children** welcome
Disabled access difficult
Pets accepted if well behaved
Closed 15 Nov to Easter
Proprietor Mme Michèle Gombert-Devals

Lot

Farmhouse hotel, Mauroux

Hostellerie Le Vert

Finding the entrance to the Hostellerie Le Vert may take a little time: this solid 17thC farmhouse has been little changed in its recent conversion (first to a restaurant, then to a hotel), and there is just a small side door to lead you inside.

Within, all is original stone walls and beams. The beamed dining-room, with elegantly laid tables, opens out on to a terrace with wide views of the countryside; through an arch at one end of the room is the small sitting-room – meant for an aperitif, not for relaxing for the evening. The bedrooms are all comfortably and tastefully modernized, and have lovely views from their small windows. The largest are quite grand and furnished with antiques. But perhaps the most attractive are those in the little annexe only a couple of yards from the entrance – the lower one stone-vaulted, the upper one massively beamed with a marble floor. The garden is lush, with chairs and tables, and improving in colour despite dry summers.

The Philippes are a friendly and hard-working couple – he cooks (interestingly and competently), she serves – whose enterprise deserves to succeed.

Nearby Bonaguil (15 km) – château; Biron castle (35 km); Monpazier (50 km) – *bastide* ; Cahors (50 km) – medieval bridge.

Mauroux 46700 Puy-l'Evêque
Tel 65.36.51.36
Location in countryside, off D5 10 km SW of Puy-l'Evêque; 10 km SE of Fumel; in garden, with ample private car parking
Meals breakfast, lunch, dinner
Prices rooms 200F-340F; breakfast 35F, menus 100F-190F
Rooms 7 double, all with bath or shower; all have central heating, phone, TV
Facilities dining-room, sitting-room, terrace
Credit cards AE, MC, V
Children welcome – children's menu 50F
Disabled no special facilities
Pets welcome at extra charge
Closed Jan to mid-Feb
Proprietors Eva and Bernard Philippe

Lot

Hôtel du Pont de l'Ouysse

The *raison d'etre* of this small *auberge* is its stunning dining terrace overlooking the little river Ouysse, shaded by a lime tree and a large horse-chestnut. It is wonderfully peaceful, as there is no nearby through-road, only an access road to the hotel. The bedrooms are prettily decorated, and there is a simple dining-room for cool days and evenings. The cooking is good, and makes use of local produce (including eel from the Ouysse), but is not confined to the ubiquitous *confit* and foie gras of which it is easy to tire in this area. The Chambons – he in the kitchen, she in charge of the front of the house – take pride in their little hotel, and are improving it all the time. The latest addition was a smart swimming-pool.

Nearby Martel (20 km); Autoire (30 km) – gorges.

Lacave 46200 Souillac
Tel 65.37.87.04
Fax 65.32.77.41
Location in countryside 9 km SE of Souillac; with terrace and car parking
Meals breakfast, lunch, dinner
Prices rooms 400F-700F; breakfast 60F, meals from 150F
Rooms 12 double, all with bath (4 twin); all rooms have phone, TV
Facilities dining-room, sitting-room; swimming-pool
Credit cards V
Children accepted
Disabled no special facilities
Pets accepted
Closed mid-Nov to end Feb
Proprietor Daniel Chambon

Auberge du Sombral

A beautifully restored house in a spectacular setting at the heart of the lovely medieval village, perched high above the Lot valley. There is a pretty dining-room with a tiled floor and rural colours – cream walls, browns, rusts and fresh flowers. Housekeeping is excellent – bedrooms are freshly decorated and spotlessly clean, with crisp linen and lots of hot water on tap. Some bedrooms are on the small side, though. Madame Hardeveld is not the most effusive hostess, but she runs her hotel (and kitchen) very well. Our inspector was very pleased with the cheapest menu. Best out of season, when the village is quiet.

Nearby Pech-Merle – caves; Cahors (35 km) – medieval bridge.

St-Cirq-Lapopie 46330 Cabrerets
Tel 65.31.26.08
Fax 65.30.26.37
Location on village square, with public car parking nearby
Meals breakfast, lunch, dinner
Prices rooms 300F-350F; breakfast 45F, menus 95F-220F
Rooms 8 double, 5 with bath, 3 with shower (2 twin); all rooms have phone
Facilities sitting-room, dining-room
Credit cards MC, V
Children accepted
Disabled access difficult
Pets accepted at extra charge
Closed mid Nov to Mar; Tue dinner and Wed except in school holidays
Proprietor Mme. Gills Hardeveld

Lot

Village hotel, St-Cirq-Lapopie

La Pélissaria

It is a long drive up to St-Cirq-Lapopie – far longer than the maps would have you believe – but it is also a beautiful one, and at the end it is not only a lovely medieval hill-top village but also this archetypal charming small hotel.

Lovingly restored by the proprietor, M. Matuchet, the 13thC house clings to the hillside. Its quirky character is such that you descend the stairs to the bedrooms – which look out on to the tiny garden and enjoy stunning views over the Lot valley. The bedrooms are light, airy and comfortable; a recent visitor remarked on the attention to detail inside her room and the 'secluded private terrace' outside. The two smallest rooms have recently been made into a suite.

Dinner, cooked by Mme Matuchet and served by Monsieur in the elegant and intimate beamed dining-room (with roaring log fire on cold, wet nights) is adventurous and in our experience delicious; bear in mind that a one-cook kitchen necessarily produces a limited range of dishes. M. Matuchet is a musician and tapes of his music provide a pleasant background to dinner. Breakfast is served al fresco or in your room if you prefer.

The excellent service and aura of tranquillity that surrounds this enchanting little hotel is only slightly marred by the difficulty in finding a parking place outside it.

Nearby Pech-Merle caves and museum; Cahors (35 km) – medieval bridge.

St-Cirq-Lapopie 46330
Cabrerets
Tel 65.31.25.14
Fax 66.30.25.52
Location in middle of village, 30 km E of Cahors; with garden; parking difficult
Meals breakfast, lunch, dinner
Prices rooms 410F-570F, suite 640F; breakfast 49F, dinner from 150F
Rooms 5 double, 3 with bath, 2 with shower (4 twin); 2 suites with bath; all rooms have phone, TV **Facilities** dining-room, sitting-room
Credit cards MC, V
Children welcome
Disabled no special facilities
Pets accepted
Closed mid-Nov to Apr; restaurant only, Thu and Fri
Proprietor Marie-Françoise Matuchet

Lot

Les Vieilles Tours

Rocamadour – the 'vertical village' – is apparently the second most visited tourist sight in France; but complete tranquillity can be had nearby in this mellow country house.

It is a beautifully restored stone building, dating from the 13th and 17th centuries, with its medieval atmosphere largely preserved. The dining-room is in the oldest part of the building, with rich pink and floral fabrics contrasting with the original stone walls, tiled floors and old timbers. The cosy sitting-room occupies the first floor of an interesting circular turret-wing. The views across open countryside are completely uninterrupted, giving a feeling of privacy and isolation to the spacious, attractively furnished rooms (most of them in a new but traditional-style building). The Zozzolis generate a relaxed but refined atmosphere. He is an artist, and his paintings (for sale) are hung throughout the hotel. Madame cooks, making full use of local produce in her three dinner menus (one changing daily) – 'very good, excellently presented and good value,' says one report.

There are spectacular walks and cycle rides in the surrounding countryside, and, for the less energetic, a swimming-pool. A recent visitor complains of astonishingly rude service, but this sounds like a hiccup – another commends Les Vieilles Tours as 'delightful and extremely accommodating'.

Nearby château; Moulin de Cougnaguet (10 km); Autoire (20 km) – village, mouth of Autoire Gorges; Carennac (20 km).

Lafage 46500 Rocamadour
Tel 65.33.68.01
Location in countryside 2.5km outside Rocamadour, on D673 to Payrac; with grounds and ample car parking
Meals breakfast, dinner; lunch by arrangement
Prices rooms 210F-440F; DB&B 250F-365F; breakfast 37F-57F; menus 115F-255F, children's 57F

Rooms 8 double, 9 family, 16 with bath, one with shower; all have phone; TV on request
Facilities 2 sitting-rooms (one with TV), dining-room; swimming-pool
Credit cards MC, V
Children welcome **Disabled** access difficult **Pets** accepted, but not in restaurant **Closed** Nov to Easter **Proprietors** M. and Mme Zozzoli

Lot/Landes

Hôtel les Falaises

Huddled below a fine cliff, at the foot of a tiny medieval village, and on the banks of the Dordogne, Les Falaises enjoys an enviable position. Despite being slightly away from the bustle of the western Dordogne, the usual holiday facilities are offered nearby – fishing, canoes and bicycles for hire. A day's activity would be well rewarded by the large and restful garden, and the excellent shady terrace where meals are served. Inside, the dining-room is light and airy (there's a sitting area, the 'coin anglais', with a large fireplace), and the simple bedrooms are light and well decorated. A good-value family-run hotel (the proprietor does the cooking, and has a high local reputation).
Nearby town hall, Raymond's Palace; Rocamadour (15 km).

Gluges, 46600 Martel
Tel 65.37.33.59
Fax 65.37.34.19
Location across small road from river, at the edge of village; garden and car parking
Meals breakfast, lunch, dinner
Prices rooms 210F-300F (280F-360F for three people)
Rooms 14 double (3 twin), one single; 11 with bath, 4 with shower; all rooms have central heating, phone
Facilities dining-room, sitting-room **Credit cards** MC, V
Children welcome
Disabled access only to dining-room and terrace
Pets not accepted in bedrooms
Closed Dec to Feb (1 Mar)
Proprietor M. Dassiou

Auberge des Pins

An excellent example of unpretentious French hotelkeeping, offering satisfactory accommodation and food in modest but well cared for surroundings at moderate prices. It is a timbered chalet-style building set deep in the forests south of Bordeaux, and catering as much to locals in its large, attractively rustic restaurant as to travellers. The rooms are simple but fresh, and although the number has increased in recent years the welcome is as personal as ever. The place has obvious appeal for families looking for a relaxing place to stay, with swings and a sand-pit, and there is a miniature railway nearby.
Nearby Marquèze Ecomuseum; Landes Forest; beaches (40 km).

Route de la Piscine 40630 Sabres
Tel 58.07.50.47
Fax 58.07.56.74
Location amid forest, 40 km NW of Mont-de-Marsan, with large garden and ample car parking
Meals breakfast, lunch, dinner
Prices rooms 180F-650F; meals 100F-350F
Rooms 26 double (7 twin), practically all with bath or shower; all rooms have central heating, phone, cable TV
Facilities bar, TV room, restaurant, conference rooms; play area
Credit cards V
Children welcome
Disabled easy access to restaurant **Pets** not accepted in hotel **Closed** January
Proprietor Lesclauze family

Landes

Les Huitrières du Lac

Hossegor is an attractive family resort amid pine forests, spreading between a lake and the nearby Atlantic coast. Les Huitrières, on the lakeside, is primarily a restaurant, specializing (of course) in fish and seafood: 'Good, very simple food without any frills', says a visitor. The large dining-room (with terrace) has a superb view over the lake, especially at sunset. 'We had a very pleasant breakfast overlooking the water,' reports a visitor who was otherwise disappointed, finding service sullen and atmosphere lacking. Bedrooms are simply furnished but large, with fair-sized bathrooms; some have balconies overlooking the lake ('well worth the small extra charge'), others face the somewhat noisy road. Pleasant setting, good value.

Nearby Bayonne (20 km); Biarritz (30 km).

1187 Ave du Touring Club 40150 Hossegor **Tel** 58.43.51.48 **Fax** 58.41.73.11 **Location** on edge of lake, just outside village; 22 km N of Biarritz; with car parking **Meals** breakfast, lunch, dinner **Prices** rooms 240F-270F; menus 95F-180F	**Rooms** 9 double (3 twin), all with bath; all rooms have central heating, phone **Facilities** sitting-room, dining-room **Credit cards** AE, MC, V **Children** accepted **Disabled** no special facilities **Pets** not accepted **Closed** Dec to Mar **Manager** Mme Eychenne

La Bergerie

Mme Clavier and her husband have made their immaculate whitewashed house – built in southern single-storey style – a calm and civilized haven where the slow pace of life is infectious. M. Clavier used to be a wine merchant and, naturally enough, tends the cellar; Madame does the cooking, and the (obligatory) set dinner is based on whatever is fresh and good at the time – she makes a point of not owning a freezer. The dining-room is small, but attractively furnished with antiques, the adjacent sitting-room cool and elegant. The bedrooms – all with fair-sized bathrooms – look on to the neat gardens, and those in the annexe have French windows.

Nearby Beaches (15 km); Léon (20 km) – boat trips down Courant d'Huchet; Dax (28 km) – cathedral; Bayonne (45 km).

Ave du Lac 40140 Soustons **Tel** 58.41.11.43 **Location** close to middle of village, 37 km NW of Biarritz; with large garden and ample car parking **Meals** breakfast, dinner **Prices** rooms 250F-350F; DB&B 350F **Rooms** 12 double, all with	bath (8 twin); all rooms have central heating, phone **Facilities** sitting-room, dining-room **Credit cards** DC, MC, V **Children** accepted **Disabled** access difficult **Pets** not accepted **Closed** Nov to end Mar **Proprietors** M. and Mme Clavier

Landes

Lakeside hotel, Mimizan

Au Bon Coin du Lac

Jean-Pierre Caule is the third generation of his family to run Au Bon Coin, and is rightly proud of it. The two-storey, stone and painted-wood house has a superb lakeside setting, with neat little footpaths inviting you to walk around the grounds. But the hotel's *raison d'être* is its Michelin-starred restaurant, and M. Caule's culinary skill as head chef (seafood is his speciality). The generally expensive feel of the place is reflected in the menu – and the prices. The dining-room has an uncluttered view of the lake and is charmingly furnished: round tables, white table-cloths, floral china and floral-covered chairs. The service is formal, as you would expect in a restaurant in this price range, but nevertheless friendly, and not overpowering.

The bedrooms are large and luxurious; not impersonal, but rather uniform. Despite the many activities on the lake – sailing, fishing – the swings nearby and the special children's menu, this is not really a place for a family holiday. But it is ideal for those who want four-star treatment, a relaxed and friendly atmosphere and excellent food.

Nearby Lakes; beaches (5 km); Landes forest (30 km); Sabres (40 km) – railway to Marquèze Ecomuseum.

34 Ave du Lac, Mimizan 40200 Landes
Tel 58.09.01.55
Fax 58.09.40.84
Location amid forests, 2 km N of Mimizan; on edge of lake, with garden and car parking
Meals breakfast, lunch, dinner
Prices rooms 350F-580F; menus 150F-350F; reduced rates for children
Rooms 5 double, all with bath and shower; 4 suites, all with bath and shower; all rooms have central heating, TV, phone, radio, minibar

Facilities sitting-room, dining-room
Credit cards AE, V
Children welcome; special meals, baby-listening available
Disabled ground-floor bedrooms
Pets not welcome
Closed Feb; restaurant only Sun dinner, and Mon in low season
Proprietor Jean-Pierre Caule

Gers

Le Ripa Alta

Set on the main square of a quiet town recently invigorated by an ambitious scheme to equip the church with a massive organ, the Ripa Alta is a simple hotel which revolves around the restaurant – and the cooking of Maurice Coscuella, which manages to combine innovation with respect for regional tradition (a reporter confirms that 'dinners are superb'). His wife and daughter manage the hotel; it is simply furnished, but there are plans to make it more comfortable. Excellent breakfasts can be had on the terrace. Front rooms, overlooking the square, can be noisy.

Nearby Aire-sur-l'Adour (30 km) – church of Ste-Quitterie.

3 Place de l'Église 32160 Plaisance	rooms have central heating, phone; 11 rooms have TV
Tel 62.69.30.43	**Facilities** dining-room, bar,
Fax 62.69.36.99	banqueting-room
Location in middle of village, 43 km N of Tarbes; with ample car parking	**Credit cards** AE, DC, MC, V
	Children welcome
	Disabled no special facilities
Meals breakfast, lunch, dinner	**Pets** accepted at extra charge
Prices rooms 175F-455F; breakfast 30F, menus 75F-300F, children's 50F	**Closed** Nov
	Proprietor Maurice Coscuella
Rooms 13 double, all with bath or shower (5 twin); all	

Hôtel des Trois Lys

'The restoration of the Trois Lys has resulted in one of the best hotels I have ever stayed in' – one of the many compliments in the guest book of this immaculate establishment in the heart of Condom. Jeannette Manet will welcome you warmly to her lovely 17thC house, with its sandy stone walls and white shutters, and restrained elegant decoration within. The bedrooms are spacious and smart, with tasteful antique or reproduction furniture and fresh flowers. Some look over the inviting swimming-pool; there is also a shaded terrace at the front of the hotel.

Nearby Armagnac cellars, cathedral, churches.

38 rue Gambetta 32100 Condom	**Facilities** breakfast-room, sitting-room, 2 bars;
Tel 62.28.33.33	swimming-pool
Fax 62.28.41.85	**Credit cards** AE, DC, MC, V
Location right in heart of town; with secure car parking	**Children** welcome
	Disabled one specially adapted room
Meals breakfast	
Prices rooms 250F-550F; breakfast 40F	**Pets** accepted
	Closed never
Rooms 9 double, all with bath; one single with shower; all rooms have central heating, phone, TV, hairdrier	**Proprietor** Jeannette Manet

Pyrénées-Atlantiques

Riverside hotel, St-Etienne-de-Baïgorry

Arcé

This white Basque hotel is a real family venture. It was founded by Jean Arcé in 1864 as humble eight-room *auberge* on the road to the Spanish border, just eight kilometres away. Since then, it has passed down through four generations of the Arcé family, each of which has left a mark on the hotel. But, despite the extensive changes, expansion and modernization, the hotel has lost none of its character.

The setting – by a river in a typical Basque village – is a magical one, best appreciated from the dining terrace, which juts out over the water and is sheltered by a canopy of chestnut trees. The food is almost as good as the view, featuring plenty of local specialities (game, fish) and rating one star from Michelin. Inside the shuttered building are spacious public rooms – a beamed sitting-room with assorted furniture and a brick fire-place, a library with books in all languages, and a smart dining-room with picture windows. Some of the bedrooms are impressively large, with an apartment-sized sitting area; others open on to small terraces with mountain views. There is a smart swimming-pool across the river.

Nearby walking, fishing, bicycling; Pyrenees; Spanish border; Atlantic coast – beaches.

64430 St-Etienne-de-Baïgorry
Tel 59.37.40.14
Fax 59.37.40.27
Location in village 10 km W of St-Jean Pied-de-Port; with garden and car parking
Meals breakfast, lunch, dinner, snacks
Prices rooms 370F-665F; breakfast 47F, menus 120F-230F
Rooms 20 double, 18 with bath, 2 with shower, (7 twin); one single with shower; 6 family rooms with bath; all rooms have central heating, phone; some rooms have TV, hairdrier **Facilities** dining-room, sitting-rooms, games room; terraces, swimming-pool, tennis court
Credit cards MC, V **Children** welcome **Disabled** no special facilities **Pets** accepted
Closed mid-Nov to mid-Mar
Proprietors M. Arcé

151

Pyrénées-Atlantiques

Village hotel, Aïnhoa

Hôtel Ohantzea

Aïnhoa is an attractive mountain village, close to the Spanish border but with adequate roads to Bayonne. Set on the main through-road, the timbered Ohantzea has been in the Ithurria family for three centuries, and old family furniture is dotted around and scattered throughout the house, which is satisfyingly rustic and tasteful throughout – uneven wooden floors, beamed ceilings. The bedrooms are notably spacious, and some have balconies. The menu may disappoint those expecting some Spanish influence but it is fair value and the dining-room is pleasant enough, looking out on to a terrace and the apple trees in the garden beyond. M. and Mme Ithurria are a charming, outgoing couple who make everyone feel at home.

Nearby St-Pée-sur-Nivelle (10 km) – old houses, galleried Basque church; Sare (10 km) – cog railway up La Rhune.

Aïnhoa 64250 Cambo-les-Bains
Tel 59.29.90.50
Location in middle of village, 10 km SW of Cambo-les-Bains; with garden and car parking behind
Meals breakfast, lunch, dinner
Prices rooms 240F-295F; menus 120F-210F
Rooms 10 double, 9 with bath and shower (3 twin); all rooms have central heating, phone

Facilities sitting-room, 2 dining-rooms
Credit cards AE, DC, MC, V
Children welcome
Disabled no special facilities
Pets accepted
Closed Dec and Jan
Proprietor M. Ithurria

Pyrénées-Atlantiques

Relais des Voyageurs

This former presbytery – its pretty, flower-filled garden used to be the cemetery of the next-door church – has been sympathetically converted into a welcoming small hotel. It is not perfect – parts of it suffer from noise from the road and some of the bedrooms are cramped. But the best of the rooms are spacious and have balconies overlooking the garden (with terrace); the dining-room (with a small sitting-area by the huge fireplace) is light and warm, with bare stone walls; and the Hermants are apparently as amiable as their predecessors.

Nearby Bidache (15 km) – château; Orthez (30 km).

Place de l'Église, Escos 64270
Tel 59.38.42.39
Location in grounds of village church, on D936 30 km NW of Navarrenx; with garden, and car parking in square nearby
Meals breakfast, lunch, dinner
Prices rooms 110F-230F; menus 60F-150F
Rooms 8 double, 2 with bath, 5 with shower (2 twin); all rooms have central heating, phone
Facilities dining-room with sitting-area
Credit cards MC, V
Children accepted
Disabled no special facilities
Pets accepted
Closed never
Proprietors M. and Mme Hermant

Le Vieux Logis

This jolly little *auberge* is not particularly *vieux* in style or in fact, but it attracts a brisk trade in lunchtime visitors on their way to or from the nearby caves of Bétharram – its traditional regional cuisine earning a red R from Michelin for quality combined with moderate prices. It is an attractive spot to stay in while exploring the foothills of the Pyrenees. With its large lawned garden dotted with wooden chalets (accommodation is in these or in the main hotel) it is particularly appealing for families.

Nearby Grottes de Bétharram; Lourdes (15 km); Pau (30 km).

Rte des Grottes 64800 Lestelle-Bétharram
Tel 59.71.94.87
Location in countryside on RN637, 3 km E of village, 12 km W of Lourdes; with garden and car parking
Meals breakfast, lunch, dinner
Prices rooms 200F-250F; menus 90F-180F
Rooms 40 double, all with bath or shower; all rooms have central heating, TV, phone
Facilities 4 dining-rooms, 2 conference rooms; swimming-pool
Credit cards AE, MC, V
Children welcome
Disabled 2 rooms accessible
Pets accepted if small and well behaved
Closed 15 Jan-1 Mar
Proprietor Pierre Gaye

Pyrénées-Atlantiques

Village hotel, Sare

Hôtel Arraya

With its timbered, white-painted houses, Sare can claim to be the prettiest of all the extremely pretty Basque villages – altogether captivating, provided the weather is right and the surrounding pastures merely lush, emerald and gleaming (not rain sodden). In the heart of the village, this 16thC house was once a hostel for religious pilgrims on their way across the Pyrenees to Santiago de Compostella; now it houses, among others, stylish Parisians who have no wish to hurry away, despite the charms of the coast (less than 16 km away) or the high mountains (a little further).

Behind the slightly severe frontage on the main square lies a country-house hotel of great character. Sitting-room, bar and dining-room – not to mention every nook and cranny on stairways or landings – are filled with glorious old Basque furniture; sofas and chairs are comfortable and inviting, and flowers are everywhere. There are more antiques in the individually decorated bedrooms (not especially spacious, but bright and beautiful); some look out over the fine garden. As if all this is not enough, the cooking is good and there is a particularly well-chosen wine list; and there is even a splendid Gâteau Basque for tea-time indulgence.

Nearby Cog railway up La Rhune; Aïnhoa (10 km) – Basque village; Ascain (5 km) – Basque church; St-Jean-de-Luz (14 km).

64310 Sare	one single with shower; all
Tel 59.54.20.46	rooms have central heating,
Location in middle of village,	phone; TV on request
14 km SE of St-Jean-de-Luz;	**Facilities** sitting-room, bar,
with garden and ample public	dining-room
car parking (private parking	**Credit cards** AE, MC, V
nearby)	**Children** welcome; special
Meals breakfast, lunch, dinner	menu available
Prices rooms 375F-540F;	**Disabled** no special facilities
breakfast 50F per person;	**Pets** accepted in restaurant
meals 135F-335F	only
Rooms 20 double, 17 with	**Closed** Nov to May
bath, 4 with shower (12 twin);	**Proprietor** Paul Fagoaga

Pyrénées-Atlantiques/Ariège

La Fayette

This little family-run hotel occupies a prime spot (in a pedestrian zone) in the very heart of the animated port and resort of St-Jean. The building is unusual – in Dutch style, all arches and red brick; it has a street terrace for outside meals, and a charming rustic dining-room. There is a small, neat and formal TV room, and small, simple but cheerful bedrooms. Guests on *pension* terms enjoy a choice of dishes; Peyo Colombet's repertoire includes his wife's special recipe for scallop and monkfish casserole (called *co'lotte*). An otherwise contented visitor warns of doggy smells on the stairs.

Nearby Church of St-Jean-Baptiste; Ciboure; Biarritz (15 km); Ascain (10 km) – Basque church; Sare (15 km) – cog railway.

18-20 Rue de la République
64500 St-Jean-de-Luz
Tel 59.26.17.74
Fax 59.51.11.78
Location in middle of old town, near beach; with free public car parking 400m away
Meals breakfast, lunch, dinner
Prices rooms 280F-320F; DB&B 300F-430F
Rooms 18 double, 10 with bath, 7 with shower (10 twin); all rooms have central heating, phone, TV
Facilities dining-room, conference room, bar
Credit cards AE, DC, MC, V
Children accepted
Disabled no special facilities
Pets dogs accepted **Closed** never **Proprietor** Mme Mayie Colombet

Auberge du Poids Public

The Lauragais is the rolling upland that forms the watershed between Aquitaine and the Midi, and St-Félix, on top of a hill, gives views in all directions, not the least impressive of them from the windows of this thoroughly well run inn. The dining-room is rustic and jolly, with a blazing fire when appropriate; bedrooms are rather grander in style. Claude Taffarello took over in early 1990 and reports suggest that he is keeping up the same high standards as his predecessor: 'Excellent service', 'superb dinner', 'tastefully decorated – everything gleamed'.

Nearby Castres (35 km); Toulouse (45 km).

31540 St-Félix-Lauragais
Tel 61.83.00.20
Fax 61.83.86.21
Location on edge of village, on D2, 40 km SE of Toulouse; with small garden, car parking and garage
Meals breakfast, lunch, dinner
Prices rooms 250F-300F; DB&B 260-320F; menus 130F-305F
Rooms 13 double, 8 with bath, 5 with shower (4 twin); all rooms have central heating, phone, TV, minibar
Facilities dining-room, bar, sitting-room
Credit cards AE, V
Children welcome; special meals available
Disabled no special facilities
Pets dogs accepted
Closed Jan and one week Feb, Sun evening in winter
Proprietor M. and Mme Claude Taffarello

Allier

Château de Boussac

The Château de Boussac lies between Vichy and Moulin, tucked away in the Bourbonnais – a region rarely included on foreign visitors' itineraries – and is quite difficult to find. There are no prominent signs or roadside posters, because this is not a hotel in the ordinary sense. Solid, turreted and moated, the château could be a tourist sight in its own right; it is built around a courtyard, and the main reception rooms, furnished with Louis XV antiques and chandeliers, open on to a vast terrace with an ornamental lake and formal gardens.

But this is no echoing monument devoid of furnishings – on the contrary, the château is very much lived-in. It is a private home where you stay as paying guests of the aristocratic owners, whose family have owned the château since the middle of the 18th century. By day the Marquis dons his overalls and works on the estate, but comes in to cook at least one course of the *table d'hote* evening meal and chat to his guests. His wife looks after the rooms with care – there are fresh flowers everywhere and the antiques are highly polished. Dinner *en famille* can be a rather formal affair, but the food is hard to fault and the Marquis, who speaks English, will make you feel at home.

Nearby Souvigny (35 km) – Gothic/Romanesque church; Vichy (40 km) – spa town; Moulins (50 km) – half-timbered houses.

Target 03140 Chantelle
Tel 70.40.63.20
Fax 70.40.60.03
Location in countryside, off D42, 12 km NW of Chantelle, 50 km W of Vichy; in large park, with ample car parking
Meals breakfast, dinner
Prices rooms 600F-1,000F; menus 210F-310F; breakfast 50F
Rooms 4 double (3 twin), 1 suite, all with bath; all rooms have central heating
Facilities dining-room, sitting-room
Credit cards MC, V
Children accepted if well behaved **Disabled** no special facilities **Pets** accepted if well behaved **Closed** Nov to Feb (except by reservation in advance) **Proprietors** Marquis and Marquise de Longueil

Allier

Country hotel, Coulandon

Le Chalet

It is the setting that lifts this *Relais du Silence* out of the ordinary – in a secluded, wooded garden (park-like in style) of which the main feature is a big fish pond perfect for strolling around, drink in hand, before dinner. Rooms (some in the chalet-style building itself, others in converted outbuildings) vary in style and size; none is notably stylish, but the best are cheerfully comfortable (with exposed beams and bright wallpaper) and sound value. There are regional specialities in the traditional-style dining-room, and the service is amiable. The kitchen is the province of M. Hulot (no relation).

Nearby Moulins – timbered houses, cathedral.

03000 Coulandon
Tel 70.44.50.08
Fax 70.44.07.09
Location in countryside 6 km W of Moulins, off D945; with large grounds and ample car parking
Meals breakfast, lunch, dinner
Prices rooms 260F-430F; breakfast 40F; menus 100-220F
Rooms 19 double, 5 with bath, 14 with shower (5 twin); 9 family rooms, 6 with bath, 3 with shower; all rooms have central heating, phone, TV
Facilities dining-room, sitting-room; fishing, swimming-pool
Credit cards AE, DC, MC, V
Children accepted
Disabled 6 ground-floor bedrooms
Pets accepted
Closed 16 Dec to 31 Jan
Proprietor M. H Hulot

Cantal

Château hotel, Ydes

Château de Trancis

A classic little Loire-style château transported to the 500-metre-high fringes of the Auvergne regional park seems an unlikely thing. It is more easily understood when you know that the Italianate architectural flourishes are of 20thC origin.

There are further surprises in store. The château is run by an English couple, travel writers Innes and Fiona Fennell, who have refurbished it to create the kind of harmonious and stylish ambience that is not hard to find in more popular areas of France but is distinctly rare in and around the Massif Central. Bedrooms are well equipped and individually decorated, with antique furniture and rugs on polished floors. Public rooms embrace an ornate Louis XIV salon, a 'German' dining-room and an 'English' library. The view from the terrace across the smart little pool is essentially pastoral, and only slightly spoilt by the little-used railway line a field away.

A house-party atmosphere prevails, encouraged by the fact that the Fennels' five-course dinners are served only to residents. The Britishness of the Fennells' operation surfaces in one other important respect that will endear the hotel to some travellers and rule it out for others: they do not normally accept children.
Nearby Dordogne gorges, Parc Régional des Volcans d'Auvergne.

15210 Ydes
Tel 71.40.60.40
Fax 71.40.62.13
Location on D15, off D22, 2 km N of village of Saignes, 3 km E of Ydes; in countryside, with car parking in grounds
Meals breakfast, dinner
Prices rooms 500F-850F, suite 1200F, including breakfast; DB&B 530F-850F
Rooms 6 double (one twin), one suite, all with bath or shower; all rooms have central heating, phone, hairdrier, TV, minibar, tea/coffee facilities, electric fan
Facilities 3 sitting-rooms, 2 dining-rooms; 2 terraces, park, swimming-pool
Credit cards MC, V
Children not accepted
Disabled difficult access
Pets no dogs **Closed** Oct to Easter **Proprietors** Innes and Fiona Fennell

Cantal

Auberge Fleurie

This delightful creeper-covered *auberge* was taken over last year by Mme Courchinoux-Barbance after 70 years or more in the caring hands of the Barral family. Thus far, little seems to have changed. Bedrooms are comfortable enough, but the two attractive dining-rooms (polished wood dressers, gleaming copper, red-check table-cloths) are the focal point; there is a bar, which is well patronised by locals. (There is a sitting-room in a cottage annexe nearby.) The menus remain good value. Reports on the new regime welcome.

Nearby Entraygues (15 km) – medieval bridge; Lot valley.

Place du Barry 15120 Montsalvy
Tel 71.49.20.02
Location on edge of village, 35 km S of Aurillac; garden and private car parking at cottage annexe, 1 km away
Meals breakfast, lunch, dinner
Prices rooms 120F-160F; meals 50F-170F; breakfast 25F
Rooms 13 double, 5 with shower (3 twin); all rooms have central heating

Facilities 2 dining-rooms, bar; sitting-room in annexe
Credit cards AE, DC, MC, V
Children welcome; special meals available
Disabled no special facilities
Pets accepted
Closed restaurant 15 Jan to 15 Feb
Proprietor Mme Courchinoux-Barbance

Hostellerie de la Maronnne

Set in a beautiful peaceful valley in the Auvergne, with a small modern swimming-pool, this 1880s country house makes a fine retreat whether you are in search of peace or of outdoor exercise. Much has changed of late: a smart dining-room has been built into the hillside, other public areas have been attractively refurbished, and newly built bedrooms have replaced the least attractive of the old ones, and others have been remodelled. 'Could easily have stayed there for weeks', says our latest reporter.

Nearby Salers (10 km); Anjony (20 km) – château.

Le Theil 15140 St-Martin-Valmeroux
Tel 71.69.20.33
Fax 71.69.28.22
Location in countryside 3 km E of St-Martin, on D37; with gardens and ample car parking
Meals breakfast, lunch, dinner
Prices rooms 350F-550F; DB&B 355F-455F; breakfast 40F-50F; menu 200F
Rooms 21 double, all with bath; all rooms have central heating, phone, minibar; 10

have balcony or terrace
Facilities dining-room, sitting-room, breakfast room, seminar room; swimming-pool, tennis, *pétanque*, sauna, garden
Credit cards MC, V
Children welcome; baby-sitting by arrangement
Disabled lift/elevator
Pets accepted but not in dining-room
Closed Nov to Mar
Proprietor Alain de Cock

Haute-Loire

Farmhouse hotel, Moudeyres

Le Pré Bossu

Moudeyres is a remote village high (1,200 metres) in the volcanic hills of the Mézenc massif, surrounded by fields of wild flowers (in the spring) and mushrooms (in the autumn). The village consists almost entirely of thatched rough-stone houses, many now beautifully restored. The Pré Bossu is no exception, although it was built as recently as 1969, but with old materials; from a distance, there is little to make you suspect it is a hotel, and inside all is appropriately simple and charming. The young Flemish owners have worked hard to create an attractive and comfortable house. Starting with beams, wood floors and inglenook fireplace, they have added fine antique dressers, lace curtains, wild flowers, plants and books. It is all fresh and well-kept. Bedrooms are rustic, too – clean and simple, with good shower rooms; tranquillity is assured.

This remote little place prompts more reports from readers than just about anywhere else – and they tell different stories. 'Absolutely delightful', says one; 'over-rated', another. If there is a common reservation, it is over an occasional lack of warmth, physical and metaphorical. Carlos Grootaert's food is ambitious and reliable, earning a Michelin star. But one recent visitor would have liked a wider choice. Keep the reports coming.

Nearby Restored 18thC farm; Le Puy – volcanic rock formations.

43150 Moudeyres
Tel 71.05.10.70
Fax 71.05.10.21
Location on edge of village, 25 km SE of Le Puy; in garden, with ample car parking
Meals breakfast, lunch, dinner
Prices rooms 325F-920F; breakfast 55F, menus 165F-360F
Rooms 10 double, 5 with bath, 5 with shower (4 twin); one family room; all rooms have central heating, phone
Facilities bar, TV room, dining-room
Credit cards AE, MC, V
Children accepted **Disabled** no special facilities **Pets** accepted in bedrooms, but not in dining-room
Closed 11 Nov to Easter
Proprietor Carlos Grootaert

Lozère

Château hotel, La Malène

Château de la Caze

This is a medieval château in the true fairytale tradition, with turrets and vaults in abundance. Converted sympathetically, it still retains an ancient atmosphere although the chapel is now the dining-room, and modern bathrooms have been added to the bedrooms. Furnishings are antique and grand, bedrooms are large. A barn annexe in the lush garden provides space for further bedrooms, and there is a sunny terrace for summer breakfasts which looks down over the moat. Cooking is traditional, and of a high standard. And then there is the setting, right by the glorious Tarn, the steep valley sides rearing above.

Nearby Gorges du Tarn; Florac; Parc National des Cévennes.

La Malène 48210 Ste-Enimie
Tel 66.48.51.01
Fax 66.48.55.75
Location beside river in Tarn gorge, on D907 48 km NE of Millau; with ample car parking and large garden
Meals breakfast, lunch, dinner
Prices rooms 575F-1,050F; breakfast 55F; menus 165F-330F
Rooms 19 double (10 twin) all with bath; all have TV, phone
Facilities sitting-room/bar, dining-room; swimming-pool
Credit cards AE, DC, MC, V
Children welcome; special meals available
Disabled 3 ground-floor rooms in annexe
Pets accepted, but not in dining-room **Closed** end Oct to 1 May **Proprietors** Simone and Martine Roux

Manor house hotel, La Malène

Manoir de Montesquiou

An attractive and rather less expensive (though by no means cheap) rival for the Château de la Caze (see above) – a 15thC manor house, complete with turrets. The setting, in the tiny village of La Malène, is slightly less impressive, but the drama of the Tarn gorge is undiminished. The conversion into a hotel has not interfered greatly with the castle-like feel of the traditionally furnished building. Your bedrooms may be in a tower; it may have a grand old four-poster; it may have splendid views of the gorge; it is sure to be comfortable and well looked after. The Guillenet family run their hotel with care and good humour.

Nearby Gorges du Tarn; Florac; Parc National des Cévennes.

48210 La Malène
Tel 66.48.51.12
Fax 66.48.50.47
Location in village in the Tarn gorge, on D907 between Millau and Florac
Meals breakfast, lunch, dinner
Prices rooms 420F-785F; breakfast 55F, menus 160F-245F
Rooms 10 double (4 twin), 2 suites, all with bath or shower; all rooms have central heating, air-conditioning, phone; some have TV
Facilities sitting-room, 2 dining rooms, bar, solarium
Credit cards DC, V
Children accepted
Disabled no special facilities
Pets dogs accepted (35F)
Closed Nov to Easter
Proprietors Bernard and Evelyne Guillenet

Aveyron

Manor house hotel, Castelpers

Château de Castelpers

This family-home-turned-hotel makes a relaxing retreat. The house dates from the 17th century and ranges from the purely rustic to the Gothic in style, with a tower, arched windows and rooms of character furnished comfortably with antiques. But it is not a château hotel in the grand manner; families can feel at ease, with swings and spacious lawns (dotted with ancient trees) for children to play on and trout streams to explore, and prices that reflect the modest size of some of the bedrooms. Good food, served in front of an open fire in winter.

Nearby Château du Bosc (10 km); Sauveterre-de-Rouergue (20 km).

Castelpers 12170 Requista
Tel 65.69.22.61
Location in countryside 9 km SE of RN88, 10 km S of Naucelle; in wooded park with private car parking
Meals breakfast, lunch, dinner
Prices rooms 240F-455F; menus 135F-260F
Rooms 7 double (4 twin), 2 family rooms; 3 with bath, 6 with shower; all rooms have phone, 5 have TV
Facilities sitting-room, 2 dining-rooms; fishing
Credit cards AE, MC, V
Children welcome if well behaved
Disabled one specially equipped ground-floor bedroom
Pets accepted, but not in dining-room
Closed 1 Oct to 1 Apr
Proprietor Mme Yolande Tapie de Celeyran

Aveyron

Hôtel Ste-Foy

Conques is a lovely old village, and at its heart is the great abbey church from which this hotel – a sturdy medieval house directly opposite – takes its name. The house has been sensitively restored and beautifully furnished with close attention to detail. Bedrooms are highly individual, tasteful and spacious, with views either over the church or the flowery courtyard garden. The cooking of Maxime Deschamps gets good reviews. Plans are afoot to create more rooms, and to extend the air-conditioning already installed in top-floor rooms.

Nearby Church of Ste-Foy (remarkable tympanum and treasury).

Conques 12320
St-Cyprien-sur-Dourdou
Tel 65.69.84.03
Location in heart of village, 40 km N of Rodez; with private car parking
Meals breakfast, lunch, dinner
Prices rooms 400F-900F; breakfast 53F; menus 160F-280F; lunch 100F
Rooms 17 double, 15 with bath, 2 with shower (10 twin); 2 single, both with shower; all rooms have central heating, phone
Facilities 3 dining-rooms, sitting-room, bar, interior patio, conference room; 2 terraces; exercise room
Credit cards MC, V
Children accepted
Disabled no special facilities
Pets accepted
Closed end Oct to Easter
Proprietors M. and Mme Garcenot

Longcol

The *long col* is a loop in the river Aveyron, below this splendid turreted medieval farmhouse, immersed in woods a few miles from Najac. The Luyckx family are keen antique collectors; the low-beamed rooms are full of beautiful pieces of furniture, tapestries and Asian artefacts. Bedrooms are equally original and comfortable, but vary in size. Meals are served in the light, airy dining-room, or on the little walled terrace in summer – or by the central angular swimming-pool, which shares the views. Seven new rooms and conference facilities were added a couple of years ago, but the polished, informal atmosphere remains unchanged.

Nearby Najac – medieval houses and castle.

La Fouillade 12270 Najac
Tel 65.29.63.36
Fax 65.29.64.28
Location in large wooded grounds near village; with garden and car parking
Meals breakfast, lunch, dinner
Prices rooms 450F-750F; meals 120F-260F
Rooms 17 double, 15 with bath, 2 with shower; all rooms have central heating, phone, TV, minibar, radio
Facilities dining-room, sitting-room, billiard room, terrace; swimming-pool, tennis court
Credit cards AE, V
Children welcome; baby-sitting available **Disabled** no special facilities **Pets** welcome **Closed** 15 Nov to Easter; restaurant only, Tue out of season
Proprietor Luyckx family

Aveyron

Village hotel, Najac

L'Oustal del Barry

High up in the pretty old village of Najac, with its medieval fortress towering above the winding River Aveyron, is this spick-and-span little country hotel offering an honest welcome and notably good value. The hotel has been in the family for five generations, and for the last 20 years in the hands of Jean-Marie, whose cooking – modern, but regionally based – has a high local reputation. Rooms are spacious but ordinary. There is a lush garden, and a sunny terrace in front of the hotel. 'Excellent food, friendly and helpful people', says our most recent report.
Nearby Castle, Gorges de l'Aveyron; Cordes (25 km).

Place du Bourg 12270 Najac
Tel 65.29.74.32.
Fax 65.29.75.32
Location in middle of village, 54 km NW of Albi and 24 km S of Villefranche-de-Rouergue; with garden and car parking
Meals breakfast, lunch, dinner
Prices rooms 324F-546F with breakfast; meals 130F-320F
Rooms 21 double, 7 with bath, 10 with shower (5 twin); one family room with shower; all have central heating, phone, TV; 4 have a small sitting-room; 2 have a large balcony
Facilities 2 dining-rooms, sitting-room with TV; boules
Credit cards AE, MC, V
Children welcome; special menus available **Disabled** lift/elevator **Pets** accepted
Closed Nov to end-Mar
Proprietors Catherine and Jean-Marie Miquel

Riverside hotel, St-Jean-du-Bruel

Hôtel du Midi

The rural *logis* at its best: a village inn amid grand countryside, run by the same family for four generations, offering welcoming rooms and excellent food at irresistible prices. It is very much a family-run place, with Mme overseeing the dining-room while Jean-Michel cooks. Vegetables come from the garden, poultry is home-raised, jams and croissants home-made. The Papillons have recently divided the dining-room in two, making one half into an intimate *salon* with leather furniture. A delighted visitor lists the swimming-pool and pretty garden as other highlights. Bedrooms vary: some are recently renovated.
Nearby Gorges de la Dourbie (10 km); Montpellier-le-Vieux.

12230 St-Jean-du-Bruel
Tel 65.62.26.04
Fax 65.62.12.97
Location by river, in village on D991, 40 km SE of Millau; with garden and garages
Meals breakfast, lunch, dinner
Prices rooms 75F-187F; menus 68F-187F
Rooms 12 double, 8 with bath (3 twin); 2 single; 5 family rooms, 3 with bath, 2 with shower; all rooms have central heating, phone
Facilities 3 dining-rooms, bar, sitting-room, TV room; swimming-pool, jacuzzi
Credit cards V
Children welcome; special menus available
Disabled access to dining-room only **Pets** accepted
Closed mid-Nov to Easter
Proprietor Papillon familly

Aveyron

Riverside hotel, St-Sernin-sur-Rance

Hôtel Carayon

St-Sernin is a handsome medieval village in hilly countryside not far from the Tarn, of which the Rance is a tributary. The Carayon (once called the France but, after a century in the same hands, now known by the family name) is a white-painted, shuttered building with café tables in front; most of the rooms are in a glossy modern extension, and they are now so numerous that the hotel should no longer have a place here.

But an enthusiastic report from a visitor convinces us otherwise. The hotel enjoys a lovely view over the valley of the Rance (shared by the restaurant and its terrace and many of the rooms), the welcome is warm and – not least – Pierre Carayon's cooking is excellent. What is more, the menu prices are modest, earning a prized red R rating from Michelin. The reputation of the Carayon is for good honest regional fare, fresh ingredients and large portions – nothing *nouvelle* about it.

The Carayons are an attractive and friendly couple (Pierre speaks good English, having worked in London hotels).
Nearby Vallée du Tarn (20 km); Monts de Lacaune (30 km).

Place du Fort 12380
St-Sernin-sur-Rance
Tel 65.99.60.26
Fax 65.99.69.26
Location in village, 50 km E of Albi, 63 km SW of Millau; with garden, car parking and garages
Meals breakfast, lunch, dinner
Prices rooms 179F-349F; menus 69F-300F
Rooms 26 double, 14 with bath, 10 with shower (8 twin); 10 family rooms/suites, 5 with bath, 3 with shower; all rooms have central heating, phone, minibar; 10 rooms have TV
Facilities 2 dining-rooms, TV room, games room; swimming-pool, mini-golf
Credit cards AE, DC, MC, V
Children welcome **Disabled** 3 bedrooms specially equipped
Pets accepted **Closed** Sun dinner and Mon out of season
Proprietor Pierre Carayon

Tarn

Medieval inn, Cordes

Le Grand Écuyer

Cordes is a glorious medieval village on an isolated hill, its main street lined by fine Gothic mansions. Le Grand Écuyer is scarcely less impressive – a former hunting lodge of the Comte de Toulouse and a classified historic monument, transformed into a comfortable, elegant and atmospheric hotel.

For many visitors, the food is the thing. Yves Thuriès, the *chef-patron*, is an excellent cook in general but as a *pâtissier* he has few equals. The dining-room is medieval in style, with old stone walls and tiled floors, dark beamed ceiling, old prints and so on, blending well with the lacy white table-cloths, shining silver, painted plates and tapestry chairs. The sitting-room and bar are more domestic, with deeply upholstered armchairs, low tables and potted plants. Bedrooms are grand but inviting – beamed ceilings, monumental stone fireplaces, rugs on expanses of polished floor – and are beautifully furnished with antiques (four-poster beds, chests and so on). Bathrooms are modern.

It could easily be too heavy and pompous, but M. Thuriès and his friendly staff ensure that a graciously informal atmosphere prevails.

Nearby Rue Droite (14thC houses); Fôret Grésigne (15 km) – marked trails; Albi – *la ville rouge*.

Rue Voltaire 81170 Cordes	**Facilities** 2 dining-rooms,
Tel 63.56.01.03	breakfast room, sitting-room,
Fax 63.56.18.83	bar
Location in middle of village,	**Credit cards** DC, MC, V
25 km NW of Albi; with public	**Children** accepted
car parking nearby	**Disabled** no special facilities
Meals breakfast, lunch, dinner	**Pets** accepted
Prices rooms 600F-850F, suite	**Closed** Nov to Easter
1,400F; menus 160F-500F	**Proprietor** Yves Thuriès
Rooms 12 double, one suite,	
all with bath; all rooms have	
central heating, phone, radio	

Tarn

Medieval inn, Cordes

Hostellerie du Vieux Cordes

If you want a simpler base than the Grand Écuyer in the old town of Cordes, here is the answer. Also owned by the exacting M. Thuriès, and managed by Mme Françoise Guibert, it compromises only slightly on his high standards of comfort and cuisine. Set at the top of the old hill town, the stone-built 13thC building has a terrace garden giving long views (shared by many of the bedrooms) over the rooftops; there are tables here and also in an interior courtyard where they are shaded by mature wisteria. Inside, stone, beams and tiled floors give it a rustic ambience – furniture is generally simple, except in the plush sitting-room, where the baronial gets out of hand.

Nearby Rue Droite (14thC houses); Fôret de Grésigne (15 km).

Rue St-Michel 81170 Cordes **Tel** 63.56.00.12	**Facilities** dining-room with bar, sitting-room
Location at top of town; with car parking nearby	**Credit cards** AE, DC, MC, V
Meals breakfast, lunch, dinner	**Children** accepted
Prices rooms 265F-420F; meals from 120F	**Disabled** no special facilities
Rooms 21 double, 7 with bath, 13 with shower (5 twin); all rooms have central heating, phone; TV	**Pets** accepted **Closed** Jan **Proprietor** Yves Thuriès

Farmhouse hotel, Mazamet

La Métairie Neuve

Mazamet is not a notably appealing town except to students of sheepskin processing, but it is practically surrounded by the grand scenery of the Parc Régional du Haut Languedoc – and Pont de Larn lies just below the pretty Gorges du Banquet. The Metairie is a tastefully renovated old farm with its heritage properly respected – exposed beams, stone walls, polished tiled-floors – and with a relaxed atmosphere. Mme Tournier is a charming hostess who keeps the antique-furnished public areas looking immaculate. Bedrooms were renovated in 1992.

Nearby Castres (15 km) – Goya museum; Carcassonne (50 km).

81660 Pont-de-Larn **Tel** 63.61.23.31	**Facilities** 2 dining-rooms, sitting-room, conference room; swimming pool
Location in countryside 2km E of Mazamet on D65, 18km SE of Castres; with private car parking	**Credit cards** DC, MC, V **Children** welcome; special menu available
Meals breakfast, lunch, dinner	**Disabled** ramp access to restaurant only
Prices rooms 340F-450F; menus 100F-250F	**Pets** accepted
Rooms 11 double (5 twin), all with bath; all rooms have central heating, phone, TV; 9 have minibar	**Closed** mid-Dec to mid-Jan; restaurant only Sat **Proprietor** Mme Tournier

Ardèche

Hôtel du Midi

The restaurant here is named after the renowned Madame Barattéro (a culinary heroine of Elizabeth David), from whom M. Perrier's parents took over in the 1950s. It remains the heart of the hotel, serving an ambitious blend of traditional and *nouvelle* dishes which earn modest awards from the gastronomic guides. The dining-room is rather plain but intimate, service helpful and friendly. Bedrooms, in a separate building a minute's walk away, are comfortably old-fashioned and spacious. Those at the front (which were rather noisy) have been double glazed.

Nearby Small steam train to Tournon (35 km); Valence (40 km).

Place Seignobos 07270
Lamastre
Tel 75.06.41.50
Fax 75.06.49.75
Location in middle of town,
40 km W of Valence; with
garden, and garage
Meals breakfast, lunch, dinner
Prices rooms 280F-425F;
menu 195F-400F
Rooms 13 double, 12 with
bath, one with shower (8
twin); all rooms have central
heating, phone, 7 have TV

Facilities 3 dining-rooms; 2
sitting-rooms
Credit cards AE, DC, MC, V
Children welcome; special
meals available
Disabled one ground-floor
bedroom **Pets** accepted
Closed 15 Dec to 1 Mar; Sun
evening and Mon
Proprietor M. and Mme
Bernard Perrier

Château d'Urbilhac

This fairytale château – 19thC but in Renaissance style, with round tower and steep slate roof – has a beautiful, peaceful, elevated setting in a very large park (much of the food comes fresh from the estate). The interior is rather ponderous in style, but it does not lack character or comfort. The bedrooms are exceptionally civilized, with plenty of space and some splendid old beds. A key feature is the smart swimming-pool, below the grand terrace. The Xomperos are a charming couple, much concerned for guests' happiness.

Nearby Tournon (33 km); Valence (40 km) – cathedral.

07270 Lamastre
Tel 75.06.42.11
Fax 75.06.52.75
Location in countryside on
D2, 2 km S of village; in large
grounds with ample car
parking and garage
Meals breakfast, lunch, dinner
Prices rooms 450F-650F;
menus from 200F; DB&B
(obligatory in season)
500F-575F
Rooms 13 double, 11 with

bath, 2 with shower (3 twin);
all rooms have phone
Facilities sitting-room, 2
dining-rooms; swimming-
pool, tennis court
Credit cards AE, DC, MC, V
Children accepted
Disabled dining-room and
one bedroom on ground floor
Pets accepted
Closed Oct to Apr
Proprietors M. and Mme
Xompero

Ardèche

Village inn, Vallon-Pont-d'Arc

Le Manoir du Raveyron

When our inspectors arrived, this rustic village inn was bursting at the seams with Sunday lunchers. The atmosphere was genuinely entertaining: any minute one expected a fiddler to appear and the clientele to start dancing. The waiters were frantically overworked, but still ready to oblige. Bedrooms are simple but not uncomfortable. Luxury, no; but atmosphere in plenty. The hotel faces an ugly modern building; but the surroundings do not intrude, because the old stone building is set well back from the street, behind gates and a large and leafy courtyard-cum-garden. The food is reported to be 'quite superb, and underpriced,' the welcome exceptionally kind.

Nearby Gorges de l'Ardèche; Pont d'Arc (5 km); Marzal (20 km)

Rue Henri Barbusse 07150
Vallon-Pont-d'Arc
Tel 75.88.03.59
Location in village on D579,
33 km S of Aubenas, 51 km
NE of Alès; with garden and
car parking
Meals breakfast, lunch, dinner
Prices rooms 165F-250F;
menus 90F-210F, children's
menu 42F
Rooms 13 double, one single,
all with shower; all rooms have
central heating
Facilities dining-room,
sitting-room/bar
Credit cards MC, V
Children welcome
Disabled no special facilities
Pets accepted
Closed 15 Oct to 15 Mar
Proprietors M. Bourdat and
M. Gauthier

Drôme

Converted castle, Dieulefit

Les Hospitaliers

Le Poët-Laval perches on a hillside overlooking the valley of the Jabron: an unspoilt medieval village dominated by the former stronghold that is now Les Hospitaliers. It is a remarkable spot.

Les Hospitaliers is now a hotel of various creature comforts, including a good restaurant and a pool and terrace from which there are splendid views. The restaurant (which shares the views) has an interesting collection of paintings; Yvon Morin was an art-dealer before becoming a hotelier. Tables are laid with fine china, white linen or lace, and candles; service is hard to fault.

Bedrooms are furnished with antiques; many share the beautiful views. Our most recent reporter 'booked for one night and stayed for three'.

Nearby Montélimar (20 km) – nougat; Viviers (30 km) – medieval town, cathedral; Valence (60 km) – cathedral, wines.

Le Poët-Laval, Dieulefit 26160 La Bégude-de-Mazenc **Tel** 75.46.22.32 **Location** at top of old village, 5 km W of Dieulefit; with gardens; car parking nearby **Meals** breakfast, lunch, dinner **Prices** rooms 520F-1,100F; meals 160F-450F **Rooms** 21 double, 20 with bath, one with shower (8 twin); 3 family rooms, all with	bath; all rooms have central heating, phone **Facilities** 2 dining-rooms, 2 sitting-rooms, bar; swimming-pool **Credit cards** AE, DC, MC, V **Children** accepted **Disabled** no special facilities **Pets** cats and dogs accepted **Closed** 15 Nov to 1 Mar **Proprietors** M. and Mme Yvon Morin

Drôme

Auberge des Quatres Saisons

St-Restitut is one of the lesser known perched villages of Provence. The vine-clad *auberge* lies in the oldest part of the village – a fascinating conversion of ancient houses, preserving many of the old stone walls. Bedrooms are quiet, rather dark and cosy – with heavy patterns and furniture, in Provençal style. In the restaurant the stone floor has been recently carpeted, but the medieval stone vaulting and period furniture remain, providing a fine setting for good regional fare. There is a small breakfast terrace on the first floor.

Nearby St-Paul-Trois-Châteaux (5 km); Bollene (7 km).

Place de l'Eglise, St-Restitut
26130 St-Restitut
Tel 75.04.71.88
Fax 75.04.70.88
Location in middle of village, 9 km NE of Bollène, on D160; with small garden, and car parking nearby
Meals breakfast, lunch, dinner
Prices rooms 325F-450F; menus 130F-195F
Rooms 8 double (6 twin), 5 with bath, 3 with shower; 2 family rooms with bath; all rooms have phone
Facilities dining-room, sitting-room
Credit cards AE, DC, MC, V
Children accepted
Disabled no special facilities
Pets accepted
Closed Jan; restaurant only, Sat lunch
Proprietors Mme Marie Therese de Guyenro and M. Bernard Fritsch

Hôtel Pic

Most tourists give Valence a miss, but there is one good reason for making a detour – the Pic. Any meal here, whether an *al fresco* lunch or dinner in the luxury of the dining-room, is a special event. The Pic is now regarded as one of the top restaurants in France – it has probably the most famous *menu dégustation* in the country, comprising five exquisite courses – but is delightfully free of any snobby atmosphere. The five comfortable bedrooms are rarely vacant.

Nearby Cathedral; L'Hermitage (15 km); Montélimar (45 km).

285 Ave Victor-Hugo 26001 Valence **Tel** 75.44.15.32
Fax 75.40.96.03
Location on S outskirts of town, east of A7 (exit Valence south); with garden and private parking
Meals breakfast, lunch, dinner
Prices rooms 650F-850F, apartments 800F-1,000F; breakfast 100F, menus 280F-620F
Rooms 3 double rooms (one twin) and two apartments; all with bath; rooms reserved for restaurant clients only; all rooms have phone, TV, central heating
Facilities dining-room, sitting-room
Credit cards AE, DC, MC, V
Children welcome
Disabled lift/elevator
Pets accepted
Closed 3 weeks Aug; Wed and Sun evening
Proprietors Pic family

Drôme

Château de Rochegude

The number (and price) of rooms in this sumptuous château are at the top end of our scale, but we cannot resist including it because of its wonderful setting – overlooking the vineyards of the Rhône plain – and its equally wonderful food (2 *toques* Gault-Millau, one star Michelin). Bedrooms are palatial, most furnished with four-posters or half-testers and requisite antiques. There are plenty of nooks to explore – a glassed-in cloister, a crumbling tower, walled gardens, a wooded park – or you can simply linger by the pool, or in one of the elegant public rooms.
Nearby Orange; Carpentras; Avignon

26790 Rochegude
Tel 75.04.81.88
Fax 75.04.89.87
Location in countryside, 8 km SE of Bollene, just off D8; with large park and ample car parking
Meals breakfast, lunch, dinner
Prices rooms 725F-1650F with breakfast; lunch 190F, dinner 250F-450F **Rooms** 23 double (12 twin), 2 single, 4 apartments, all with bath; all rooms have central heating, air-conditioning, phone; most rooms have TV, minibar; some have jacuzzi
Facilities sitting-room, bar, dining-room
Credit cards AE, DC, MC , V
Children welcome; baby-sitting available
Disabled no special facilities
Pets accepted in restaurant
Closed Jan to Feb
Manager André Chabert

La Capitelle

A rough-stone Logis de France, dating from Renaissance times, with stone-mullioned windows, in a backwater setting in a walled medieval village. The whole operation has an air of confident good taste, with a stylishly traditional feel to the individually furnished and boldly decorated bedrooms and the vaulted dining-room, and modern sofas in the sitting-area. Both the public rooms have splendid stone fireplaces. Only a few minutes' drive from the Autoroute du Soleil, La Capitelle makes an excellent stopover on the way to or from the south.
Nearby Montélimar (17 km); Valence – cathedral (30 km); lavender fields – late summer harvest (20 km).

Le Rempart 26270 Mirmande
Tel 75.63.02.72
Fax 75.63.02.50
Location on edge of village, 30 km S of Valence on D204, E of N7; private garage (50F)
Meals breakfast, lunch, dinner
Prices rooms 220F-410F; breakfast 40F, meals 125F-175F; children's meals 52F
Rooms 9 double (4 twin), 2 with bath, 7 with shower; one family room; all rooms have central heating, phone
Facilities dining-room, sitting-room, TV room
Credit cards DC, MC, V
Children tolerated
Disabled no special facilities
Pets accepted (30F charge)
Closed mid-Nov to mid-Jan; restaurant Tue and Wed lunch
Proprietor Mme Boucher

Gard

Country hotel, La Favède

A l'Auberge Cévenole

The usual approach to this neat country hotel is through the disagreeably industrialized valley which runs north from Alès; but don't be put off. The *auberge*, set in a little circle of hills, is as peaceful and alluring as any you could wish to find. The building – a much-expanded 1950s villa, opened as a hotel in 1960 – is white, with a red-tiled roof and a shady, creeper-clad terrace. It is set in an exceptional garden: informal, full of flowers, with plenty of secluded corners in which to read, plus a fair-sized (unheated) swimming-pool. Inside the pace is slow (though not the service, except on occasions when the waitresses are over-stretched), the atmosphere quietly old-fashioned. A rash of shepherds and shepherdesses covers many of the walls; bedrooms and bathrooms range from adequate to very comfortable without being luxurious (with the exception of the two apartments, which are).

The Burlons took over a professional and flourishing enterprise from M. Chabaud four years ago. A visitor found a very friendly welcome, the food 'adequate but not outstanding'.

Nearby Château de Rousson (20 km); St-Jean-du-Gard and Corniche des Cévennes (25 km); Grotte de Trabuc (25 km).

La Favède 30110 Les Salles-du-Gardon
Tel 66.34.12.13
Fax 66.34.50.50
Location in hamlet on D283 off N106 14 km N of Alès; with large garden, ample car parking
Meals breakfast, lunch, dinner
Prices rooms 300F-600F; breakfast 45F, menus 165F-265F
Rooms 19 double (7 twin), all with bath or shower; all have central heating, phone
Facilities dining-room, bar/sitting-room, TV room; swimming-pool, mini-tennis, table-tennis
Credit cards MC, V
Children accepted
Disabled 8 ground-floor rooms
Pets not accepted
Closed mid-Oct to Mar
Proprietors M. and Mme Burlon

Gard

Restaurant with rooms, Tavel

Hostellerie du Seigneur

Surrounded by vineyards, Tavel is known for its rosé wines. Those seeking a simple base for a night or two will be pleased to find this congenial little restaurant with rooms in the centre of the village. Perched above the main road, the Hostellerie is a cosy place, with a pleasant little terrace overlooking a square. Inside, a bar-cum-reception area leads into the hotel's hub: an intimate stone-vaulted dining-room where *cuisine bourgeoise* is offered – incorporating, naturally, the wines of Tavel at every opportunity. Upstairs, bedrooms are plain, old-fashioned but entirely adequate.

Nearby Avignon (15 km); Orange (15 km) – Roman theatre.

Place du Seigneur 30126 Tavel
Tel 66.50.04.26
Location in middle of village, 10 km NW of Avignon; with public car parking
Meals breakfast, lunch, dinner
Prices rooms 170F-280F; menus 90F-136F
Rooms 6 double (one twin); one family room; all rooms have central heating

Facilities dining-room, sitting-room, bar
Credit cards MC, V
Children accepted
Disabled no special facilities
Pets not accepted
Closed 15 Dec to 15 Jan
Proprietors Ange and Juliette Bodo

Restaurant with rooms, Les Angles

L'Ermitage-Meissonnier

It was Michel Meissonnier's father, Paul-Louis, who built up the reputation of L'Ermitage for fine food. Although no longer awarded a star by Michelin, pay no heed: the menus are still mouth-watering, the execution of them still way above average and the prices still reasonable by these elevated standards. It is a relaxing place to stay; bedrooms lack charm but are spacious, comfortable and peaceful. The stone-walled dining-room has been done out in green and pink, but it is the delightful terrace that steals the show – shaded by mulberry trees, lit by candles on the tables. Beyond it is an inviting swimming-pool.

Nearby Avignon – Palais de Papes, cathedral; Nîmes (39 km).

Ave de Verdun 30133 Les Angles
Tel 90.25.41.02
Fax 90.25.11.63
Location on NW fringes of Avignon, 3 km from middle on RN900; with garden, terrace and private car parking
Meals breakfast, lunch, dinner
Prices rooms 260F-480F; menus 160F-450F, children's menu 120F

Rooms 16 double (6 twin), most with bath; all rooms have central heating, phone
Facilities dining-room, sitting-area; swimming-pool
Credit cards AE, DC, V
Children welcome
Disabled no special facilities
Pets accepted at extra charge
Closed Jan and Feb;
Proprietor M. Meissonnier

Gard

Hostellerie la Magnaneraie

There are several hotels to choose from in Villeneuve-lès-Avignon – a pleasant and historically interesting base from which to explore nearby Avignon. The largest of them, the Prieuré, is also the best known; it is luxurious (and expensive), but it lacks the friendliness of the Magnaneraie – a solid, rectangular stone building in a well-heeled residential corner of the town.

Eliane Prayal and her husband Gérard – a talented and committed chef – continue to make improvements to their hotel. Having added entirely new bedrooms next to the magnificent swimming-pool, they then turned their hand to renovating and enlarging the 'old' bedrooms in the main house, adding air-conditioning but retaining an elegant and refined style. Now that bedrooms, garden and restaurant have been attended to, the energetic Prayals have turned their attention to the sitting-room. Despite all this up-grading, and the sense of elegance that prevails, the easy-going atmosphere that the Prayals have prided themselves on still exists: many of the bedrooms can accommodate families (some have charming bunk beds), and (well behaved) children are much in evidence.

Nearby Tour Phillipe-le-Bel, Chartreuse du Val-de-Bénédiction; Avignon – Palais des Papes, cathedral, Pont St-Bénézat.

Rue du Camp-de-Bataille
30400 Villeneuve-lès-Avignon
Tel 90.25.11.11
Fax 90.25.46.37
Location in residential area on fringe of village, across the Rhône from Avignon; with garden and car parking
Meals breakfast, lunch, dinner
Prices rooms 450F-950F, menus 180F-350F
Rooms 27 double, all with bath; all rooms have central heating, TV, phone, minibar;
many rooms with private terrace and/or air-conditioning
Facilities dining-room, sitting-room, bar, conference room; swimming-pool, tennis
Credit cards AE, DE, MC, V
Children accepted
Disabled access easy but no special facilities
Pets accepted
Closed never
Proprietors Gérard and Eliane Prayal

Gard/Vaucluse

Hôtel de l'Atelier

In a quaint side street fairly near the main square, this old town house makes a complete contrast to our other recommendation in Villeneuve. It has nothing like the bustle of the Magnaneraie (there is no restaurant), but the welcome is sincere. The building has been sympathetically restored – original stone walls much in evidence – with careful attention to detail. Breakfast is served in a pleasant room, and there is a picturesque courtyard at the back – enclosed by a jumble of old buildings, and an ideal place in which to sit and drink muscat before dinner.

Nearby Avignon – Palais des Papes, cathedral, Pont St-Bénézet.

5 Rue de la Foire 30400
Villeneuve-lès-Avignon
Tel 90.25.01.84
Fax 90.25.80.06
Location in town, 2 km N of middle of Avignon; with garden and public parking only
Meals breakfast
Prices rooms 220F-400F
Rooms 19 double, 13 with bath, 6 with shower (8 twin); all rooms have central heating, phone; 11 rooms have TV
Facilities breakfast room, sitting-room with TV, terrace, garden
Credit cards AE, DC, MC, V
Children welcome
Disabled 3 bedrooms on ground floor
Pets accepted
Closed Nov to Dec
Proprietors M. and Mme Gounaud

Auberge la Fontaine

La Fontaine gets its name from the magnificent fountain beside it, in the heart of the perched village of Vénasque. The stone village house has been run as a restaurant for over 30 years, and in 1987 Ingrid and Christian Soehlke added five lovely suites to their two dining-rooms. Each suite has its own kitchen and terrace overlooking Provençal tiled roofs and bell-towers. The rooms are decorated in rustic style – stone-flagged floors, wooden furniture, dried flowers. The excellent restaurant is still the main focus of attention, though a *bistro* opened in 1993.

Nearby Carpentras; Avignon (30 km).

Place de la Fontaine, 84210
Vénasque
Tel 90.66.02.96
Fax 90.66.13.14
Location in heart of Vénasque, 10 km SE of Carpentras; no private car parking
Meals breakfast, dinner
Prices rooms 700F; breakfast from 50F; dinner 200F
Rooms 5 suites, all with bath; all have central heating, air-conditioning, phone, TV, minibar, radio, hairdrier
Facilities dining-room
Credit cards MC, V
Children welcome
Disabled access very difficult
Pets well-behaved dogs welcome
Closed restaurant only, mid-Nov to mid-Dec
Managers Christian and Ingrid Soehlke

Vaucluse

Converted mill, Les Beaumettes

Le Moulin Blanc

This ancient mill, opened as a hotel in 1981, makes an attractive
(though not cheap) base for an extended stay, equipped as it is
with extensive lawns and a glamorous pool. Bedrooms are large,
with restrained decoration and handsome antiques. Those on
the garden side are preferable to those at the back – an otherwise satisfied visitor complains of road noise. The main dining-
room is light and lofty, the sitting-room a rough-stone vault with
rugs on a polished floor. Pretty courtyard for summer dining.
Nearby Village des Bories (5 km), Gordes (10 km).

Les Beaumettes 84220 Gordes
Tel 90.72.34.50
Location in countryside 40 km
E of Avignon, on RN100; with
garden and ample car parking
Meals breakfast, lunch, dinner
Prices rooms 450F-920F;
menus 195F-320F; breakfast
60F
Rooms 18 double, all with
bath; connecting rooms
available; all rooms have TV,
phone, minibar, radio alarm;
some rooms have terraces

Facilities 2 dining-rooms,
sitting-room; swimming-pool,
tennis
Credit cards AE, DC, MC, V
Children welcome; special
meals available
Disabled no special facilities
Pets dogs accepted
Closed never
Proprietors Mireille Diez

Vaucluse

Les Géraniums

Well off the beaten track, at the edge of a small medieval village near Mont Ventoux, this is the sort of simple and peaceful *auberge* that is becoming increasingly hard to find. It is well cared for, with comfortable rustic-style bedrooms and smart bathrooms, and an attractive, lofty, beamed dining-room. There are two terraces for meals and drinks, and a sunbathing area with views over the unspoiled countryside. Cooking is uncomplicated, and concentrates on local produce. 'Bustling', 'friendly', 'excellent service', 'good value for money' comment recent satisfied customers.

Nearby Mont Ventoux, Vaison-la-Romaine, vineyards.

Le Barroux, 84330 Caromb
Tel 90.62.41.08
Fax 90.62.56.48
Location at edge of quiet old village, 12 km NE of Carpentras; with car parking
Meals breakfast, lunch, dinner
Prices rooms 200F-240F; breakfast 30F, dinner 80F-250F
Rooms 20 double, 8 with bath, 12 with shower; 2 family rooms, both with shower; all rooms have central heating, phone
Facilities dining-room, sitting-room, bar, TV room; terrace
Credit cards AE, DC, MC, V
Children welcome
Disabled easy access to restaurant only **Pets** accepted
Closed restaurant only, 5 Jan to 10 Feb
Proprietor M. Roux

Les Florets

Les Florets lies in the heart of the Gigondas wine region, at the feet of the Dentelles de Montmirail – spectacular jagged peaks which are a paradise for hikers and rock-climbers. The hotel is small, family-run and appropriately named: floral bedrooms ('décor appalling,' says one reporter), flowers on the tables, and (at the right time of year) a riot of blossom covering the nearby hills. The bedrooms in an annexe on the hill behind the hotel are recommended. The great asset of Les Florets is surely the idyllic terrace, shaded by plane trees and with a view of the vineyards and mountains. Food is reportedly excellent.

Nearby Vineyards; Vaison-la-Romaine (15 km) – Roman remains.

Route des Dentelles 84190 Gigondas
Tel 90.65.85.01
Fax 90.65.83.80
Location in countryside 1.5 km E of Gigondas, 18 km E of Orange; with ample car parking
Meals breakfast, lunch, dinner
Prices rooms 345F-410F; breakfast 40F, meals 155F-210F, children's menu 57F
Rooms 12 double, 9 with bath, 3 with shower (5 twin); 2 single; one family room with bath; all rooms have central heating, phone; 7 rooms have TV **Facilities** dining-room, bar **Credit cards** AE, DC, MC, V **Children** welcome
Disabled no special facilities
Pets accepted
Closed Jan, Feb; Wed
Proprietor Mme Bernard

Vaucluse

Hostellerie de Crillon le Brave

The old vicarage of the hilltop village of Crillon-le-Brave has made a luxurious hotel of quite exceptional appeal. The rambling 16thC stone-built house is solid and calm, but most of the credit for the resounding success of the hotel – open only since late 1989 – must go to the patron, Peter Chittick, a Canadian lawyer with exceptionally clear ideas about hotelkeeping. A considerable share goes also to the perched location, giving uninterrupted views of a landscape of olive groves and vineyards that to northern European eyes seems a close approximation to heaven.

The central trick that Mr Chittick and his collaborator Craig Miller have pulled off is to provide luxury without erasing character. Despite the designer fabrics, fitted carpets and smart bathrooms, the exposed beams, white walls and rustic furniture dominate both in the sitting-rooms and the spacious bedrooms.

You eat beneath stone vaults, or out on the pretty terrace. Chef Philippe Monti produces refined Provençale food that is in perfect harmony with this blissful setting. The wine-list concentrates on the Rhône and other nearby wine areas.

Nearby Mont Ventoux; Orange (35 km); Avignon; Gordes.

Place de l'Eglise, 84410
Crillon-le-Brave
Tel 90.65.61.61
Fax 90.65.62.86
Location in hilltop village
35km NE of Avignon, on D138
off D974, with garden, private
car parking and garages
Meals breakfast, lunch,
dinner, snacks
Prices rooms 750F-1,250F,
suites 1,250F-1,450F; breakfast
75F, dinner about 300F
(including wine)
Rooms 17 double (6 twin),
one with shower, the rest with
bath; 4 suites; all rooms have
central heating, phone,
hairdrier, minibar
Facilities 3 sitting-rooms,
dining-room; swimming-pool
Credit cards AE, MC, V
Children welcome; babysitting
available **Disabled** access
difficult **Pets** accepted
Closed Jan, Feb, Mar;
restaurant only, Tue and Wed
lunch in Nov and early Dec
Proprietors Peter Chittick and
Craig Miller

Vaucluse

Table du Comtat

Séguret is a tiny medieval village, looking out over the rocky Dentelles de Montmirail. Built against the hillside, this hotel blends well into the surroundings. The much modernized interior is light, airy and spacious, with attractive fabrics and furniture, and masses of flowers in the restaurant, which has large windows giving wonderful views shared by the terrace and some bedrooms – all of which are very pleasant, with well equipped bathrooms. Franck Gomez prepares light and original dishes. A delightful place, though not cheap.

Nearby Gigondas (5 km) – vineyards; Orange (25 km).

Le Village, Séguret 84110 Vaison-la-Romaine
Tel 90.46.91.49
Fax 90.46.94.27
Location above tiny village on D23, 8 km SW of Vaison-la-Romaine; small garden, with car parking in front
Meals breakfast, lunch, dinner
Prices rooms 420F-600F; meals 225F-450F
Rooms 8 double, all with bath (3 twin); all rooms have central heating, phone
Facilities 2 dining-rooms, sitting-room; swimming-pool
Credit cards AE, DC, MC, V
Children accepted; special menu available
Disabled access difficult
Pets accepted in bedrooms only
Closed Tue night and Wed, except Jul, Aug, Easter and Christmas
Proprietor M. Franck Gomez

La Ferme de la Huppe

'Well worth a visit. Very comfortable room in a converted stable. Beautiful pool and a lovely courtyard garden. Very well run by a French/Swiss family. Food very good.' So runs the reader's report that earns a place here for this huddle of old farm buildings – rough stone and pale tiles without, rough stone, plain walls and beams within. Furnishings are stylishly rustic, with occasional antiques and tasteful fabrics. Competent cooking, geared to the markets.

Nearby Sénanque Abbey (4 km); Fontaine-de-Vaucluse (13 km); Avignon – cathedral, Papal palace (40km); Parc du Luberon.

Les Pourquiers 84220 Gordes
Tel 90.72.12.25
Fax 90.72.01.83
Location in countryside 2km SE of Gordes, off D2 on D156, 40km NE of Avignon; in gardens, with private car parking
Meals breakfast, lunch, dinner
Prices rooms 400F-500F; breakfast 25F, menus 145F-190F, children's menu 110F
Rooms 7 double (3 twin), 1 single, all with bath; all rooms have central heating, phone, TV, minibar, hairdrier
Facilities sitting-room, dining-room; swimming-pool
Credit cards MC, V
Children welcome
Disabled access to ground-floor rooms
Pets not accepted
Closed early Nov to late Mar
Proprietor Mme A Konings

Vaucluse

Country villa, Roussillon

Mas de Garrigon

This ochre-coloured building was purpose-built by the Rech-Druarts in the late 1970s, though you might not guess it: the traditional Provençal farmhouse style has been carefully reproduced, with a multiplicity of rough-tiled roofs facing this way and that, as if built at random over the years.

The hotel stands in a rather isolated rural position among pines and scrub, facing the Lubéron hills – not surprisingly, it is a Relais du Silence. In front of the house is a neat sheltered swimming-pool with country views, and all of the bedrooms (done out in restrained modern style, and thoroughly equipped) have a sunny private terrace sharing the views.

The place is run on house-party rather than conventional hotel lines. Guests are encouraged to browse in the well-stocked library or listen to classical music in the comfortable salon – before an open fire in winter. Philippe Anzallo's cooking is ambitious and competent, and Mme Rech-Druart is much involved in the menu-planning and daily food shopping. Lunch can be had by the swimming-pool.

Nearby Gordes (7 km) – château; Village des Bories (5 km).

Rte de St-Saturnin d'Apt, Roussillon 84220 Gordes
Tel 90.05.63.22
Fax 90.05.70.01
Location in countryside, on D2 3 km N of Roussillon, 7 km E of Gordes; in grounds with ample car parking
Meals breakfast, lunch, dinner
Prices rooms 700F-900F; breakfast 70F, meals 170F-325F
Rooms 7 double (2 twin), two family rooms, all with bath; all rooms have phone, TV, minibar

Facilities 3 dining-rooms, bar, library, sitting-room; swimming-pool
Credit cards AE, DC, V
Children older ones accepted if well behaved
Disabled ground-floor bedrooms
Pets accepted if well behaved
Closed restaurant only 15 Nov to 27 Dec; Sun dinner and Mon
Manager Mme Christiane Rech-Druart

Vaucluse

La Chaumière

The village of Lauris lies in the heart of Provence, overlooking the Durance valley. La Chaumière, in the upper part of the village, is a group of buildings clustered around a flowery terrace with broad views, where meals are served in summer. In 1989 the hotel was totally refurbished with some style, and the bedrooms are attractively decorated and very comfortable. Many are spacious and have fine views; some cater for families. This is a very well run establishment, well liked by its many British guests. Food is above average.

Nearby Lubéron Nature Park; Lourmarin Château (5 km).

Place du Portail 84360
Lauris-sur-Durance
Tel 90.08.20.25
Fax 90.08.35.24
Location in small village, 5 km NW of Cadenet; with ample car parking
Meals breakfast, lunch, dinner
Prices rooms 400F-750F; breakfast 55F; menus 175F-275F
Rooms 15 double, 9 with bath, 6 with shower; all rooms have

central heating, phone, TV
Facilities 2 dining-rooms, sitting-room, meeting-room
Credit cards AE, MC, V
Children accepted
Disabled access easy
Pets accepted in bedrooms only
Closed 15 Nov to 15 Dec
Manager Mme A Diamant

Auberge de Cassagne

Although this Provençal-style *auberge* in a leafy suburb of Avignon is at the top end of our size scale, there is still ample space for relaxing – a swimming-pool, a shady terrace for meals, manicured lawns and paved courtyards surrounded by bungalow-style bedrooms with traditional furniture and fabrics. There are more bedrooms in the main building, along with a cosy sitting-room and a beamed dining-room overlooking the garden. The young chef, trained by two of France's best, is making his own mark.

Nearby Avignon – Palais des Papes, Pont St-Bénèzet.

84130 Le Pontet
Tel 90.31.04.18
Fax 90.32.25.09
Location in rural suburb of Avignon, 4 km NW of middle, 3 km W of A7; with gardens and ample car parking
Meals breakfast, lunch, dinner
Prices rooms 490F-1,080F; menus 210F-440F, under-10's 110F
Rooms 22 double, 20 with bath, 2 with shower; 4 family rooms, all with bath; all rooms

have central heating, TV, phone, minibar, safe-box, air-conditioning
Facilities dining-room, 2 sitting-rooms, bar; swimming-pool
Credit cards AE, DC, MC, V
Children welcome
Disabled no special facilities
Pets accepted; 60F charge
Closed never
Proprietors Jean-Michel Gallon, Philippe Boucher and André Trestour

Alpes-de-Haute-Provence

Town inn, Château-Arnoux

La Bonne Etape

The setting of this 18thC coaching inn (on a busy road in an unremarkable town) is not auspicious, and the outside gives little hint of what lies within – one of the most satisfactory blends of refinement and hospitality to be found in France.

Where to start? Perhaps in the kitchen, where Pierre and Jany Gleize (father and son) make innovative and stylish use of largely home-grown ingredients, earning 2 stars from Michelin and 3 *toques* from Gault-Millau. Among their specialities is Sisteron lamb (raised on fragrant Provençal pastures). The light, warm dining-room is a supremely comfortable and relaxing place to savour their cooking, with well-spaced round tables.

But this is no restaurant-with-rooms. Bedrooms are more than comfortable – beautifully decorated and furnished with a tasteful mix of modern and antique pieces; some of the bathrooms, too, are delightfully individual. And even on the stairs and in the corridors there is attention to decorative detail. The swimming-pool is a superb sun-trap, with an attractive terrace surround.

To cap it all, the Gleize family are warmly welcoming hosts, happily committed to their work.

Nearby Les Mées (10 km) – rock formation; Sisteron – citadel; Ganagobie priory (20 km).

Chemin du Lac 04160 Château-Arnoux
Tel 92.64.00.09
Fax 92.64.37.36
Location in country town, on main RN 85 14 km SE of Sisteron (motorway 3 km); with car parking, garage and garden
Meals breakfast, lunch, dinner
Prices rooms 400F-900F, suites 800F-1,200F; breakfast 85F; menus 190F-490F
Rooms 11 double, 7 suites, all with bath; all rooms have air-conditioning, phone, TV, radio, minibar
Facilities 2 dining-rooms, sitting-room, bar, conference room, all with air-conditioning; heated swimming-pool
Credit cards AE, DC, MC, V
Children accepted
Disabled no special facilities
Pets accepted
Closed Tue; 3 Jan to 15 Feb
Proprietors Gleize family

Alpes-de-Haute-Provence

Auberge de Reillanne

This country *auberge* excites much enthusiasm in visitors, and it is not difficult to see why. Converted from a magnificent old *bastide*, it is no ordinary hotel; here you really do feel like a guest in a private mansion. The *auberge* is no newcomer to the public eye: it has featured extensively in guidebooks and the national press, inspiring journalists with its sober good taste.

Despite the grandeur of the building, it is not a place of four-star sophistication. There are seven very large bedrooms with stone walls and beamed ceilings, and rows of books take the place of the usual mod cons – there are no radios or TVs. In the dining-room, paintings, sculpture and flower bouquets seem in perfect harmony with the setting.

Maurice Bellaiche, who took over the hotel four years ago, is now firmly established and the hotel appears to be going from strength to strength. He is also in charge in the kitchen and his simple honest dishes are gaining a good local reputation. One reporter describes him as a 'brilliantly inventive self-taught cook'. Recent Belgian visitors were 'wildly enthusiastic' about the Auberge, describing the atmosphere and service as 'perfection'.

Nearby Lubéron Park – marked trails; St-Michel observatory (10 km); Aix-en-Provence (70 km); Avignon (80 km).

04110 Reillanne
Tel 92.76.45.95
Location in countryside, 1 km from village, 19 km SW of Forcalquier; in garden, with car parking
Meals breakfast, lunch, dinner
Prices rooms 325F; breakfast 40F; meals 115F-200F
Rooms 5 double, all with bath (2 twin); 2 family rooms, both with bath; all rooms have central heating, phone, minibar
Facilities sitting-room, 2 dining-rooms
Credit cards AE, MC, V
Children welcome
Disabled no special facilities
Pets welcome if well behaved
Closed never
Proprietor Maurice Bellaiche

Alpes-Maritimes

Château Eza

This former home of Prince William of Sweden, formed from houses at the top of the dramatically perched medieval village of Èze, was opened in 1985 as a luxury hotel. The bedrooms and suites are magnificent, with priceless antiques, exquisite Oriental carpets, open fireplaces, marble bathrooms and terraces with spectacular views. Most have private entrances on to the narrow winding streets of the village. The renowned restaurant – one of several Michelin-starred places in Èze – has equally stunning views, notably from the glass-sheltered terrace.

Nearby Èze village, Nice (12 km).

Rue de la Pise, 06360 Èze-Village, Côte d'Azur
Tel 93.41.12.24
Fax 93.41.16.64
Location on edge of cliff overlooking Riviera, in medieval village; with car parking
Meals breakfast, lunch, dinner
Prices rooms 1,200F-3,500F; breakfast 80F, lunch 150F-230F, dinner from 430F
Rooms 5 double, 3 suites, all with bath; all rooms have central heating, air-conditioning, phone, TV, hairdrier, minibar, radio
Facilities dining-room, tea salon, bar, terraces
Credit cards AE, DC, MC, V
Children welcome; baby-sitting available
Disabled access difficult
Pets small dogs accepted
Closed Nov to Apr
Proprietor André Rochat

Les Muscadins

Mougins, an old hill-village, is something of a gastronomic Mecca, with no less than four Michelin-starred restaurants since Les Muscadins was promoted. The hotel – a white-washed building surrounded by tropical vegetation – has been thoroughly revamped with great style; the American owner M. Bianchini has filled it with memorable antiques, many from the lavish homes of 18thC fops called *Muscadins*. The luxurious bedrooms are highly individual and beautifully coordinated and have impeccable bathrooms; most also have views of the coast. Elegantly furnished terrace.

Nearby Cannes; Grasse; Vallauris (10 km) – Picasso museum.

18 bd Courteline 06250 Mougins
Tel 93.90.00.43
Fax 92.92.88.23
Location on E road into old village, 2 km N of A8 motorway, 6 km N of Cannes; with car parking
Meals breakfast, lunch, dinner
Prices rooms 750F-950F, suite 1,250F; breakfast 60F, menus 135F-165F
Rooms 7 double, one suite; all rooms have central heating, air-conditioning, phone, TV, minibar
Facilities sitting-room, dining-room, bar **Credit cards** AE, DC, MC, V **Children** welcome **Disabled** access difficult **Pets** welcome
Closed Feb to mid-Mar
Proprietor Edward Bianchini

Alpes-Maritimes

Medieval inn, Haut-de-Cagnes

Le Cagnard

Perched along the ramparts of this old hill village (and awkward to reach in a large car), Le Cagnard has been smartly converted from a series of medieval houses. Thanks to expert restoration and period furnishings the atmosphere is distinctly medieval. Food here is some of the best in the area, and the restaurant has regained its Michelin star; meals are eaten by candle-light in the vaulted dining-room or on the terrace (with its wonderful views). A recent reporter complains of slow service.

Nearby Château Grimaldi – modern art museum, with Renaissance courtyard; Nice (15 km); Grasse (30 km) – perfumes.

Rue Pontis-Long,
Haut-de-Cagnes 06800
Cagnes-sur-Mer
Tel 93.20.73.21
Fax 93.22.06.39
Location in middle of hill village, 2 km above main town of Cagnes; car parking at entrance to village
Meals breakfast, lunch, dinner
Prices rooms 380F-1,500F; meals 300F-520F
Rooms 18 double, 10 apartments, all with bath; all rooms have central heating, air-conditioning, TV, phone, minibar
Facilities dining-room, bar
Credit cards AE, DC, MC, V
Children accepted
Disabled no special facilities
Pets accepted
Closed restaurant only, Thu lunch and 1 Nov to 20 Dec
Proprietor Barel Laroche family

Village hotel, St-Paul-de-Vence

Le Saint-Paul

Yet another captivating place to stay in captivating St-Paul – a pricey one regrettably (Relais & Châteaux), though not the most expensive. The bedrooms have been individually done out with real panache, and the public areas are equally welcoming. You may be hoping to eat out on the terrace, squeezed between the old buildings, but the vaulted dining-room makes a good atmospheric substitute. There is a comfortable country-house air about the sitting-room. Above-average cooking.

Nearby Maeght Foundation – modern art; Cagnes-sur-Mer (5 km) – château-museum; Nice; Grasse (25 km) – perfumes.

86 Rue Grande 06570
Saint-Paul-de-Vence
Tel 93.32.65.25
Fax 93.32.52.94
Location in centre of village, on D7, 3.5km S of Vence, 25km W of Nice; with small garden and valet parking in public car park
Meals breakfast, lunch, dinner
Prices rooms 700F-1,200F, suites 1,100F-1,700F; breakfast 85F, menus 170F-290F
Rooms 15 double (3 twin), 3 suites, all with bath; all rooms have satellite TV, air-conditioning, minibar, safe
Facilities dining-room, sitting-room, function room
Credit cards AE, DC, MC, V
Children welcome
Disabled one specially converted room
Pets accepted
Closed never
Manager Olivier Borloo

Alpes-Maritimes

Village inn, Peillon

Auberge de la Madone

You may think that you have taken a wrong turning as you first spy the village of Peillon, perched impossibly above, with little sign of any road leading up. But access is possible; and once there you will be thankful that you have taken the trouble to venture into this rugged landscape, just 20 km from Nice.

In Peillon, time stands still. This medieval village, as yet delightfully uncommercialized, consists of a few dark and dank cobbled alleys leading up to the church, and tall, grey stone houses with small windows looking out over rocky crests and distant forests. The *auberge* is set just outside the walled village itself, although it shares the views. Behind, paths lead off into the hills, past the grazing sheep with their tinkling bells; in front is the village car park and *boules* area.

The *auberge*, while retaining a certain simplicity, provides pleasant accommodation. The rather small bedrooms (with equally small balconies) were completely refurbished a few years ago, and are now attractive and comfortable with stylish, all-white bathrooms. Meals are served on the pretty, sunny terrace, under a large awning, or in the welcoming Provençal-style dining-room. Cooking is above average, and the menus are fair value – though one visitor wished for more variety in the *en pension* menu. An all-weather tennis court is another of the hotel's many attractions.

Nearby Monaco – Palace, museums, exotic gardens.

06440 Peillon-Village
Tel 93.79.91.17
Location on edge of perched village, 19 km NE of Nice; with ample car parking
Meals breakfast, lunch, dinner
Prices rooms 400F-750F; meals 130F-360F
Rooms 20 double, 15 with bath, 5 with shower; all rooms have central heating, TV, phone

Facilities bar, 2 dining-rooms; tennis court
Credit cards MC, V
Children very welcome
Disabled no special facilities
Pets accepted by arrangement
Closed 20 Oct to 20 Dec
Proprietors Millo family

Alpes-Maritimes

Country hotel, Roquefort-les-Pins

Auberge du Colombier

This is an old *mas*, low and white, whose chief attraction is its setting – amid large gardens with lawns and tall shady trees, and views over wooded hills towards the sea. There is also an especially attractive terrace for summer eating, a tennis court, and plenty of space around the swimming-pool for lounging. The bedrooms (some with balconies and views) are plainly furnished and on the small side, but reportedly comfortable. A useful base for seeing the sights of the Côte d'Azur – though you may be tempted to stay put instead; the Wolffs and their young staff are charming hosts.

Nearby St-Paul (10 km); Grasse – perfumeries.

06330 Roquefort-les-Pins **Tel** 93.77.10.27 **Fax** 93.77.07.03 **Location** in countryside off D2085, 15 km E of Grasse, 18 km N of Cannes; with large garden and car parking **Meals** breakfast, lunch, dinner **Prices** rooms 160F-650F, apartments 550F-950F; breakfast 50F; menus 145F-180F	**Rooms** 18 double (7 twin), 2 apartments, all with bath; all rooms have phone, TV **Facilities** 2 dining-rooms, sitting-room, bar, conference room; swimming-pool, tennis court, private night-club **Credit cards** AE, DC, MC, V **Children** accepted **Disabled** no special facilities **Pets** accepted **Closed** Jan **Proprietor** M. Wolff

Villa guest-house, St-Jean-Cap-Ferrat

Clair Logis

It is not easy to find a reasonable, cheap hotel in an area such as the exclusive and leafy Cap, near the pleasure port of St-Jean-Cap-Ferrat. It is even harder to find one like this, which has the charm of a turn-of-the-century private villa (it was turned into a hotel in 1950 by Pierre Melon's grandmother) and is set in lush, secluded gardens. Bedrooms are simple (those in the more recently built annexe are not particularly spacious) and four can accommodate families. Breakfast is taken in the cosy breakfast room/TV lounge in the main building – there is no restaurant, but that is no hardship in this area.

Nearby beaches, marinas; Villa-Museum Ile de France; Peillon (20 km) – one of many hilltop villages in this area; Monte Carlo.

12 Ave Centrale 06230 St-Jean-Cap-Ferrat **Tel** 93.76.04.57 **Fax** 93.76.11.85 **Location** in middle of Cap Ferrat promontory, 5 km from Nice; in large garden with ample car parking **Meals** breakfast **Prices** rooms 280F-680F, extra bed 120F; breakfast 40F	**Rooms** 18 double (8 twin), all with bath, 8 also with shower; all rooms have central heating, phone; 12 have TV **Facilities** sitting-room **Credit cards** AE, DC, MC, V **Children** welcome **Disabled** access to annexe possible **Pets** welcome **Closed** 15 Nov to 15 Dec **Proprietor** Pierre Melon

Alpes-Maritimes

La Gardiole

The views and beaches of the 'exclusive' Cap d'Antibes are open to all, and there are modest hotels – of which the unassuming pink-washed Gardiole, right in the middle of the promontory, is the pick. It is furnished simply but effectively – dark-wood chairs and rugs on polished tiled floors, white walls hung with ornaments and paintings – and family-run in friendly fashion. The dining-room is light and airy but the terrace, surrounded by flowers and shaded by wisteria, is where everyone wants to sit. The sound regional cooking is 'not cheap but very good'.

Nearby Beach, pine forest, Thuret gardens; Antibes (5 km).

Chemin de la Garoupe 06600 Cap d'Antibes
Tel 93.61.35.03
Location in woody residential area 500 m from beach, in middle of Cap; with large terrace
Meals breakfast, lunch, dinner
Prices rooms 360F-650F menus 100F-175F
Rooms 14 double (7 twin), 4 single, 3 family rooms; all with bath or shower; all rooms have central heating, phone, safe, air-conditioning; TV on request
Facilities dining-room, sitting-room, TV room
Credit cards AE, DC, V
Children welcome
Disabled no special facilities
Pets accepted
Closed Nov to Feb
Proprietor Mme Anne-Marie Arama

Galerie des Arcades

This is a simple village café in a 15thC building offering good value for money. The bedrooms (some with four-poster beds) are refreshingly uncontrived. Pungent Provençal dishes are eaten under the arcades of the village square, or in the two dining-rooms crammed with modern paintings (M. Brothier has a fine collection of modern works of art, including Vasarely, which he is only too pleased to show his guests). Our most recent reports are conflicting: one was delighted, and warns visitors to book well in advance, the other was extremely disappointed and found the 'the service and ambience non-existent'. More reports please.

Nearby Potters, glass-blowers and Legér Museum; Nice (15 km).

16 Place des Arcades 06410 Biot
Tel 93.65.01.04
Location in centre of village, 18 km NE of Cannes, near N7
Meals breakfast, lunch, dinner
Prices rooms 250F-450F (30%-50% reduction for children under 10); breakfast 30F, menus 160F-200F
Rooms 12 double, 7 with bath, 5 with shower (4 twin), 4 can take extra beds; all rooms have central heating, phone
Facilities 2 dining-rooms
Credit cards AE
Children accepted
Disabled no special facilities
Pets accepted
Closed restaurant only, mid-Nov to mid-Dec, Sun dinner and Mon
Proprietor Andre Brothier

Alpes-Maritimes

Village hotel, St-Paul-de-Vence

La Colombe d'Or

A famous, chic small hotel, distinguished by a considerable collection of modern art, but also a delightful place to stay. All is simple and in exquisite 'country' taste – white walls and bed-spreads, vases of bright flowers, quarry-tiled floors, huge old stone fireplaces. Outside there is a creeper-surrounded terrace (with huge white umbrellas). The dining-room has a wonderful carved fireplace, a lovely painted ceiling, and walls hung with the works of Matisse, Picasso, Utrillo and so on. The food wins no awards, but that hardly matters.

Nearby Maeght Foundation – modern art; Cagnes-sur-Mer (5 km) – château-museum; Nice; Grasse (25 km) – perfumes.

Place de Gaulle 06570
St-Paul-de-Vence
Tel 93.32.80.02
Fax 93.32.77.78
Location in village, 20 km NW of Nice; with gardens and ample car parking
Meals breakfast, lunch, dinner
Prices rooms 1,100F-1,300F; breakfast 60F, meals 300F-400F
Rooms 15 double (12 twin), 10 family rooms; all with bath;
all rooms have air-conditioning, central heating, phone, TV, radio
Facilities sitting-room, dining-room; sauna, swimming-pool, gardens
Credit cards AE, DC, MC, V
Children welcome
Disabled access difficult
Pets accepted
Closed mid-Nov to mid-Dec
Proprietors Roux family

Country villa, St-Paul-de-Vence

Les Orangers

The formula of Les Orangers is simple – a traditional Provençal house in a fine hillside setting, furnished with simple good taste and immaculately kept. In the sitting-room there are exposed beams, solid antiques, fresh flowers, an open fire, colourful rugs on polished floors. The charming bedrooms are much the same, and most have balconies or terraces sharing the lovely view of St-Paul-de-Vence and the hills of the Alpilles. In the gardens there are olive and orange trees. The hotel is much favoured by American visitors, and the English owner lends a relaxed air to the proceedings.

Nearby Maeght Foundation – modern art; Cagnes-sur-Mer (5 km) – château-museum; Nice; Grasse (25 km) – perfumes.

Chemin des Fumerates 06570
St-Paul-de-Vence
Tel 93.32.80.95
Fax 93.32.00.32
Location on edge of town, 20 km W of Nice; with garden and car parking
Meals breakfast
Prices rooms 390F-690F; breakfast 40F
Rooms 8 double (5 twin), one
single, all with bath; all rooms have central heating, phone, minibar
Facilities sitting-room
Credit cards MC, V
Children accepted
Disabled no special facilities
Pets accepted
Closed never
Proprietor M. Franklin

Alpes-Maritimes

Country villa, St-Paul-de-Vence

Le Hameau

St-Paul-de-Vence is among the best-preserved hill villages in France. Its ramparts, rising above green terraces of vineyards and bougainvillea, provide panoramic views of the hills and valleys of the Alpes-Maritimes; and its old streets, lined by galleries, workshops and chic boutiques, attract numerous day-trippers in high season.

Of the few hotels in and around the village, Le Hameau is certainly one of the most desirable – an unusually stylish and notably relaxed place run by a friendly and eager-to-please young couple. It consists of a cluster of red-roofed Provençal villas, surrounded by orange, lemon and other fruit trees. Bedrooms are rustic in style, with beams, dark-wood furniture and rugs on red-tiled floors; they vary in size and price considerably – many have their own terrace or balcony. There is a cool, neat breakfast room, but you will be hoping to have no need of it – one of Le Hameau's great delights is breakfast (with home-made jam) taken in the large terraced garden.

Our two most recent reporters were delighted with the hotel and both stayed longer than they had planned.

Nearby Maeght Foundation – contemporary arts; Cagnes-sur-Mer (5 km) – château-museum (Renaissance courtyard); Nice (15 km); Grasse (25 km) – perfumes.

528 Rte de la Colle 06570
St-Paul-de-Vence
Tel 93.32.80.24
Fax 93.32.55.75
Location one km outside village, 20 km from Nice; with gardens and ample car parking
Meals breakfast
Prices rooms 350F-520F, apartments 650F; breakfast 45F
Rooms 13 double (5 twin), one single, one suite; all with bath or shower; one children's room ; all rooms have central heating, phone, minibar; 4 have air-conditioning
Facilities sitting-room, dining-room
Credit cards AE, MC, V
Children accepted if well behaved **Disabled** no special facilities **Pets** accepted if well behaved **Closed** 15 Nov to 24 Dec, mid-Jan to mid-Feb
Manager Xavier Huvelin

Bouches-du-Rhône

L'Abbaye de Ste-Croix

For over seven hundred years, Cistercian monks were the only ones to enjoy the panoramic views of the Provençal countryside from this beautiful 12thC abbey. In 1969 the Bossard family rescued it from ruin and turned it into a luxury hotel. A maze of stone passageways leads through low arches to a beamed dining-room (with fabulous views), a cosy vaulted sitting-room, and bedrooms named after saints. Some of these are cavernous, but others, originally monks' cells, are very small and dark – and cold, according to one visitor. Michelin-starred food.

Nearby château, museum; Aix-en-Provence (30km); Arles (40km).

Route de Val de Cuech, 13300 Salon-de-Provence **Tel** 90.56.24.55 **Fax** 90.56.31.12
Location in sweeping countryside, 3 km NE of Salon on D16; with garden and ample car parking
Meals breakfast, lunch, dinner
Prices rooms 595F-1,110F; breakfast 98F, meals 180F-455F
Rooms 19 double, 17 with bath, 2 with shower; 5 apartments, all with bath; all rooms have central heating, phone, minibar; some rooms have TV
Facilities dining-room, bar, TV room; swimming-pool (unheated), table-tennis
Credit cards AE, DC, MC, V
Children accepted
Disabled no special facilities
Pets not accepted in restaurant
Closed 31 Oct to 1 Mar; restaurant only, Mon lunch
Proprietor Bossard family

Mas de la Brune

Since 1987 the Mas de la Brune has been Stefan Gagg's consuming passion; he considers his guests lucky to stay there, and only accepts those who have made reservations. It is a superb Renaissance period mansion, formerly the consul's residence and now a listed historical monument. In summer, meals are served on the terrace, overlooking the park. The dining-room and salon are both stone-vaulted; one has a grand open fireplace, the other houses a traditional olive press. All bedrooms and public rooms have been carefully furnished, with antiques, colourful fabrics, modern conveniences, fresh flowers. Cuisine is highly regarded.

Nearby Cavaillon (13 km); Avignon (25 km).

13810 Eygalières-en-Provence **Tel** 90.95.90.77 **Fax** 90.95.99.21
Location near village, 8 km E of St Rémy on D99; in grounds, with guarded car park **Meals** breakfast, lunch, dinner
Prices DB&B 845F-1,025F
Rooms 10 double, all with bath (5 twin); all rooms have central heating, phone, air-conditioning, hairdrier, TV, minibar, safe
Facilities dining-room, sitting-room, terrace; swimming-pool
Credit cards MC, V
Children accepted over 12 years
Disabled no special facilities
Pets accepted in bedrooms
Closed Jan to Mar and Nov/Dec
Proprietor Stefan Gagg

Bouches-du-Rhône

Converted mill, Fontvieille

La Régalido

At the heart of Provence, the little town of Fontvieille is excellently situated for sightseeing, lying between the ancient cities of Avignon and Arles and close to many more fine sights. Down the road is the windmill about which the 19thC novelist Alphonse Daudet wrote in his *Lettre de Mon Moulin*.

At the edge of town, the Régalido is a former oil mill, built in the early 19th century, which has been converted into a fine *auberge*. It is extremely attractive, in a thoroughly Provençal style, decorated with great flair by Madame Michel. There is a charming sitting-room full of flowers, and a log fire lit on chilly days. Tables are beautifully set in the spacious dining-room, and there is an atmosphere of well-being which suits the excellent cooking of Jean-Pierre Michel. His style is classic, but he has a penchant for Provençal dishes (seafood, olive oil, herbs and garlic). Bedrooms are individually decorated, and 'very comfortable', according to a reporter. Friendly staff and a pretty, flowery garden, complete the pleasant picture, marred only by the steep prices.

Nearby Montmajour Abbey; Arles; the Camargue (10 km) – flamingoes, white horses; Tarascon (15 km) – château.

Rue Frederic-Mistral 13990 Fontvieille
Tel 90.54.60.22
Fax 90.54.64.29
Location in middle of village, 9 km NE of Arles; with gardens and ample car parking
Meals breakfast, lunch, dinner
Prices rooms 600F-1,350F; breakfast 80F; menus 290F-390F
Rooms 14 double, 12 with bath, 2 with shower; all rooms have central heating, phone, minibar, air-conditioning
Facilities dining-room, 2 sitting-rooms, bar
Credit cards AE, DC, MC, V
Children accepted
Disabled one specially equipped ground-floor bedroom
Pets accepted (at a charge)
Closed Jan; restaurant only, Tue lunch, and Mon lunch (and dinner in low season)
Proprietor Jean-Pierre Michel

Bouches-du-Rhône

Auberge de la Benvengudo

The creeper-clad Benvengudo is a welcoming *auberge* with its own large garden and swimming-pool, much more affordable than most places in or near Les Baux. Rooms are furnished in the manner of a private country house: a cosy sitting-room with beams, fireplace and robust antiques, intimate dining-room and bedrooms with carefully chosen antiques and pretty patterned curtains. Weather permitting, breakfast and dinner are served on the terrace. Recent visitors found their suite not comfortably furnished – but we have news of recent refurbishment.

Nearby Montmajour abbey (15 km); Arles and the Camargue (15 km); Tarascon (20 km) – château; Avignon (40 km).

Vallon de l'Arcoule 13520 Les Baux-de-Provence
Tel 90.54.32.54
Location in valley below village, towards Arles; in gardens, with garages
Meals breakfast, dinner
Prices rooms 495F-650F, suites 750F-920F
Rooms 17 double (10 twin); 3 suites; all rooms have central heating, phone, TV

Facilities dining-room, sitting-rooms; swimming-pool, tennis
Credit cards MC, V
Children accepted
Disabled some ground-floor rooms
Pets accepted in bedrooms; 50F charge
Closed 1 Nov to 15 Feb, restaurant Sun
Managers M. and Mme Rossi

Mas de la Chapelle

The surroundings are uninspiring, but this 16thC house between Arles and Tarascon is happily secluded in a lush little park. The chapel from which it takes its name is the centrepiece. Built by the Knights of Malta, it now forms the impressive dining-room; Aubusson tapestries hang on the pale stone walls above immaculately set tables. The sitting-room is less grand but similarly medieval in atmosphere, with its heavily beamed ceiling, as are some of the bedrooms. Others have less character, but compensate with huge dimensions.

Nearby Camargue; Nîmes (30 km); Avignon (40 km).

Petite Route de Tarascon, 13200 Arles
Tel 90.93.23.15
Fax 90.96.53.74
Location in countryside W of N570, 4 km N of town, in secluded grounds with large car park
Meals breakfast, lunch, dinner
Prices rooms 470F-670F; breakfast 50F, menus 145F-280F, children 50F
Rooms 15 double, all with

bath; all rooms have central heating, phone, TV, minibar
Facilities dining-room, sitting-room; 3 tennis-courts, 2 swimming-pools, table-tennis; golf and horse-riding available
Credit cards MC, V
Children accepted
Disabled no special facilities
Pets accepted
Closed Feb
Proprietors M and Mme Remillieux

Bouches-du-Rhône

Ranch hotel, Les Stes-Maries-de-la-Mer

Mas de la Fouque

Located near the main resort of the Camargue, the Mas de la Fouque is a ranch-like hotel with a herd of the famous white horses for hire. Rooms throughout are smartly decorated – white walls, tiled floors, timbered ceilings – but the bedrooms are the epitome of comfort, with private terraces built over the lagoon. Despite the four-star luxuries (and prices), this is very much a family-run hotel with a friendly, relaxed atmosphere. 'Delicious food; nothing but good memories,' says a visitor.

Nearby The Camargue; Aigues-Mortes (25 km); Arles (38 km).

Rte du Petit Rhône 13460 Les Stes-Maries-de-la-Mer
Tel 90.97.81.02
Fax 90.97.96.84
Location in the Camargue, 4 km NW of Les Stes-Maries-de-la-Mer; with ample car parking
Meals breakfast, lunch, dinner
Prices rooms 1,340F-1,910F; lunch 170F-220F, dinner 220F-380F
Rooms 12 double, all with bath (6 twin); 3 family rooms, 2 with bath; all rooms have TV, phone, minibar
Facilities 2 sitting-rooms, bar, dining-room; tennis, swimming-pool, putting
Credit cards AE, DC, MC, V
Children welcome if well supervised
Disabled access easy; all on ground floor
Pets dogs accepted
Closed Jan to mid-Mar
Proprietor Jean-Paul Cochat

Bouches-du-Rhône

L'Oustaloun

The village of Maussane-les-Alpilles is close to the famous tourist sight of Les Baux, and makes a much cheaper base to stay. L'Oustaloun is to be found on the church square – a village *hostellerie* with masses of old-world charm and character. Stone walls, exposed beams and quarry tiles are all features of the downstairs rooms. The restaurant is housed in three 16thC rooms with stone-vaulted ceilings; tables are embellished with flowers and candelabra. The food is honest, regional fare: lamb *en croûte* and fillet of sea bass are typical dishes. Bedrooms are simple in style but furnished with handsome antiques.

Nearby Montmajour Abbey (15 km); Arles (15 km) and the Camargue; Tarascon (20 km) – château; Avignon (40 km).

Place de l'Église 13520
Maussane-les-Alpilles
Tel 90.54.32.19
Fax 90.54.45.57
Location in middle of village, 2 km S of Les Baux; with street car parking and garage
Meals breakfast, lunch, dinner
Prices rooms 250F-380F; breakfast 32F; menus 120F-165F

Rooms 9 double, 3 with bath, 6 with shower (4 twin); all rooms have phone, TV
Facilities 3 dining-rooms, sitting-room with TV
Credit cards AE, MC, V
Children accepted; smaller portions available **Disabled** no special facilities **Pets** accepted
Closed Jan and Feb
Proprietor Eric Fabregoul

Château des Alpilles

This is an elegant, upright early 19thC manor house just outside St-Rémy, set in large grounds with venerable trees, offering an atmosphere of gracious living combined with the facilities of a modern luxury hotel. The bedrooms are spacious and furnished with antiques, the bathrooms marble and modern, the salon and bar richly decorated. Full meals are not served, but snacks are available all day, and in summer there is a poolside grill.

Nearby Tarascon (15 km); Avignon (25 km); Arles (25 km).

Route Départmentale 31
13210 St-Rémy-de-Provence
Tel 90.92.03.33
Fax 90.92.45.17
Location in countryside 2 km W of village, on D31; in large grounds, with ample private car parking
Meals breakfast; light snacks available by arrangement
Prices rooms 760F-980F, suite 1,150-1,460F; breakfast 65F; meals 150F-250F
Rooms 16 double (8 twin), 4 suites; all with bath; all rooms

have central heating, satellite TV, phone, radio, minibar; air-conditioning in suites
Facilities sitting-room, bar, dining-room, conference room; swimming-pool, tennis, sauna
Credit cards AE, DC, MC, V
Children very welcome if well behaved
Disabled lift/elevator
Pets accepted on lead at extra charge **Closed** Jan to Mar
Proprietors Françoise and Catherine Bon

Bouches-du-Rhône

Manor house hotel, Noves

Auberge de Noves

The name is a joke: this is no *auberge*, but a luxurious and pricey hotel (four red gables in Michelin) in a splendid house, isolated in the Provençal countryside. Of course, there are elegant antiques everywhere, and the bedrooms are splendid. Of course, the cooking is exquisite, and breakfast extraordinary. Of course, the service is polished to perfection. What comes as a bonus is the charming attention of the suave M. Lalleman, who displays a genuine interest in his guests despite the amounts they are paying him. 'Worth every penny', says a recent report.

Nearby Avignon – Palais des Papes, cathedral; Nîmes (40 km).

13550 Noves
Tel 90.94.19.21
Fax 90.94.47.76
Location in countryside off D28, 2 km NW of Noves, 11 km SE of Avignon; in grounds, with car parking
Meals breakfast, lunch, dinner
Prices rooms 1,100F-1,400F, suites 1,700F; breakfast 100F; menus 250F-475F
Rooms 19 double, 4 apartments, all with bath; all rooms have central heating, TV, phone, air-conditioning
Facilities dining-room, sitting-room/bar, conference room; swimming-pool, tennis, helipad
Credit cards AE, DC, V
Children welcome
Disabled 10 bedrooms accessible
Pets accepted
Closed 2 Jan to 3 Feb; restaurant only, Wed lunch
Proprietors Lalleman family

Bouches-du-Rhône

Hôtel des Arts

For both locals and tourists, the shady pavement tables of this unpretentious place have long been a happy spot to sit and watch the Provençal world go by. Inside, the restaurant serves, at a reasonable price, well cooked, simple food (liberally laced with the region's herbs). Tables are crammed together, and loud greetings fill the air at lunch and dinner; paintings cover the walls at random, floors are stone-flagged, chairs and tables simple wood – but there are vases of fresh flowers and crisp linen, too. Bedrooms seem secondary, but they are neatly done out in the local rustic style, and prices are modest.

Nearby Ruines de Glanum and Les Antiques – Roman remains.

30 Blvd Victor-Hugo 13210
St-Rémy-de-Provence
Tel 90.92.08.50
Fax 90.92.55.09
Location on main street in middle of town, 18 km S of Avignon; with small car park
Meals breakfast, lunch, dinner
Prices rooms 160F-300F; menus 90F-160F
Rooms 12 double, all with bath (8 twin); 3 single, one with bath; 2 family rooms; all rooms have central heating, phone **Facilities** dining-room, TV room, bar
Credit cards AE, V, MC
Children accepted
Disabled access to restaurant and one bedroom
Pets accepted
Closed Feb; restaurant Wed
Proprietor Mme Nicole Caritoux

Mas des Carassins

Of all the Provençal hotels that call themselves *mas*, this is one of the few authentic examples: a farmhouse built in 1854, which is both mellow and peaceful, set in large and rambling gardens where you can be sure of finding a secluded spot to sit. Almost all the bedrooms have views of the rocky Alpilles and there is a cosy sitting-room with books and plenty of local information. There is no restaurant, but in the evening you can order simple dishes – ham, *charcuterie*, eggs, cheese, yoghurts – and drinks. M. Ripert and his wife are attentive, friendly hosts.

Nearby Tarascon (15 km); Avignon (30 km); Arles (30 km).

1 Chemin Gaulois 13210
St-Rémy-de-Provence
Tel 90.92.15.48
Location 800m SW of middle of town; with gardens and ample car parking
Meals breakfast, simple evening meal on request
Prices rooms 350F-550F, family rooms 600F-750F
Rooms 10 double, all with bath (7 twin); 5 family rooms, all with bath; all rooms have central heating, phone
Facilities 2 sitting-rooms
Credit cards MC, V
Children accepted if well behaved
Disabled no special facilities
Pets not accepted
Closed 15 Nov to 15 Mar
Proprietors M. and Mme Claude Ripert

Bouches-du-Rhône

Château bed and breakfast, St-Rémy-de-Provence

Château de Roussan

This beautiful château on the outskirts of St Rémy was built by a grandson of Nostradamus (Catherine de Medici's famous astrologer) at the beginning of the 18th century. An impressive avenue of trees leads to a gracious building with a mellow exterior and fine rooms carefully and beautifully furnished with antiques. The bedrooms vary in size but are all furnished in an appropriate style (though bathrooms are modern) and are enormously atmospheric. There is a formal library/salon in the oldest part of the house, and a vaulted breakfast room which also houses a television.

The McHugo family took over the château a couple of years ago, and aim to maintain the period style and family atmosphere that old hands will remember from the days of the Roussels (who still own the property). But they have upgraded the catering, installing both a new kitchen and a new chef to prepare food 'to equal the best in St-Rémy'. Meals and drinks can be had on the terrace. In the grounds there is plenty of room to sit in perfect solitude, overlooking a pool or fountain, or perhaps the 16thC farmhouse which belonged to Nostradamus himself. A recent visitor particularly enthuses over the friendliness and the 'superb, informal gardens'.

Nearby Tarascon (15 km) – château; Avignon (30 km); Arles (30 km) and the Camargue.

Rte de Tarascon 13210 St-Rémy-de-Provence
Tel 90.92.11.63
Location in countryside, 2 km W of town; in large park, with ample car parking
Meals breakfast, dinner
Prices rooms 360F-750F; menu 70F-140F
Rooms 20 double (7 twin), 16 with bath, 4 with shower; all rooms have phone, central heating
Facilities TV room, library
Credit cards AE, MC, V
Children welcome
Disabled 2 ground-floor bedrooms
Pets accepted
Closed restaurant only, Wed
Proprietors Judy and Brian McHugo

Bouches-du-Rhône

Mas d'Entremont

Just outside Aix stands this stylish old Provençal farmhouse – low red-roofed buildings clustered around a courtyard. Within are wooden beams and pillars, rustic furniture, tiled floors and open fireplaces. Bedrooms (most in separate bungalows in the grounds) are more modern in style, but clean, comfortable and quite stylish. The gardens are a delight – a swimming-pool shielded by cypresses, a covered dining-terrace looking over a pond, and plenty of secluded corners. Cuisine is classic and competent. 'An excellent hotel,' comments a recent visitor.
Nearby Aix-en-Provence; Abbaye de Silvacane (25 km).

Montée d'Avignon 13090 Aix-en-Provence
Tel 42.23.45.32
Fax 42.21.15.83
Location in countryside just off N7, 2 km NW of Aix; with large grounds and car parking
Meals breakfast, lunch, dinner
Prices rooms 600F-900F; breakfast 55F; menus 190F-220F; DB&B 550F-660F
Rooms 17 double (7 twin); all with bath; all rooms have air-conditioning, satellite TV, phone, minibar, safe, private terrace
Facilities dining-room, sitting-areas; swimming-pool, tennis **Credit cards** MC, V
Children accepted; some rooms have side-rooms
Disabled lift/elevator **Pets** accepted **Closed** hotel, Nov to mid-Mar; restaurant, Sun evening and Mon lunchtime
Proprietors Marignane family

Relais de la Magdeleine

Despite elegant furnishings, this 18thC *bastide* is one of those rare hotels which caters equally well for grown-ups who want pampering and children who want nothing more than plenty of open space and a lovely swimming-pool. It is a tricky balancing act, which the charming Marignanes carry off with great flair and warmth. Sound Provençal meals cooked by the son of the household are served in refined dining-rooms or on a peaceful gravelled terrace. Bedrooms are spacious, decorated with restraint and furnished with antiques; fresh flowers abound.
Nearby Cassis (15 km) – coastal inlets; La Ste-Baùme massif.

13420 Gémenos
Tel 42.82.20.16
Fax 42.32.02.26
Location on outskirts of town, 23 km E of Marseilles; with garden and ample car parking
Meals breakfast, lunch, dinner
Prices rooms 395F-750F; menu 240F
Rooms 24 double, 20 with bath, 4 with shower (12 twin); 4 family rooms, all with bath; all rooms have central heating, phone, TV
Facilities sitting-rooms, dining-rooms; swimming-pool
Credit cards MC, V
Children accepted
Disabled no special facilities
Pets accepted, except near swimming-pool
Closed mid-Jan to mid-Mar
Proprietors M. and Mme Marignane

Bouches-du-Rhône

Farmhouse hotel, Les Baux-de-Provence

Mas d'Aigret

In a fine setting with views over peaceful countryside, this old farmhouse – simpler than most hotels of Les Baux – attracts rave reviews from visitors. There is a fine, shady dining terrace and an extraordinary restaurant carved out of the rock; all is fresh and pretty, decorated in rustic Provençal style. Some of the bedrooms are quite small, but all open out on to a terrace or balcony. Englishman Pip Phillips and his wife Chantal have improved the *mas* in various ways – notably by employing a very talented chef.
Nearby Ruined fortress-village; Arles (15 km) and the Camargue.

13520 Les Baux-de-Provence
Tel 90.54.33.54
Fax 90.54.41.37
Location just below fortress, on D27A 500 m E of Les Baux; in large grounds with private car parking
Meals breakfast, lunch, dinner
Prices rooms 450F-850F; lunch 90F, dinner 180F-350F
Rooms 12 double (6 twin), 3 family rooms, all with bath; all rooms have central heating,

TV, phone, minibar
Facilities dining-room, sitting-room, bar; swimming-pool,
Credit cards AE, DC, MC, V
Children welcome
Disabled no special facilities
Pets welcome (40F), but not in restaurant
Closed Jan and Feb; restaurant only, Wed lunch
Proprietors Pip Phillips and family

Var

Village hotel, Grimaud

Coteau Fleuri

This attractive stone house, built into the hillside at the edge of the fashionable perched village of Grimaud, is about a hundred years old and retains a simple Provençal style. There is a rambling garden with olive trees, and a small flowery terrace in front of the hotel. The spotless bedrooms have pretty furnishings and prints, and smart tiled bathrooms; most are rather small, though this matters little because many have a splendid view of vineyards and the Maures massif (others look out over the garden and the ruins of Grimaud castle and chapel). The public rooms are attractive and relaxing: there is a small bar, a dining-room in two parts (both of which extend on to the terrace and benefit from the view), and a spacious sitting-room with tiled floor and grand piano. Throughout the hotel are masses of fresh flowers. In winter there are log fires.

Monsieur Minard, formerly of the Mas de Chastelas in St Tropez, took over the hotel in 1988 and has created a friendly, professional and smooth-running operation. Food is a highlight; *nouvelle* in style but not in quantity, theatrically presented by attentive staff – 'the most delicious meal of our holiday'. Three young visitors particularly recommend the *mousse au chocolat*.

Nearby St-Tropez (10 km); Pampelonne (15 km).

Place des Pénitents, Grimaud
83310 Cogolin
Tel 94.43.20.17
Fax 94.43.33.42
Location in middle of village behind chapel; with car parking in front
Meals breakfast, lunch, dinner
Prices rooms 300F-450F; breakfast 45F; menus from 190F
Rooms 13 double, 8 with bath, 5 with shower (4 twin); one family room with bath; all rooms have phone

Facilities dining-room, sitting-room, bar
Credit cards AE, DC, MC, V
Children welcome
Disabled no special facilities
Pets accepted if well behaved
Closed 1 to 20 Dec, 3 to 18 Jan; restaurant only, Tue (except Jul and Aug)
Proprietors Jacline and Jacques Minard

Var

Hôtel Belle-Vue

This hotel lives up to its name, looking out from its slightly elevated setting to St-Clair beach and across the bay towards the yachts at Le Lavandou. The Belle-Vue (a *Relais du Silence*) offers unpretentious but comfortable accommodation. Bedrooms are simply but attractively decorated and furnished, and have smart modern bathrooms. A few have private balconies where you can take a drink in the evening sun – but there is also a pleasant gravelled garden dotted with shaded tables. The dining-room is bright and spacious, with large picture windows and plenty of plants; fish is, of course, a speciality. This is a well-run and welcoming family hotel, with high standards throughout.

Nearby Le Lavandou – harbour, boat trips to Îles d'Hyères.

Blvd du Four des Maures, St-Clair 83980 Le Lavandou
Tel 94.71.01.06
Fax 94.71.64.72
Location a short distance from beach in small resort, 1.5 km from Le Lavandou, 35 km W of St Tropez
Meals breakfast, lunch, dinner
Prices rooms 350F-750F; meals 160F-210F

Rooms 19 double, 11 with bath, 8 with shower (6 twin); all rooms have central heating, phone
Facilities dining-room, bar
Credit cards AE, DC, MC, V
Children accepted
Disabled no special facilities
Pets not accepted
Closed Nov to Mar
Proprietors Clare family

Le Logis du Guetteur

The Logis du Guetteur was originally the Château of Villeneuve – an 11thC fort, built to ward off invasions from the Saracens. It still looks more or less as it must have done nine centuries ago, with rough stone walls, plain rooms, and a tower from where the *guetteur* (watchman) surveyed the plain, all with appropriate period furnishings. The bedrooms, overlooking the rooftops of Les Arcs, are quiet, with lovely views. But the main emphasis here is on food. The medieval cellar restaurant offers a choice of reasonably priced menus or, if you prefer, gastronomic specialities – among them *foie gras frais*, truffle soufflé and quail *flambé* in Armagnac.

Nearby Other villages – Lorgues (10 km); St-Tropez (45 km).

Place du Château 83460 Les Arcs **Tel** 94.73.30.82
Fax 94.73.39.95
Location 12 km S of Draguignan, not far from RN7; with car parking
Meals breakfast, lunch, dinner
Prices rooms 450F; breakfast 48F; meals 125F-260F
Rooms 10 double, 6 with bath, 4 with shower; one single with shower; all rooms have central heating
Facilities dining-room, sitting-room, terrace; swimming-pool
Credit cards AE, DC, MC, V
Children accepted
Disabled no special facilities
Pets accepted
Closed mid-Nov to mid-Dec
Proprietor Max Callegari

Var

Mas des Brugassières

This modern (1974) 'farmhouse' blends well into the surrounding countryside, in its garden among the vineyards. Bedrooms have tiled floors and traditional furniture; some open out directly on to the garden and swimming-pool (and are ventilated only by the door). There is one public room – a sitting-room-cum-bar with simple wooden furniture and vast French windows – but from Easter to October most sitting will be done outside. The hotel also has a tennis court, but in 1991 a visitor considered it 'badly in need of resurfacing' and we have no word of improvement.

Nearby Ste-Maxime – beach resort; Port-Grimaud (15 km).

Plan-de-la-Tour 83120 Ste-Maxime **Tel** 94.43.72.42 **Fax** 94.43.00.20 **Location** in countryside 8 km NW of Ste-Maxime; with gardens and ample car parking **Meals** breakfast **Prices** rooms 420F-550F; breakfast 38F **Rooms** 14 double, all with bath and shower (5 twin); all	rooms have central heating, phone **Facilities** sitting-room/bar; swimming-pool, tennis **Credit cards** MC, V **Children** accepted **Disabled** ground-floor bedrooms **Pets** dogs accepted at extra charge (60F) **Closed** Nov to mid-Mar **Proprietors** Steve and Annick Geffine

Var

Le Verger

'Our friends call this place "Little Normandy" because it is so green, unlike most of the Côte d'Azur,' says Anne Zachary, highlighting only one attractive aspect of Le Verger. Harmoniously decorated bedrooms open directly on to the lawn, and so the pool. Meals are served outside in summer – varied and satisfying dishes in the Mediterranean style, with no pretensions. The Zacharys have kept the scale and feel of the private house they converted in 1987, which comes heartily recommended by an experienced reporter.

Nearby Provence countryside; St-Tropez (12 km).

Route de Collobrières 83360 Grimaud
Tel 94.43.25.93
Fax 94.43.33.92
Location in countryside 1 km W of Grimaud, on D14 off D558, 12 km W of St-Tropez; in spacious gardens with private car parking
Meals breakfast, lunch, dinner
Prices rooms 500F-850F; breakfast 60F, meals 185F-375F
Rooms 6 double, all with bath; 2 single, one with bath, one with shower; all rooms have central heating, phone, TV
Facilities sitting-room, dining-room; swimming-pool
Credit cards MC, V
Children accepted, but no special facilities
Disabled not very suitable
Pets welcome **Closed** Nov to Easter; restaurant over Christmas and New Year
Proprietor Mme Zachary

Le Yaca

This smart little hotel has been cleverly converted from three 200-year-old buildings. There is a confusing mix of styles, but rustic-chic predominates. Bedrooms are furnished with antiques, simply decorated in a typical southern style, but with all the comforts including air-conditioning; some have private terraces and look over the sea – others over the garden, with its figs and palms, and splendid pool, around which tables are set. Josiane Aknine takes care to get to know her guests and to make sure they have everything they need. She no longer serves dinner, but this is no particular hardship in a place like St-Tropez.

Nearby Beaches – la Bouillabaisse (1 km), Tahiti (4 km).

1 Blvd d'Aumale 83990 St-Tropez
Tel 94.97.11.79
Fax 94.97.58.50
Location in middle of town; in pedestrian area, with car parking nearby
Meals breakfast
Prices rooms 1,100F-2,000F; breakfast 70F
Rooms 23 double, one suite, all with bath; all have central heating, air-conditioning, TV, phone, radio, minibar
Facilities dining-room, bar
Credit cards AE, DC, MC, V
Children accepted if well behaved
Disabled no special facilities
Pets accepted if well controlled
Closed 15 Oct to 27 Dec, 4 Jan to Easter
Manager Josiane Aknine

Var

Village mansion, Seillans

Hôtel des Deux Rocs

This captivating hotel in a famously captivating hill village seems to have largely recovered from its exposure on British TV a few years back.

The hotel's setting (it is an 18thC mansion, just outside the medieval walls) remains its chief drawback as well as one of its main attractions: parking close to the hotel is impossible. But for most visitors that counts for little compared to the pleasure of breakfast or an evening drink beside the fountain on the shady little cobbled square in front, looking across the green valley.

Inside there are two inviting little *salons*, one serving as a bar, and a long wood-and-stone dining-room. The food is traditional and excellent – though what is offered to guests on *pension* terms may be unexciting. Bedrooms vary in size and standard. Those at the back of the house are rather cramped, while some of those at the front are marvellously spacious and light, with vigorous colour schemes. Mme Hirsch is ever-present, overseeing the scrupulous housekeeping – first-class linen and towels – taking the orders at dinner with chiffon scarf trailing, advising on sightseeing excursions.

Nearby Cascade de Bresque (15 km); Tourtour (10 km); Thoronet Abbey (20 km); Gorges du Verdon (30 km).

Place Font d'Amont 83440 Seillans
Tel 94.76.87.32
Fax 94.76.88.88
Location at top of small village, 30 km W of Grasse; with terrace
Meals breakfast, lunch, dinner
Prices rooms 240F-500F; breakfast 40F, menus 135F-210F
Rooms 15 double (5 twin), all with bath or shower; all rooms have central heating, phone, minibar
Facilities dining-room, bar, sitting-room
Credit cards MC, V
Children accepted
Disabled no special facilities
Pets dogs accepted but not in dining-room
Closed Nov to mid-Mar
Proprietor Mme Hirsch

Var

Converted castle, Trigance

Château de Trigance

In the remote limestone hills that surround the dramatic Gorges du Verdon, there are few villages and even fewer hotels; if you are touring this region, it is a relief to know that you have a room booked at the Château de Trigance, for it is hard to imagine where else to stay. On arrival, you might be taken aback. Is this fortress perched high on a rocky hilltop really your hotel? (Yes.) And if it is, how are you going to penetrate its defences? (By climbing a steep flight of rocky stairs – don't worry, your luggage will be carried up for you.)

Once inside, you are in the Middle Ages. Stone by stone, M. Thomas has painstakingly rebuilt his 11thC castle (it was largely destroyed in the Revolution, and for many years served as a quarry for the local villagers); he will be delighted to show you before-and-after photographs to prove it. The impressive stone-vaulted, candle-lit dining-room, and the sitting-room below, are windowless and highly atmospheric, furnished in appropriate medieval style. Most of the bedrooms (cut into the hill) are similar, with canopied beds, antique furniture, tapestries and banners – and fine views from their windows. The cooking is surprisingly good, considering the remoteness of the place. A romantic and unusual hotel, renovated in 1989.

Nearby Verdon gorge – Europe's 'Grand Canyon'.

83840 Trigance
Tel 94.76.91.18
Fax 94.47.58.99
Location overlooking tiny village, 10 km NW of Comps-sur-Artuby; with terrace, and private car parking
Meals breakfast, lunch, dinner
Prices rooms 500F-700F, suites 830F; menus 190F-320F
Rooms 8 double, all with bath; 2 suites; all rooms have central heating, phone, TV
Facilities dining-room, sitting-room
Credit cards AE, DC, MC, V
Children welcome
Disabled access very difficult
Pets accepted
Closed Nov to mid-Mar
Proprietor Jean-Claude Thomas

Var

Le Manoir

This large whitewashed, green-shuttered 19thC manor house stands on a lush, secluded island a few km off the south coast. The whole island used to belong to Pierre Buffet's family; today it is a state-owned nature reserve (the island appeals more to botanists than sun-worshippers), and the charming Buffets run their home as a hotel – along house-party lines, with many regularly returning guests. White-walled bedrooms are furnished with 19thC pieces – simple but stylish and comfortable. Since the departure of chef Gérard Ré, we lack reports on the food, but are confident that it will remain of a high standard. Meals are served in the peaceful garden full of palm and eucalyptus trees.

Nearby Marked trails to various points, scuba diving.

Ile de Port-Cros 83400 Hyères
Tel 94.05.90.52
Fax 94.05.90.89
Location in lush gardens close to port (boats from Le Lavandou or Port d'Hyères)
Meals breakfast, lunch, dinner
Prices DB&B 890F-1,900F; FB 1,050F-2,200F
Rooms 23 double, 13 with bath, 10 with shower; 4 family rooms with bath; all rooms have central heating, phone
Facilities 2 dining-rooms, 2 sitting-rooms, bar
Credit cards MC, V
Children children accepted if well behaved
Disabled no special facilities
Pets not accepted
Closed mid-Oct to Apr
Proprietor Pierre Buffet

La Ponche

Tucked away in a tiny square overlooking the small fishing port and tiny beach of La Ponche, this cluster of 17thC houses is an oasis of quiet. It is very much a family enterprise; Margerite Barbier started her fishermen's bar in 1937. She was later joined by her daughter, Simone Duckstein, who steadily transformed it into a stylish, arty little hotel. The open-air restaurant on the square is comfortable and civilized; there is a small but sophisticated dining-room, too. The food is memorable and there is an inexpensive lunch menu. Bedrooms were thoroughly revamped in 1993.

Nearby Beaches – La Bouillabaisse (1 km); Tahiti (4 km).

3 Rue des Remparts 83990 St-Tropez
Tel 94.97.02.53
Fax 94.97.78.61
Location in heart of old town, overlooking Port des Pêcheurs; with car parking
Meals breakfast, lunch, dinner
Prices rooms 950F-1,350F, suites 1,350F-2,100F; breakfast 60F, lunch 115F, dinner from 200F **Rooms** 13 double with bath; 2 family rooms with bath; 3 suites; all have air-conditioning, central heating, phone, satellite TV, minibar
Facilities TV room, bar, 2 dining-rooms
Credit cards AE, MC, V
Children accepted
Disabled access difficult
Pets accepted
Closed end Oct to end Mar
Proprietor Mme Barbier

Var

Converted mill, Fayence

Moulin de la Camandoule

This lovingly restored olive-mill lies at the foot of the hill town of Fayence, in extensive private grounds divided in half by the low Roman aqueduct which used to bring water to the mill. The existing building dates from the 19th century, and was rescued from ruin thirty years ago. Shirley and Wolf Rilla (an English/German couple) moved here in 1986.

Food is a highlight, at least for most visitors. Meals are served outside in summer – on a terrace overlooking the cherry orchard – or in the delightfully rustic dining-room decorated with original mill trappings. Between the dining-room and the lofty, beamed sitting-room (with its adjoining 'snuggery') is the ancient water wheel, now preserved behind glass. Bedrooms, named after pieces of mill machinery, are individually decorated and generally spacious. Personal touches such as books, family paintings, ornaments and fresh flowers add to the welcoming (rather than luxurious) atmosphere.

It is clear from reports both new and old that Wolf Rilla is not a naturally welcoming host. But our latest reporters are happy to overlook his eccentricities, such are the attractions of the hotel. Half-board terms are said to offer poor value.

Nearby Grasse (30 km) – perfumes; Cannes (30 km).

Chemin Notre-Dame-des-Cyprès 83440 Fayence
Tel 94.76.00.84
Fax 94.76.10.40
Location at foot of village, 30 km NW of Cannes; in large grounds with ample car parking
Meals breakfast, lunch, dinner
Prices rooms 250F-675F, DB&B 450F-555F; breakfast 45F, menus 165F-285F
Rooms 9 double with bath (4 twin); 2 single with shower; all rooms have central heating, phone, TV
Facilities dining-room, sitting-room with bar; swimming-pool
Credit cards MC, V
Children welcome
Disabled no special facilities
Pets accepted (40F)
Closed never
Proprietors Wolf and Shirley Rilla

Var

La Bastide de Tourtour

This country house was built by M. Laurent in the late 1960s in traditional style, with lovely honey-coloured stone but without much inspiration. What the hotel lacks in architectural elegance it makes up for in comfort and attentive service (it is in the Relais & Château group), and the food is excellent, if not in the first rank. But for many visitors the key attraction is the secluded setting, high up amid pine forests with a sun-trap swimming-pool and wonderfully long views.

Nearby Salernes (10 km); Cascade de Bresque (15 km).

Rte de Draguignan, Tourtour 83690 Salernes
Tel 94.70.57.30
Fax 94.70.54.90
Location on outskirts of village, 22 km NW of Draguignan; with gardens and ample car parking
Meals breakfast, lunch, dinner
Prices rooms 370F-1,260F; lunch 170F, menus 310F-390F
Rooms 23 double, all with bath (12 twin); 2 single, both with bath; all rooms have

central heating, TV, phone, minibar
Facilities sitting-room, dining-room, bar, billiards, jacuzzi; tennis, swimming-pool, table tennis, pétanque
Credit cards AE, DC, V
Children accepted; prices on request
Disabled some facilities
Pets accepted
Closed 1 Nov-10 Mar
Proprietor M. Laurent

Auberge St-Pierre

Just outside the hill-top village of Tourtour in its own rolling acres, the Auberge St-Pierre is a peaceful, unpretentious retreat – a 16thC manor-house run as a welcoming hotel by the helpful Marcellins. The public rooms preserve something of a medieval feel, with stone floors and a fountain in the dining-room, and great bay windows providing views over the terrace, where meals are served. The spacious bedrooms are newly refurbished. Most of the food – expertly cooked in classic and local styles by M. Marcellin – comes from the home farm.

Nearby Salernes (10 km); Cascade de Bresque (15 km).

Tourtour 83690 Salernes
Tel 94.70.57.17
Location 3 km E of Tourtour; in large grounds with ample car parking
Meals breakfast, lunch, dinner
Prices rooms 400F-520F; breakfast 50F; menus 170F-220F
Rooms 18 double, 14 with bath, 4 with shower (5 twin); all rooms have central heating, phone

Facilities 2 dining-rooms, sitting-room, TV room, bar; swimming-pool, sauna, fishing, archery, tennis
Credit cards not accepted
Children accepted
Disabled no special facilities
Pets accepted; food not provided
Closed mid-Oct to Apr; restaurant only, Wed
Proprietors Marcellin family

Var

Lou Calen

One of the more authentic examples of a Provençal-style hotel – a fine town house on the village square, furnished in a home-like blend of antique and rustic styles, with plenty of flowers, plants, paintings and bric-a-brac. Bonuses are the swimming-pool in a luxuriant shady garden and the delightful dining terrace. Bedrooms vary considerably in size, style and price, but all feel welcoming. The cooking is simple but hearty, and the menu flexible. Standards can slip under high-season pressure.

Nearby Cascade de Bresque (5 km); Thoronet (20 km) – abbey; Tourtour (25 km) – village; Gorges du Verdon (25 km).

1 Cours Gambetta 83850 Cotignac
Tel 94.04.60.40
Fax 94.04.76.64
Location in middle of village, 20 km N of Brignoles; in garden, with public car parking nearby
Meals breakfast, lunch, dinner
Prices 280F-460F, suites 480F-580F; meals 140F-240F
Rooms 6 double, 5 with bath, one with shower; 10 family rooms, all with bath; all rooms have central heating, phone, TV
Facilities sitting-room, meeting-room; swimming-pool
Credit cards AE, DC, MC, V
Children accepted
Disabled no special facilities
Pets accepted
Closed Jan to late Mar; Wed except in Jul and Aug
Manager J. R. Mendes

Domaine de Châteauneuf

For golfing bon viveurs, this takes some beating – a polished little Relais & Châteaux hotel beside the recently opened but 'superbe' golf course of Sainte-Baume. The four-square 17thC house, white-painted and red-roofed, stands surrounded by pines and other tall trees. On one side, secluded by the trees, is the pool area; on the other, behind the house, a courtyard garden enclosed by villas containing two of the hotel's large suites. Inside, the style of the public areas is grandly traditional; the elegantly furnished sitting-room is distinguished by impressive murals and a 17thC piano. Bedrooms have a fresh, designer style.

Nearby Aix-en-Provence.

Au Logis de Nans, 83860 Nans-les-Pins
Tel 94.78.90.06
Fax 94.78.63.30
Location in countryside 3.5 km N of village, 40 km SE of Aix, in own grounds with ample car parking, helipad
Meals breakfast, lunch, dinner
Prices rooms 600F-2,250F; breakfast 70F, meals 230F-410F
Rooms 30 (5 suites), all with bath or shower; all rooms have minibar, satellite TV, phone, hairdrier
Facilities dining-room, sitting-room; swimming-pool, tennis, golf, boules
Credit cards AE, MC, DC, V
Children accepted
Disabled no special facilities
Pets dogs accepted (50F charge)
Closed 30 Nov to 28 Feb
Proprietor Jeanne Malet

Var/Hérault

Château de Ponderach

In 1963 Mme Counotte successfully transformed this solid country house – in the family since its construction over 200 years ago – into an intimate and relaxing hotel. It is completely secluded in extensive wooded grounds, and the spacious bedrooms have private terraces which look out over the forest. The family-home atmosphere is retained – the dining-room is full of family pieces and flowers, and Madame is a welcoming and gracious hostess. Good classic cuisine, including a *menu régional Occitan*. Some modest expansion of both the bedrooms and the public rooms is planned.

Nearby St-Pons – cathedral; Grotte de la Devèze (5 km).

Rte de Narbonne 34220
St-Pons-de-Thomières
Tel 67.97.02.57
Location in countryside 1 km
S of St-Pons and 50 km NW of
Narbonne; with large grounds,
ample car parking and garage
Meals breakfast, lunch, dinner
Prices rooms 400F-470F;
DB&B 660F-700F; breakfast
75F, menus 175F-375F,
children's 80F

Rooms 9 double (4 twin), all
with bath and shower; all
rooms have phone
Facilities sitting-room,
dining-room, bar
Credit cards AE, DC, MC, V
Children welcome
Disabled no special facilities
Pets accepted
Closed Oct to Apr
Proprietor Mme Pierre
Counotte

Château de Madières

The magnificent semi-ruined building, perched above the Vis river gorge, and the surrounding wild countryside proved irresistible to the Brucys when they first visited this 14thC fortress in 1982. Undaunted, they set about the task of restoring it to its former glory – creating comfortable rooms within the existing framework of medieval walls and arches. No two bedrooms are alike, though all are decorated in traditional style and have modern bathrooms. Key attractions are the dining-rooms – one galleried with a vast Renaissance fireplace, the other vaulted and jutting out of the main building, with spectacular valley views.

Nearby Cirque de Navacelles; Grotte des Demoiselles; Ganges.

Madières 34190 Ganges
Tel 67.73.84.03
Fax 67.73.55.71
Location on hillside
overlooking village, on
crossroads of D48 and D25;
with shady park and ample car
parking
Meals breakfast, lunch, dinner
Prices rooms 530F-890F;
breakfast 75F, menus
190F-350F, children's 110F

Rooms 7 double (one twin), 3
apartments, all with bath; all
rooms have central heating,
phone, TV, minibar
Facilities 3 sitting-rooms, bar,
2 dining-rooms, 3 terraces,
swimming- pool **Credit cards**
AE, MC, V **Children** accepted
Disabled no special facilities
Pets accepted **Closed** Nov to
Easter **Proprietors** Bernard
and Françoise Brucy

Aude

Le Domaine d'Auriac

A calm and relaxing country house of which the primary attractions are outdoors: golf and tennis on the doorstep, a pool surrounded by beautifully manicured gardens and mature trees, and a dining terrace with a blissfully verdant view. But conditions indoors are harmonious and confortable too – this, after all, is a member of Relais & Chateaux. Spacious rooms overlook either the gardens or the golf course.

Nearby Carcassonne (3km) – cathedral, fortified town; vineyards.

Route de Saint-Hilaire 11009 Carcassonne
Tel 68.25.72.22
Fax 68.47.35.54
Location in countryside, 3km S of Carcassonne on D104 off D118; in extensive gardens, with secure car parking
Meals breakfast, lunch, dinner
Prices rooms 660F-1,300F; breakfast 80F, menus 170F-350F, children's menu 120F
Rooms 23 double (12 twin), 22 with bath, one with shower; all have central heating, phone, TV, minibar, hairdrier, tea/coffee kit
Facilities breakfast room, sitting-room, bar, dining-room, billiard room, bridge room; swimming-pool, tennis, 9-hole golf course
Credit cards AE, DC, MC, V
Children accepted; babysitting available **Disabled** lift/ elevator **Pets** welcome (70F)
Closed late Jan to Feb; Sun night (and restaurant Mon lunch) winter **Proprietor** Bernard Rigaudis

Le Relais du Val d'Orbieu

A carefully converted old mill plus associated buildings, encircled by trees. Most of the rooms, simply but neatly furnished, are at ground level, opening directly on to a grassy courtyard. The public rooms are warmly inviting. Our enthusiastic reporter judged the fixed-price menus 'excellent', eating from the *carte* 'fabulous'. There is a notable cellar, concentrating on local wines. But the key ingredient is the warmth of welcome.

Nearby Narbonne – unfinished cathedral (14 km), Fontfroide Abbey (12 km), Canal du Midi (15km), coast (15km).

11200 Ornaisons
Tel 68.27.10.27
Fax 68.27.52.44
Location in countryside 3 km NE of Ornaisons, on D24 off N113, 14 km W of Narbonne; in wooded grounds with private car parking
Meals breakfast, lunch, dinner, snacks
Prices rooms 450F-950F; breakfast 65F, meals 165-300F; children's menu 90F
Rooms 14 double (6 twin), 6 family rooms, all with bath; all have central heating, phone, TV, radio, minibar, hairdrier
Facilities dining-room, bar, sitting-room; swimming-pool, tennis, golf
Credit cards AE, DC, MC, V
Children welcome **Disabled** 1 specially equipped room on ground floor **Pets** accepted
Closed Feb; restaurant only Sun evening Nov to Mar
Proprietors Agnès and Jean-Pierre Gonzalvez

Pyrénées-Orientales

La Terrasse au Soleil

This Catalan-style hotel has a lovely setting, with the splendid Canigou as backdrop on a fine day (320 days of sun per year are claimed, so you should be lucky). As you might expect, it has a terrace, where you can eat out or just observe the view (as Picasso is said to have done). Inside, a relaxed and casual atmosphere prevails. The food is good (Gault-Millau *toque*); the rooms have been recently refurbished, furniture replaced and bathrooms enlarged. A good base for excursions in the area.

Nearby Perpignan; beaches (30 km); Castelnou (30 km).

Rte de Fontfrède 66400 Céret
Tel 68.87.01.94
Fax 68.87.39.24
Location in Pyrenean foothills above town, 26 km SW of Perpignan; with gardens and car parking
Meals breakfast, lunch, dinner
Prices rooms 520F-730F, suites 1,045F-1,150F; breakfast 70F
Rooms 25 double, all with bath; 2 family rooms with bath; all rooms have air-conditioning, TV, phone, minibar, hairdrier

Facilities dining-room, sitting-room, bar; ping-pong, swimming-pool, tennis-court, petanque, golf practice area
Credit cards MC, V
Children accepted
Disabled no special facilities
Pets accepted
Closed 2 Jan-2 Mar
Proprietor M. Leveille-Nizerolle

Mouli del Riu

St-Pierre is a satellite of Font-Romeu, the major ski resort in this part of the Pyrenees, and has its own skiing on the massive Cambre d'Aze. This is a fast-developing area, and skiers' chalets have altered beyond recognition the area around the Mouli – itself a modern and undistinguished house, despite the traditional-sounding name. It is a simple and rather quirky place, which has recently changed hands. We hope that M. Mauran will continue the good work of his predecessors, the Saillarde family.

Nearby Mountain and forest walks.

St-Pierre-dels-Forcats 66210 Mont-Louis
Tel 68.04.20.36
Location in valley 3.5 km S of Mont-Louis by D32, near Spanish border; with gardens and ample car parking
Meals breakfast, lunch, dinner
Prices rooms 180F-250F, extra bed 50F; menus 80F-125F
Rooms 10 double (4 twin), 5 family rooms, all with bath; all rooms have central heating

Facilities dining-room, sitting-room, TV room
Credit cards V
Children accepted
Disabled access difficult
Pets accepted
Closed Oct to mid-Dec; Wed
Proprietor Jean-François Mauran

Pyrénées-Orientales

Village inn, Llo

Auberge Atalaya

Llo is an attractive pastoral village with château ruins and an old watch-tower. It lies high up in the Pyrenees, at an altitude of 1,450m, close to the border, and is typical of the Cerdagne – a high sun-drenched plateau of pastures and pine forests, now popular for summer and winter sports. The Atalaya, occupying a prime spot in the village, is a delightful small inn, expertly converted by the Toussaints from an old farmhouse in 1971. The bedrooms are quiet, comfortable and intimate, with romantic fabrics and soft lighting. Local specialities are served either in the rustic dining-room – gleaming antiques against stone walls – or on a charming flowery terrace.

Nearby Odeillo (10 km) – solar furnace; Font-Romeu (15 km).

Llo 66800 Saillagouse
Tel 68.04.70.04
Fax 68.04.01.29
Location in middle of village, 2 km E of Saillagouse and 10 km E of Bourg-Madame; ample car parking
Meals breakfast, lunch, dinner
Prices rooms 480F-680F; breakfast 55F, menus 145F-185F
Rooms 12 double, 10 with bath, 2 with shower (3 twin); one suite; all rooms have central heating, phone, TV, minibar
Facilities sitting-room, bar, dining-room; swimming-pool
Credit cards MC, V
Children welcome if well behaved **Disabled** no special facilities **Pets** accepted in bedrooms only
Closed early Nov to mid-Dec
Proprietors M. and Mme H Toussaint

Corse

La Giraglia

The village of Barcaggio lies at the northern extremity of the Cap Corse peninsula, well off the tourist track. There is not much to see except the pretty cluster of fishermen's houses and the little port, but the beach is excellent and seldom crowded; and for anyone seeking a peaceful and simple base, the Giraglia is an excellent choice. From the terrace and garden you can practically dangle your feet in the water, and there are pretty views towards the centre of the village. The rooms are quiet and rustic, though not without modern conveniences. The hotel no longer has a restaurant, but several places in Barcaggio serve a variety of simply cooked fish and seafood.

Nearby Rogliano – stronghold (castles, churches, hamlets); Centuri-Port (15 km) – marina.

Barcaggio 20275 Essa
Tel 95.35.60.54
Location just outside village, 50 km N of Bastia; with garden and car parking
Meals breakfast
Prices rooms 357F-410F with breakfast
Rooms 14 double, 12 with shower (4 twin); 2 single, one with shower; one family room; all rooms have central heating, phone
Facilities 3 sitting-rooms, bar, breakfast room **Credit cards** not accepted **Children** accepted **Disabled** no special facilities **Pets** accepted **Closed** late Sep to mid-Apr
Proprietor M. Duhoux

A Pasturella

Just inland from the resort of L'Ile Rousse, in a charming old hill village, A Pasturella sits on the village square at the very heart of local life. It is a traditional place, though much enlarged since the days when M. Martini's parents ran a bar here in 1937; first a restaurant, then bedrooms were added (scattered in converted annexes, some of them rather small). Now he sees to the running of the hotel while his wife does the cooking; children and grandfather help too. All is well-cared for, cheerful and friendly. Food is wholesome and generous. Some of the rooms have wonderful views – worth booking well ahead.

Nearby Ile Rousse (3 km); Calvi (25 km); Asco Valley (50 km).

Monticello 20220 l'Ile-Rousse
Tel 95.60.05.65
Location on main square of village 3 km S of L'Ile Rousse and the sea; with ample car parking
Meals breakfast, lunch, dinner
Prices rooms 300F-320F; meals 140F
Rooms 15 double (4 twin), all with shower; 4 double with bath in annexe
Facilities bar, 2 dining-rooms; terraces
Credit cards DC, MC, V
Children accepted
Disabled no special facilities, access difficult
Pets accepted
Closed Nov; hotel 6 Nov to 6 Dec; restaurant Sun evening Dec-Feb
Proprietors M. and Mme Georges Martini

Index of hotel names

In this index, hotels are arranged in order of the most distinctive part of their name; very common prefixes such as 'Auberge', 'Hôtel', 'Hostellerie' and 'Le/La/Les' are omitted, but more significant elements such as 'Château' are retained.

33 Rue Thiers, La Rochelle **96**

A
Abbaye, Annecy-le-Vieux **121**
Abbaye, Beaugency **84**
Abbaye, Le Bec-Hellouin **27**
Abbaye, St-Cyprien **138**
Abbaye St-Michel, Tonnerre **102**
Abbaye de Ste-Croix,
  Salon-de-Provence **192**
Agora, Paris **58**
Alisiers, Lapoutroie **79**
Angleterre, Châlons-sur-Marne **76**
Angleterre, Paris **55**
Arcé, St-Étienne-de-Baïgorry **151**
Argouges, Bayeux **25**
Armes de Champagne, L'Épine **76**
Arraya, Sare **154**
Arts, St-Rémy-de-Provence **198**
Artzenheim, Artzenheim **79**
Atalaya, Llo **215**
Atelier, Villeneuve-lès-Avignon **176**

B
Bannière de France, Laon **75**
Banville, Paris **66**
Bas-Breau, Barbizon **70**
Bastide de Tourtour, Tourtour **210**
Beaubourg, Paris **48**
Belle Gasconne, Poudenas **140**
Belle-Vue, Le Lavandou **203**
Benvengudo, Les Baux-de-Provence **194**
Bergerie, Soustons **148**
Bersoly's St-Germain, Paris **59**
Bois Joli, Bagnoles-de-l'Orne **33**
Bois Prin, Chamonix **122**
Bon Coin du Lac, Mimizan **149**
Bonne Étape, Château-Arnoux **183**
Bonnet, Beynac-et-Cazenac **128**
Bourgogne, Cluny **112**
Bretonne, La Roche-Bernard **42**
Bretonnerie, Paris **61**

C
Cagnard, Haut-de-Cagnes **186**
Capitelle, Mirmande **172**
Carayon, St-Sernin-sur-Rance **165**
Cassagne, Le Pontet **182**
Castel, Mailly-le-Château **101**
Castel de Bray et Monts, Bréhémont **88**
Castel de Valrose,
  Montmerle-sur-Saône **119**
Cathédrale, Rouen **20**
Cerf, Marlenheim **78**
Cévenole, La Favède **173**

Chalet, Coulandon **157**
Chapelle St-Martin, St-Martin-du-Fault **99**
Charmes, Meursault **108**
Château, Châteauneuf **109**
Château, Lalinde **129**
Château des Alpilles,
  St-Rémy-de-Provence **196**
Château d'Artannes, Artannes **90**
Château de la Beuvrière, Vierzon **92**
Château de Boussac, Target **156**
Château de Castelpers, Castelpers **162**
Château de la Caze, La Malène **161**
Château de Chissay, Montrichard **81**
Château de Coatguélen, Pléhédel **36**
Château de Commarque, Sauternes **127**
Château Cordeillan-Bages, Pauillac **126**
Château des Crayères, Reims **77**
Château Eza, Èze **185**
Château de Fleurville, Fleurville **114**
Château d'Igé, Igé **111**
Château de Madières, Ganges **212**
Château de la Menaudière,
  Montrichard **83**
Château de Montreuil,
  Montreuil-sur-Mer **73**
Château de Nieuil, Nieuil **97**
Château de Ponderach,
  St-Pons-de-Thomières **212**
Château de Pray, Amboise **88**
Château de la Râpée, Gisors **29**
Château de Remaisnil, Doullens **74**
Château de Rochecotte, Langeais **90**
Château de Rochegude, Rochegude **172**
Château de Roussan,
  St-Rémy-de-Provence **199**
Château de Teildras,
  Cheffes-sur-Sarthe **86**
Château de Trancis, Ydes **158**
Château de la Treyne, Lacave **142**
Château de Trigance, Trigance **207**
Château d'Urbilhac, Lamastre **168**
Château de la Vallée Bleue,
  St-Chartier **91**
Château de Vault-de-Lugny, Avallon **104**
Château de Vieux Mareuil,
  Vieux-Mareuil **138**
Chatenet, Brantôme **132**
Chaumière, Lauris-sur-Durance **182**
Chez Camille, Arnay-le-Duc **110**
Chez Pierre, Raguenès-Plage **41**
Clair Logis, St-Jean-Cap-Ferrat **188**
Clarion, Aloxe-Corton **106**
Clé d'Or, Barbizon **70**
Cléry, Hesdin-L'Abbé **73**
Clos, Chablis **105**

Index of hotel names

Clos, Verneuil-sur-Avre **32**
Clos du Montvinage, Etréaupont **75**
Clos Normand, Martin-Église **19**
Clos St-Médard, Thouars **94**
Clos St-Vincent, Ribeauvillé **80**
Cochon d'Or, Beuzeville **27**
Colombe d'Or, St-Paul-de-Vence **190**
Colombier, Roquefort-les-Pins **188**
Conquérant, Barfleur **24**
Côte d'Or, Châtillon-sur-Seine **108**
Coteau Fleuri, Grimaud **202**
Crillon le Brave, Crillon-le-Brave **179**
Croix Blanche,
    Chaumont-sur-Tharonne **82**
Croix Blanche, Souvigny-en-Sologne **83**
Croix-Fry, Manigod **123**
Cucheron, St-Pierre-de-Chartreuse **124**

D

Daille, Florimont-Gaumiers **128**
Danemark, Paris **46**
Demeure de Chavoire,
    Veyrier-du-Lac **121**
Deux Iles, Paris **57**
Deux Magots, La Roche-Bernard **42**
Deux Rocs, Seillans **206**
Diderot, Chinon **89**
Domaine d'Auriac, Carcassonne **213**
Domaine de Chateauneuf,
    Nans-les-Pins **211**
Domaine de Clairefontaine,
    Chonas-l'Amballan **125**
Domaine de la Rhue, Rocamadour **141**
Donjon, Étretat **18**
Duc de St-Simon, Paris **68**

E

Eber Monceau, Paris **46**
Ermitage Meissonnier, Les Angles **174**
Esmeralda, Paris **44**
Esplanade, Domme **130**
Étoile Pereire, Paris **52**

F

Falaises, Gluges **147**
Fayette, St-Jean-de-Luz **155**
Ferme de la Huppe, Gordes **180**
Fleurie, Montsalvy **159**
Florets, Gigondas **178**
Fontaine, Carpentras **176**
Fontaine aux Muses, La
    Celle-St-Cyr **105**
France, Riberac **135**
France et des Fuschias,
    St-Vaast-la-Hougue **22**
Frontière, Auberge sans, Dégagnac **142**

G

Gaillon Opéra, Paris **62**
Galerie des Arcades, Biot **189**
Gardiole, Cap d'Antibes **189**
Géraniums, Le Barroux **178**

Giraglia, Barcaggio **216**
Glycines, Les Eyzies-de-Tayac **134**
Grand Écuyer, Cordes **166**
Grande Chaumière, St-Florentin **102**
Grandes Écoles, Paris **60**
Grands Crus, Gevrey-Chambertin **109**
Grands Hommes, Paris **68**
Grenouillère, Montreuil-sur-Mer **71**
Gros Marronnier, Senlisse **43**

H

Halle, Givry **114**
Hameau, St-Paul-de-Vence **191**
Haye-le-Comte, Louviers **29**
Hospitaliers, Dieulefit **170**
L'Hôtel, Paris **45**
Huitrières du Lac, Hossegor **148**

J

Jardin des Plantes, Paris **51**
Jeanne de Laval, Les
    Rosiers-sur-Loire **87**
Jeu de Paume, Paris **50**

K

Kastell Dinec'h, Tréguier **38**
Korrigane, St-Malo **39**

L

Lameloise, Chagny **111**
Landes, Ouchamps **82**
Lenox, Paris **58**
Lièvre Amoureux, St-Lattier **125**
Loges de l'Aubergade, Puymirol **140**
Logis du Guetteur, Les Arcs **203**
Longcol, Najac **163**
Lord Byron, Paris **65**
Lou Calen, Cotignac **211**
Lutèce, Paris **54**

M

Madone, Peillon **187**
Magdeleine, Gémenos **200**
Magnaneraie,
    Villeneuve-lès-Avignon **175**
Magnolias, Meursault **107**
Malouinière, Blois **81**
Manoir, Fontenay-Trésigny **69**
Manoir, Ile de Port-Cros **208**
Manoir de Bellerive, Le
    Buisson-de-Cadouin **137**
Manoir d'Hautegente, Coly **129**
Manoir de Lan-Kerellec, Trébeurden **38**
Manoir du Lys, Bagnoles-de-l'Orne **33**
Manoir de Moëllien, Plonévez-Porzay **40**
Manoir de Montesquiou, La Malène **161**
Manoir du Raveyron,
    Vallon-Pont-d'Arc **169**
Manoir de Rochecourbe, Vézac **135**
Marais, Coulon **94**
Marais St-Jean, Chonas-l'Amballan **124**
Marceau, Doussard **123**
Maronne, St-Martin-Valmeroux **159**

Index of hotel names

Marronniers, Paris **65**
Mas d'Aigret, Les Baux-de-Provence **201**
Mas des Brugassières,
   Plan-de-la-Tour **204**
Mas de la Brune, Eygalières **192**
Mas des Carassins,
   St-Rémy-de-Provence **198**
Mas de la Chapelle, Arles **194**
Mas d'Entremont, Aix-en-Provence **200**
Mas de la Fouque, Les
   Stes-Maries-de-la-Mer **195**
Mas de Garrigon, Roussillon **181**
Maurandière, Sourdeval **23**
Mayflower, Paris **51**
Métairie Neuve, Mazamet **167**
Meysset, Sarlat-en-Périgord **130**
Midi, Lamastre **168**
Midi, St-Jean-du-Bruel **164**
Mouli del Riu, St-Pierre-dels-Forcats **214**
Moulin, Flagy **69**
Moulin de l'Abbaye, Brantôme **133**
Moulin de la Beune, Les
   Eyzies-de-Tayac **134**
Moulin Blanc, Les Beaumettes **177**
Moulin de la Camandoule, Fayence **209**
Moulin de Chaméron, Bannegon **93**
Moulins du Duc, Moëlan-sur-Mer **40**
Moulin de la Gorce, La
   Roche-l'Abeille **99**
Moulin d'Hauterive,
   St-Gervais-en-Vallière **116**
Moulin de Marcouze, Mosnac **97**
Moulin du Prieuré,
   Bonnevaux-le-Prieuré **118**
Moulin du Roc,
   Champagnac-de-Belair **131**
Moulin des Templiers, Avallon **100**
Moulin du Vey, Clécy **26**
Moulin de Villeray, Villeray **34**
Muscadins, Mougins **185**

N
Normandie, Caudebec-en-Caux **19**
Noves, Noves **197**

O
Ohantzea, Aïnhoa **152**
Orangers, St-Paul-de-Vence **190**
Oustal del Barry, Najac **164**
Oustaloun, Maussane-les-Alpilles **196**

P
Parc, Levernois **110**
Parc des Maréchaux, Auxerre **100**
Pasturella, Monticello **216**
Pélissaria, St-Cirq-Lapopie **145**
Petit Coq aux Champs, Campigny **28**
Pic, Valence **171**
Pins, Sabres **147**
Place des Vosges, Paris **48**
Plage, Ste-Anne-la-Palud **41**
Plaisance, St-Émilion **127**
Poids Public, St-Félix-Lauragais **155**

Ponche, St-Tropez **208**
Pont de l'Ouysse, Lacave **144**
Pontoise, Pons **96**
Pontot, Vézelay **103**
Poste, Charolles **112**
Pré Bossu, Moudeyres **160**
Prieuré, Ermenonville **74**
Prieuré, St-André d'Hébertot **25**
Prieuré, Tonnay-Boutonne **95**
Prima-Lepic, Paris **66**
Prince Albert, Paris **62**

Q
Quatres Saisons, St-Restitut **171**

R
Récamier, Paris **50**
Récollets, Marcigny **115**
Régalido, Fontvieille **193**
Régence Etoile, Paris **64**
Regent's Garden, Paris **67**
Reillanne, Reillanne **184**
Repaire de Kerroc'h, Paimpol **36**
Rhône, Seyssel **120**
Riboutté Lafayette, Paris **55**
Ripa Alta, Plaisance **150**
Rivage, Gien **84**
Rostaing, Passenans **117**

S
St-Dominique, Paris **63**
St-Germain, Paris **59**
St-Germain-des-Prés, Paris **47**
St-Grégoire, Paris **54**
St-Jacques, Cloyes-sur-le-Loir **35**
St-Jacques, St-Saud-en-Périgord **136**
St-Louis, Paris **47**
St-Louis Marais, Paris **60**
St-Merry, Paris **64**
St-Paul, St-Paul-de-Vence **186**
St-Pierre, La Bouille **20**
St-Pierre, Le Mont-Saint-Michel **24**
St-Pierre, St-Pierre-du-Vauvray **31**
St-Pierre, Tourtour **210**
Ste-Beuve, Paris **49**
Ste-Catherine, Montbron **98**
Ste-Foy, Conques **163**
Sarthe, Châteauneuf-sur-Sarthe **86**
Seigneur, Tavel **174**
Sélune, Ducey **21**
Solférino, Paris **56**
Solognote, Brinon-sur-Sauldre **92**
Sombral, St-Cirq-Lapopie **144**

T
Table du Comtat, Vaison-la-Romaine **180**
Taillard, Goumois **118**
Terrasse au Soleil, Céret **214**
Thoumieux, Paris **52**
Ti Al-Lannec, Trébeurden **37**
Tonnellerie, Beaugency **85**
Trois Lys, Condom **150**
Trois Mousquetaires, Aire-sur-la-Lys **72**

Index of hotel names

Tuileries, Paris **44**

U
Université, Paris **56**

V
Val d'Or, Mercurey **113**
Val d'Orbieu, Ornaisons **213**
Val-Suzon, Val-Suzon **107**
Verger, Grimaud **205**
Verneuil-St-Germain, Paris **53**
Vert, Mauroux **143**
Verte Campagne, Trelly **23**
Vieilles Tours, Rocamadour **146**
Vieux Cordes, Cordes **167**
Vieux Logis, Lestelle-Bétharram **153**
Vieux Logis, Trémolat **139**
Vieux Pérouges, Pérouges **120**
Vieux Puits, Pont-Audemer **30**
Vosges, Ribeauvillé **80**
Voyageurs, Escos **153**

Y
Yaca, St-Tropez **205**

Index of hotel locations

In this index, hotels are arranged by the name of the city, town or village they are in or near. Hotels located in a very small village may be indexed under the name of a larger place nearby.

A

Aïnhoa, Ohantzea **152**
Aire-sur-la-Lys, Trois Mousquetaires **72**
Aix-en-Provence, Mas d'Entremont **200**
Aloxe-Corton, Clarion **106**
Amboise, Château de Pray **88**
Les Angles, Ermitage Meissonnier **174**
Annecy-le-Vieux, Abbaye **121**
Les Arcs, Logis du Guetteur **203**
Arles, Mas de la Chapelle **194**
Arnay-le-Duc, Chez Camille **110**
Artannes, Château d'Artannes **90**
Artzenheim, Artzenheim **79**
Auxerre, Parc des Maréchaux **100**
Avallon, Château de Vault-de-Lugny **104**
Avallon, Moulin des Templiers **100**

B

Bagnoles-de-l'Orne, Bois Joli **33**
Bagnoles-de-l'Orne, Manoir du Lys **33**
Bannegon, Moulin de Chaméron **93**
Barbizon, Bas-Breau **70**
Barbizon, Clé d'Or **70**
Barcaggio, Giraglia **216**
Barfleur, Conquérant **24**
Le Barroux, Géraniums **178**
Les Baux-de-Provence, Benvengudo **194**
Les Baux-de-Provence, Mas d'Aigret **201**
Bayeux, Argouges **25**
Beaugency, Abbaye **84**
Beaugency, Tonnellerie **85**
Les Beaumettes, Moulin Blanc **177**
Le Bec-Hellouin, Abbaye **27**
Beuzeville, Cochon d'Or **27**
Beynac-et-Cazenac, Bonnet **128**
Biot, Galerie des Arcades **189**
Blois, Malounière **81**
Bonnevaux-le-Prieuré, Moulin du Prieuré **118**
La Bouille, St-Pierre **20**
Brantôme, Chatenet **132**
Brantôme, Moulin de l'Abbaye **133**
Bréhémont, Castel de Bray et Monts **88**
Brinon-sur-Sauldre, Solognote **92**
Le Buisson-de-Cadouin, Manoir de Bellerive **137**

C

Campigny, Petit Coq aux Champs **28**
Cap d'Antibes, Gardiole **189**
Carcassonne, Domaine d'Auriac **213**
Carpentras, Fontaine **176**
Castelpers, Château de Castelpers **162**
Caudebec-en-Caux, Normandie **19**
La Celle-St-Cyr, Fontaine aux Muses **105**
Céret, Terrasse au Soleil **214**
Chablis, Clos **105**

Chagny, Lameloise **111**
Châlons-sur-Marne, Angleterre **76**
Chamonix, Bois Prin **122**
Champagnac-de-Belair, Moulin du Roc **131**
Charolles, Poste **112**
Château-Arnoux, Bonne Étape **183**
Châteauneuf, Château **109**
Châteauneuf-sur-Sarthe, Sarthe **86**
Châtillon-sur-Seine, Côte d'Or **108**
Chaumont-sur-Tharonne, Croix Blanche **82**
Cheffes-sur-Sarthe, Château de Teildras **86**
Chinon, Diderot **89**
Chonas-l'Amballan, Domaine de Clairefontaine **125**
Chonas-l'Amballan, Marais St-Jean **124**
Clécy, Moulin du Vey **26**
Cloyes-sur-le-Loir, St-Jacques **35**
Cluny, Bourgogne **112**
Coly, Manoir d'Hautegente **129**
Condom, Trois Lys **150**
Conques, Ste-Foy **163**
Cordes, Grand Écuyer **166**
Cordes, Vieux Cordes **167**
Cotignac, Lou Calen **211**
Coulandon, Chalet **157**
Coulon, Marais **94**
Crillon-le-Brave, Crillon le Brave **179**

D

Dégagnac, Frontière, Auberge sans **142**
Dieulefit, Hospitaliers **170**
Domme, Esplanade **130**
Doullens, Château de Remaisnil **74**
Doussard, Marceau **123**
Ducey, Sélune **21**

E

L'Épine, Armes de Champagne **76**
Ermenonville, Prieuré **74**
Escos, Voyageurs **153**
Etréaupont, Clos du Montvinage **75**
Étretat, Donjon **18**
Eygalières, Mas de la Brune **192**
Les Eyzies-de-Tayac, Glycines **134**
Les Eyzies-de-Tayac, Moulin de la Beune **134**
Èze, Château Eza **185**

F

La Favède, Cévenole **173**
Fayence, Moulin de la Camandoule **209**
Flagy, Moulin **69**
Fleurville, Château de Fleurville **114**
Florimont-Gaumiers, Daille **128**

Index of hotel locations

Fontenay-Trésigny, Manoir 69
Fontvieille, Régalido 193

G

Ganges, Château de Madières 212
Gémenos, Magdeleine 200
Gevrey-Chambertin, Grands Crus 109
Gien, Rivage 84
Gigondas, Florets 178
Gisors, Château de la Râpée 29
Givry, Halle 114
Gluges, Falaises 147
Gordes, Ferme de la Huppe 180
Goumois, Taillard 118
Grimaud, Coteau Fleuri 202
Grimaud, Verger 205

H

Haut-de-Cagnes, Cagnard 186
Hesdin-L'Abbé, Cléry 73
Hossegor, Huitrières du Lac 148

I

Igé, Château d'Igé 111

L

Lacave, Château de la Treyne 142
Lacave, Pont de l'Ouysse 144
Lalinde, Château 129
Lamastre, Château d'Urbilhac 168
Lamastre, Midi 168
Langeais, Château de Rochecotte 90
Laon, Bannière de France 75
Lapoutroie, Alisiers 79
Lauris-sur-Durance, Chaumière 182
Le Lavandou, Belle-Vue 203
Lestelle-Bétharram, Vieux Logis 153
Levernois, Parc 110
Llo, Atalaya 215
Louviers, Haye-le-Comte 29

M

Mailly-le-Château, Castel 101
La Malène, Château de la Caze 161
La Malène, Manoir de Montesquiou 161
Manigod, Croix-Fry 123
Marcigny, Récollets 115
Marlenheim, Cerf 78
Martin-Église, Clos Normand 19
Mauroux, Vert 143
Maussane-les-Alpilles, Oustaloun 196
Mazamet, Métairie Neuve 167
Mercurey, Val d'Or 113
Meursault, Charmes 108
Meursault, Magnolias 107
Mimizan, Bon Coin du Lac 149
Mirmande, Capitelle 172
Moëlan-sur-Mer, Moulins du Duc 40
Le Mont-Saint-Michel, St-Pierre 24
Montbron, Ste-Catherine 98
Monticello, Pasturella 216
Montmerle-sur-Saône, Castel de
  Valrose 119

Montreuil-sur-Mer, Grenoullière 71
Montreuil-sur-Mer, Château de
  Montreuil 73
Montrichard, Château de Chissay 81
Montrichard, Château de la
  Menaudière 83
Montsalvy, Fleurie 159
Mosnac, Moulin de Marcouze 97
Moudeyres, Pré Bossu 160
Mougins, Muscadins 185

N

Najac, Longcol 163
Najac, Oustal del Barry 164
Nans-les-Pins, Domaine de
  Chateauneuf 211
Nieuil, Château de Nieuil 97
Noves, Noves 197

O

Ornaisons, Val d'Orbieu 213
Ouchamps, Landes 82

P

Paimpol, Repaire de Kerroc'h 36
Paris, Agora 58
Paris, Angleterre 55
Paris, Banville 66
Paris, Beaubourg 48
Paris, Bersoly's St-Germain 59
Paris, Bretonnerie 61
Paris, Danemark 46
Paris, Deux Iles 57
Paris, Duc de St-Simon 68
Paris, Eber Monceau 46
Paris, Esmeralda 44
Paris, Étoile Pereire 52
Paris, Gaillon Opéra 62
Paris, Grandes Écoles 60
Paris, Grands Hommes 68
Paris, L'Hôtel 45
Paris, Jardin des Plantes 51
Paris, Jeu de Paume 50
Paris, Lenox 58
Paris, Lord Byron 65
Paris, Lutèce 54
Paris, Marronniers 65
Paris, Mayflower 51
Paris, Place des Vosges 48
Paris, Prima-Lepic 66
Paris, Prince Albert 62
Paris, Récamier 50
Paris, Régence Etoile 64
Paris, Regent's Garden 67
Paris, Riboutté Lafayette 55
Paris, St-Dominique 63
Paris, St-Germain 59
Paris, St-Germain-des-Prés 47
Paris, St-Grégoire 54
Paris, St-Louis 47
Paris, St-Louis Marais 60
Paris, St-Merry 64
Paris, Ste-Beuve 49

Index of hotel locations

Paris, Solférino **56**
Paris, Thoumieux **52**
Paris, Tuileries **44**
Paris, Université **56**
Paris, Verneuil-St-Germain **53**
Passenans, Rostaing **117**
Pauillac, Château Cordeillan-Bages **126**
Peillon, Madone **187**
Pérouges, Vieux Pérouges **120**
Plaisance, Ripa Alta **150**
Plan-de-la-Tour, Mas des
    Brugassières **204**
Pléhédel, Château de Coatguélen **36**
Plonévez-Porzay, Manoir de Moëllien **40**
Pons, Pontoise **96**
Pont-Audemer, Vieux Puits **30**
Le Pontet, Cassagne **182**
Ile de Port-Cros, Manoir **208**
Poudenas, Belle Gasconne **140**
Puymirol, Loges de l'Aubergade **140**

R
Raguenès-Plage, Chez Pierre **41**
Reillanne, Reillanne **184**
Reims, Château des Crayères **77**
Ribeauvillé, Clos St-Vincent **80**
Ribeauvillé, Vosges **80**
Riberac, France **135**
Rocamadour, Domaine de la Rhue **141**
Rocamadour, Vieilles Tours **146**
La Roche-Bernard, Bretonne **42**
La Roche-Bernard, Deux Magots **42**
La Roche-l'Abeille, Moulin de la
    Gorce **99**
Rochegude, Château de Rochegude **172**
La Rochelle, 33 Rue Thiers **96**
Roquefort-les-Pins, Colombier **188**
Les Rosiers-sur-Loire, Jeanne de
    Laval **87**
Rouen, Cathédrale **20**
Roussillon, Mas de Garrigon **181**

S
Sabres, Pins **147**
St-André-d'Hébertot, Prieuré **25**
St-Chartier, Château de la Vallée
    Bleue **91**
St-Cirq-Lapopie, Pélissaria **145**
St-Cirq-Lapopie, Sombral **144**
St-Cyprien, Abbaye **138**
St-Émilion, Plaisance **127**
St-Étienne-de-Baïgorry, Arcé **151**
St-Félix-Lauragais, Poids Public **155**
St-Florentin, Grande Chaumière **102**
St-Gervais-en-Vallière, Moulin
    d'Hauterive **116**
St-Jean-Cap-Ferrat, Clair Logis **188**
St-Jean-de-Luz, Fayette **155**
St-Jean-du-Bruel, Midi **164**
St-Lattier, Lièvre Amoureux **125**
St-Malo, Korrigane **39**
St-Martin-Valmeroux, Maronne **159**
St-Martin-du-Fault, Chapelle St-Martin **99**

St-Paul-de-Vence, Colombe d'Or **190**
St-Paul-de-Vence, Hameau **191**
St-Paul-de-Vence, Orangers **190**
St-Paul-de-Vence, St-Paul **186**
St-Pierre-de-Chartreuse, Cucheron **124**
St-Pierre-dels-Forcats, Mouli del Riu **214**
St-Pierre-du-Vauvray, St-Pierre **31**
St-Pons-de-Thomières, Château de
    Ponderach **212**
St-Rémy-de-Provence, Arts **198**
St-Rémy-de-Provence, Château des
    Alpilles **196**
St-Rémy-de-Provence, Château de
    Roussan **199**
St-Rémy-de-Provence, Mas des
    Carassins **198**
St-Restitut, Quatres Saisons **171**
St-Saud-en-Périgord, St-Jacques **136**
St-Sernin-sur-Rance, Carayon **165**
St-Tropez, Ponche **208**
St-Tropez, Yaca **205**
St-Vaast-la-Hougue, France et des
    Fuschias **22**
Ste-Anne-la-Palud, Plage **41**
Les Stes-Maries-de-la-Mer, Mas de la
    Fouque **195**
Salon-de-Provence, Abbaye de
    Ste-Croix **192**
Sare, Arraya **154**
Sarlat-en-Périgord, Meysset **130**
Sauternes, Château de Commarque **127**
Seillans, Deux Rocs **206**
Senlisse, Gros Marronnier **43**
Seyssel, Rhône **120**
Sourdeval, Maurandière **23**
Soustons, Bergerie **148**
Souvigny-en-Sologne, Croix Blanche **83**

T
Target, Château de Boussac **156**
Tavel, Seigneur **174**
Thouars, Clos St-Médard **94**
Tonnay-Boutonne, Prieuré **95**
Tonnerre, Abbaye St-Michel **102**
Tourtour, Bastide de Tourtour **210**
Tourtour, St-Pierre **210**
Trébeurden, Manoir de Lan-Kerellec **38**
Trébeurden, Ti Al-Lannec **37**
Tréguier, Kastell Dinec'h **38**
Trelly, Verte Campagne **23**
Trémolat, Vieux Logis **139**
Trigance, Château de Trigance **207**

V
Vaison-la-Romaine, Table du Comtat **180**
Val-Suzon, Val-Suzon **107**
Valence, Pic **171**
Vallon-Pont-d'Arc, Manoir du
    Raveyron **169**
Verneuil-sur-Avre, Clos **32**
Veyrier-du-Lac, Demeure de
    Chavoire **121**
Vézac, Manoir de Rochecourbe **135**

Index of hotel locations

Vézelay, Pontot **103**
Vierzon, Château de la Beuvrière **92**
Vieux-Mareuil, Château de Vieux
  Mareuil **138**
Villeneuve-lès-Avignon, Atelier **176**
Villeneuve-lès-Avignon,
  Magnaneraie **175**
Villeray, Moulin de Villeray **34**

Y
Ydes, Château de Trancis **158**

17/9

24/9 - SAT
25/9 - SUN